The Exodus Itinerary Sites

Studies in Biblical Literature

Hemchand Gossai
General Editor

Vol. 55

PETER LANG
New York • Washington, D.C./Baltimore • Bern
Frankfurt am Main • Berlin • Brussels • Vienna • Oxford

Michael D. Oblath

The Exodus Itinerary Sites

Their Locations from the Perspective of the Biblical Sources

PETER LANG
New York • Washington, D.C./Baltimore • Bern
Frankfurt am Main • Berlin • Brussels • Vienna • Oxford

Library of Congress Cataloging-in-Publication Data

Oblath, Michael D.
The Exodus itinerary sites: their locations
from the perspective of the biblical sources / Michael D. Oblath.
p. cm. — (Studies in biblical literature; v. 55)
Includes bibliographical references (p.) and index.
1. Exodus, The. I. Title. II. Series.
BS1199.E93O25 222'.11091—dc21 2003003740
ISBN 0-8204-6716-2
ISSN 1089-0645

Bibliographic information published by **Die Deutsche Bibliothek**.
Die Deutsche Bibliothek lists this publication in the "Deutsche
Nationalbibliografie"; detailed bibliographic data is available
on the Internet at http://dnb.ddb.de/.

To my sons

Noah and Aron…

for their patience, compassion, intelligence, understanding...
and love…

just because…

dumu nu-íl giri₁₇-zal-šè nu-íl
...he who has not raised a child
has not achieved happiness

Sumerian Proverb

TABLE OF CONTENTS

TABLES

MAPS

EDITOR'S PREFACE

More than ever the horizons in biblical literature are being expanded beyond that which is immediately imagined; important new methodological, theological, and hermeneutical directions are being explored, often resulting in significant contributions to the world of biblical scholarship. It is an exciting time for the academy as engagement in biblical studies continues to be heightened.

This series seeks to make available to scholars and institutions, scholarship of a high order, and which will make a significant contribution to the ongoing biblical discourse. This series includes established and innovative directions, covering general and particular areas in biblical study. For every volume considered for this series, we explore the question as to whether the study will push the horizons of biblical scholarship. The answer must be *yes* for inclusion.

In this very fine volume Michael Oblath investigates with great clarity and with a requisite level of detail the localization of the particular Exodus sites as they are mentioned in the Bible. He employs what he refers to as "literary based historical-geography." In this regard, he casts his study in an important direction that does not attend particularly to the issue of archaeology. Defining history as an investigation of how people live their lives, in every way, and as challenging as it is to locate with certitude the events of an ancient time, he argues that this is the manner in which one must read the Bible. With this in mind, Michael Oblath provides in this volume a detailed and copious study of the various biblical sites associated with Exodus, and it is surely a volume that scholars will find enormously helpful.

The horizon has been expanded

Hemchand Gossai
Series Editor

PREFACE

The distance is nothing; it is only the first step that is difficult.
Mme Du Deffand (1697–1780) Commenting on the legend that
St. Denis, carrying his head in his hands, walked two leagues.
Letter to d'Alembert, 7 July 1763

There are moments in our lives that are defining. Some of them we never notice. Others shine with crystal clarity. To take hold of them and make them our own can open new paths to new understandings, new perceptions. Such moments existed in a course I took with Professor Kah-Jin (Jeffrey) Kuan on the history of Israel and Judah.

I had hoped to deepen my understanding of the origins and evolution of ancient Judah and the early Davidic Dynasty. Instead, it was the sweeping and overwhelming permeation of the exodus narrative within the biblical text that stimulated my curiosity. I was once again asking the same troubling questions. With only the most meager circumstantial evidence, how could this story have become so thoroughly embedded within the traditions of Israel, and eventually Judah? Through my research, writing and discussions it became apparent that this narrative describes some event that was perceived and felt on the level of a national psyche. It was an event, or the memory of an event, which caused the creation of a national origin tale. My own research appears to have brought me full-circle, returning to the period of David and Solomon. I have come to understand and suggest this period as the foundational era out of which the exodus story was created and given its original life.

It is not possible within the scope of this work to delve into the intricacies of the United Monarchy. Nevertheless, the study may prompt further research along new avenues, with new awareness. It supports the Israelite origin of the exodus narrative with subsequent later editing and reworking by Judean authors. Moreover, this calls into question the relationship between Israel and Judah vis à vis the development and ownership of various traditions. These include, but are not limited to, the exodus, "possession" of the land of Israel/Judah, legitimization as bearers of the covenant with YHWH, inheritance rights regarding the traditions of Israel and implications concerning the relationship between the J and E pentateuchal sources. In this regard it may be possible to support the late dating of J as well as suggesting the need to reconfigure the criteria by means of which these two sources are defined.

There are many to whom I am grateful for their guidance and inspiration. My teachers, Dr. Stanley Gevirtz, z"l and Dr. Michael Signer, opened the doors to the appreciation and critical study of primary texts, and thus to the world of antiquity. Michael, in addition, led me to the Joint Program in Near Eastern Religions of the Graduate Theological Union and the University of California, Berkeley. Because of his friendship and guidance I was introduced to a remarkable family of faculty and colleagues, with whom it has been a privilege to study and work. They provided an appreciated framework within which intellectual growth is possible.

I was fortunate to have been guided by a wonderful dissertation committee in the initial writing of this study: Dr. Jeffrey Kuan, Dr. Robert B. Coote, Dr. David Henkin, Dr. Anne Draffkorn Kilmer, and Dr. David Stronach. In blending scholars from both Cal and GTU, I could not have been more fortunate than to work with these committee members. Their teaching and scholarship inspired me. Their encouragement, support, guidance and, most importantly, their integrity, was a true gift.

The Mishnah teaches:

יהי כבוד תלמידך חביב עליך כשלך
Let the honor of your student be as dear to you as your own. *m. 'Abot* 4:12

Moreover, the Mishnah instructs that it is one's obligation to obtain a teacher...

To have had Jeffrey Kuan as the chair of my dissertation committee, and to have been his student, has been a cherished honor. His openness in confronting new and challenging ideas is inspirational. His guidance and care for all his students is a pleasure to experience. Jeffrey teaches through the example of his life, intellect and compassion. I thank him for the opportunity he afforded me to create and develop my dissertation under the guidance of a true friend and *Mensch*.

Finally, there are, indeed, moments in our lives that are defining. Some of them we never notice. Others shine with crystal clarity. This past year has brought to light the most remarkable teachers in my life, my wonderful guides and sources of continual blessing and inspiration...my sons Aron and Noah. This is for them...just because...

ABBREVIATIONS

ABD	D. N. Freedman (ed.), *Anchor Bible Dictionary*
Ant.	Josephus, Jewish Antiquities
BA	*Biblical Archaeologist*
BAR	*Biblical Archaeology Review*
BASOR	*Bulletin of the American Schools of Oriental Research*
BHS	Biblia Hebraica Stutgartensia
BR	*Bible Review*
CBQ	*Catholic Biblical Quarterly*
FHG	Fragmenta Historicorum Graecorum
GGM	Geographi Graeci Minores
HUCA	*Hebrew Union College Annual*
IEJ	*Israel Exploration Journal*
JAOS	*Journal of the American Oriental Society*
JBL	*Journal of Biblical Literature*
JCS	*Journal of Cuneiform Studies*
JEA	*Journal of Egyptian Archaeology*
JNES	*Journal of Near Eastern Studies*
JPOS	*Journal of the Palestine Oriental Society*
JQR	*Jewish Quarterly Review*
JSOT	*Journal for the Study of the Old Testament*
JSOTSupp	*Journal for the Study of the Old Testament, Supplement Series*
JTS	*Journal of Theological Studies*
Paulys	Paulys Real-Encyclopädie der Classischen Altertumswissenschaft
PEQ	*Palestine Exploration Quarterly*
RB	*Revue Biblique*
VT	*Vetus Testamentum*
VTSup	Vetus Testamentum, Supplements
ZAW	*Zeitschrift für die alttestamentliche Wissenschaft*
ZDMG	*Zeitschrift der Deutschen Morgenländischen Gesellschaft*

INTRODUCTION

ויסעו בני ישראל מרעמסס סכתה...

And the Israelites journeyed from Rameses toward Succoth...

Exod 12:37

So begins the exodus from Egypt. In the various verses, chapters and books that follow Exod 12:37 the numerous itinerary sites visited by the Israelites are described. Some are mentioned in detail, others just in passing. Some have been discovered and detailed by archaeologists, some exist solely as products of speculation and conjecture, while others remain totally, and perhaps forever, hidden from us.

The question under discussion is not the archaeological identification of these sites. That blending of archaeological discovery with biblical text is usually identified as historical-geography. Many scholars have attempted to make the connection between biblical narrative and archaeological discovery. Often the connection is forced, but to what degree depends upon the intensity of the scholars' agendas to prove the veracity of the biblical text. With the proliferation of written material supporting views from one extreme to another, it is important to justify a somewhat different approach.

This investigation asks, instead, whether within the text the biblical authors are consistent in their localization of these particular sites, identified at some time as associated with the exodus. Stated as a hypothesis: *if the geographical sites that pertain to the exodus are known to the various biblical sources, then they may be described on occasion in relative proximity to known regional locales*. In contraposition to an archaeologically based historical-geography, I am proposing the utilization of a literary based historical-geography. This process ultimately focuses on a definition of "history" that is more than a chronological progression of dates and events.

The study of history is the investigation into a record of human experiences. It is a study of people and how they live their lives. How does one eat, worship, travel, get along with others and with oneself? How does one relate to that which is incomprehensible? The telling of these stories may occur within time and marked periods of time, but chronological progression is only a framework within which we may study the experiences of societies and people of ages past.

How can we hope to understand a society, culture or way of life as one so far removed in time and in place? The link we seek is with the people of that distant time and place. As a species, humans are always faced with basic problems. We must live within nature, find sustenance and protection for ourselves, our families and communities. We must thus learn to live with our fellow humans as well as with the surrounding environment, and learn to live with ourselves as well as with the incomprehensible. Thus we may define issues of origins, economic concerns, environmental issues, social and legal needs and concerns on psychological and spiritual levels.

I propose that this is the history one studies when investigating the biblical text. To attempt to understand this ancient history, scholars make the effort to enter the world it represents. It is hoped that such scholarship is as free from preconceptions as can be humanly possible. Recognizing the inherent difficulty in that attempt, we recognize that preconceptions will exist within the stories being studied as well.

Nevertheless, it is possible to read beneath the presuppositions, especially when dealing with *geographical* concerns. Clarifying analogies may be helpful at this juncture. Consider two early 19th century histories relating the story of the American War for Independence, both written by Americans. One source is pro-British, the other pro-United States. Both stories may relate clearly different perspectives on the events of the war, their causes and motivations, examples of heroism and treachery, stories of trust and betrayal. Given all the presuppositions, given the political, religious and social agendas that would obviously be evident within the stories, at least one underlying consistency would be evident within both sources. That is, the battles at Lexington and Concord would not be described as having taken place in the Carolinas; New York will be located consistently in both histories; the Potomac River will not be portrayed as flowing through Maine.

Furthermore, unless a community, city or state is later relocated, future historians and/or storytellers will maintain the consistency in their own geographical representations of the period. The events may be altered to fit a particular bias, but the geography will remain fixed.

This is also to be expected with writers of fiction. Middle Earth, as described by Tolkien, would make no sense if Hobbiton were located in Eriador in *The Fellowship of the Ring*, inexplicably shifted to the Sea of Rhûn in *The Two Towers*, and just as inexplicably moved to Mordor in *The Return of the King*. No reader would be able to comprehend the flow of the story in such a case. It is also true that when future authors critique and discuss the writings of Tolkien they will describe the geography of Middle Earth with the accuracy of the original.

The same may be true for the exodus narrative. Whether or not the story is historically accurate, it permeates the biblical text. Generation after generation of authors related the story in oral and written form. The sites visited by the Israelite ancestors were described on various occasions and in various contexts. Those who wrote, edited and amplified the story maintained the tradition that the Israelites moved from Egypt through the wilderness to Canaan. The locales they describe as itinerary sites must be included therefore within the geographical perspective of their understanding of the route taken. If the sites were not relocated, then whenever these sites are mentioned in the biblical text, in relationship to other locales (in any context), we should have a consistent literary representation of where these sites were located.

Hence this study represents a literary based historical-geography, attempting to determine if the various biblical sources, vis à vis the exodus from Egypt, present a consistent geographical picture of their region within the literature of the Hebrew Bible. As will have appeared obvious from the preceding discussion, I assume a certain consistency in geographical memory, perception and/or experience on the part of the biblical authors. This assumption, however, is not necessarily absolute. The purpose of much of this investigation is to study whether or not the *map* of the biblical geography is consistent with itself. It may be that the authors place a particular site in strikingly different locales so that it is not possible even to conceive just where they thought the site was located. If this phenomenon recurs often with numerous sites, then the assumption of *geographical consistency* will be proven inadequate.

Another assumption tested within this investigation is that the biblical geography will consistently fit (when it can be determined) within the boundary of contemporary geographical knowledge. Again, this is not an absolute assumption, but should be evident as a result of analyzing the textual data. The comparison between the biblical geography and that of the ancient geographers studied here will often divide between two extremes. First is the "real" portrayal of the region by the ancient geographers. My assumption is that this geographical picture forms the underlying foundation of the geography within which the biblical authors wrote.

Second is what I will refer to as "canonical." This is a specific reference to the particular understanding that the exodus proceeded out of Egypt proper. Admittedly, a 21st century canonical portrayal of the exodus is that the ancient Israelites came out of the Nile Delta region of Egypt, crossed a body of water (either the Gulf of Suez or some locale to the north), fled from Egypt into the wilderness using one of several routes, came to Mt. Sinai and eventually settled at Kadesh-barnea for a number of years.

When studying the earliest prophets, however, it is clear that in the 8th century B.C.E., Amos, Hosea, Micah and Isaiah presented a certain conception of the exodus. These texts represent the earliest, non-pentateuchal sources that describe the exodus, but they make infrequent reference to the exodus itself (Amos 3:1; 9:7; Hos 2:15; 11:1; 12:9, 13; 13:4; Mic 6:2–4; Isa 11:16) and mention the slavery in Egypt only once (Mic 6:4). There are no references to any miracles or conflict between YHWH and Pharaoh, no establishment of a Passover ritual nor crossing of any body of water. Isolating these prophets, all we may say is that the "exodus" refers to the Israelites coming forth out of the land of Egypt.

This presupposition, that Egypt was the source of the exodus, is what I refer to as the "canonical perspective." A single example of its effect can be seen in the acknowledged introduction by the Septuagint translators of the identification of the Gulf of Suez (or some body of water in the western Sinai Peninsula) as the "Red Sea" (see Chapter Three, pp. 58–61). As these translators accepted the canonical perspective they were "forced" therefore to view the sea crossing as occurring near the origin of the Israelites' exodus, i.e., somewhere west of the Sinai Peninsula.

Related to the existence of these presuppositions is a specific geographic focus of this investigation. As will be evident, much emphasis is placed upon the location of the itinerary sites prior to Sinai and Kadesh-barnea. It is these sites concerning which much archaeological/textual argument and controversy occurs. As will be shown, the biblical sources consistently identify these locations as situated in the eastern Sinai Peninsula. This bears tremendous influence on locating the origins of the exodus away from the Nile Delta.

It is also important to recognize the role played by the sources in consistently locating the remaining majority of itinerary and non-itinerary sites (see Summary and Conclusions, pp. 189–93). The conclusion may be drawn that if the textual sources are consistent in situating the non-"Egypt-to-Sinai" sites, then the consistency they show in situating the "Egypt-to-Sinai" sites is strengthened. This geographic credibility will itself lend plausible support to the exodus site-map I derive. Thus, the presentation of all itinerary sites is vital to gain an understanding of the location of those that are perhaps the most important.

CHAPTER ONE

SETTING THE STAGE: EXODUS HISTORICITY, MYTHOLOGY AND PRESUPPOSITIONS

The story of the exodus is wonderfully poignant and inspirational. The ancient Israelites, achieving prominence in Egyptian society through their ancestor Joseph, fall victim to the maniacal whims of a paranoid pharaoh. They are brutally enslaved, forced to work at hard labor for many years and persecuted by this unnamed pharaoh and his son. And yet, YHWH hears their cry, defeats Pharaoh with the assistance of the human Moses, and redeems His people, Israel, with wonders and might. Moses leads them out from Egypt, stopping at numerous sites along the way. He eventually brings them to the eastern bank of the Jordan River and Dead Sea, many years later.

The exodus from Egypt is unknown to history save what is written in the Hebrew Bible. Outside of the most meager of circumstantial evidence we possess nothing to substantiate the text.[1] And yet, this story gradually evolved to become the national origin myth of ancient Israel (and eventually Judah as well). It permeates the biblical text, from mirrored patriarchal journeys to Egypt and back (Gen 12:10–13:1), to ethics of interpersonal behavior (Lev 19:34), to notions defining the right of humans to rest one day in the week (Deut 5:12–15), to justifications for the relationship between Israel and its God (Exod 20:2), etc.

Prior to the rapid advancements in the archaeological methods witnessed during the last century, the biblical tale of divine intervention and marked progress from Egypt through Moab, one site at a time, was generally accepted as historical reality. Archaeological research has tended to chip

away the mythological underpinnings of the story. On the other hand, as proposed by B. Batto and others, perhaps the effect has been to render the
mythological motifs more prominently visible and perceptible.[2] Scholars
have recognized the absolute importance and prominence of the exodus
within ancient Israel's history. They have struggled to explain the story's
origins, from the descent into slavery to the flight from Egypt, to the wandering in the wilderness, to the conquest and settlement of Canaan.

Historical-geographers have attempted to identify the exodus itinerary
sites with known, archaeological discoveries. This is true for all the itinerary
sites, but much discussion and posturing takes place concerning the sites
early in the travels, those located in or near Egypt. Many scholars define
their opinions concerning the historicity of the exodus based upon an acceptance or rejection of a particular proposed identification of Rameses, Pithom,
Migdol, Baal-zephon or Succoth, for example.

Often, the same material and textual evidence is viewed differently due
to the existence of underlying presuppositions and opinions. These biases
exist for modern scholars as well as for the ancient sources. They must be
overcome in order to gain a clearer understanding of the historicity and
origin of the exodus.

SUPPORTERS OF HISTORICITY

As noted above, the textual evidence is often used in concert with
archaeological evidence either to support or oppose exodus historicity. This
is certainly the case with the two songs considered amongst the oldest texts
in the Hebrew Bible: the Song of Deborah (Judges 5) and the Song of the
Sea (also referred to as the Song of Moses/Miriam—Exod 15:1–21).

Song of Deborah

Considered to be old and accurate, as supported by W. F. Albright and
D. N. Freedman, this song mentions the presence of Israelite tribes in the
land of Canaan.[3] Thus the early occupation of Canaan by the Israelites is
supported.

Albright's position regarding the Song of Deborah is based in his analysis of the poem's form. He perceives the poem as being old and accurate.

The metrical analysis indicates a regular and "rather elaborate" style, charac-
teristic of "pure Semitic verse."[4] It does not resemble the later Hebrew verse
forms that are related in form to the late Assyrian and Babylonian poetry.

Because the Song of Deborah mentions the presence of Israel within
Canaan at such an early period, Albright believes that the conquest and
occupation of Canaan could not have been too recent an event vis à vis the
song's composition.[5] Through an analysis of the building of Rameses and
Pithom, a critique of Exod 12:40–41 (430 years of slavery), and his analysis
of the Hyksos era (all discussed below) he concludes that the exodus
occurred around 1262–1260 B.C.E.[6]

Freedman also dates the Song of Deborah early, between 1200–900
B.C.E.[7] In comparison with the Song of the Sea, Freedman wrote:

> Even though the march from the south is not directly related to the battle at the
> Kishon river, it forms a necessary part of the story of the Conquest, and serves also
> as the link between the Exodus and Wanderings on the one hand, and the Wander-
> ings and the Conquest on the other. The sequence of events is closely knit, and
> while the poems emphasize only the most important occurrences, there are no sig-
> nificant gaps, from the beginning with the Exodus from Egypt until the final dis-
> placement of the Canaanites.[8]

Understanding the exodus to have played an integral role in the events
leading up to the composition of the song, Freedman was able to fine-tune
his dating of the events:

> According to the chronology...not more than one or two generations were involved,
> perhaps only forty to sixty years. If the Exodus and initial settlement in the south are
> to be dated around 1200 or shortly thereafter, then the march from the sacred
> mountain north should be placed in the second quarter of the same century....[9]

He then dates the Song of the Sea to around 1175 B.C.E. and the Song of
Deborah to about 1125 B.C.E.

Critique. I accept the antiquity of the Song of Deborah, within the range initially suggested by Freedman, i.e., 1200–900 B.C.E. The song would also
appear to suggest the presence of Israel within Canaan. As I will discuss

later, it would seem apparent that these early Israelite "tribes" also dwell within the Negeb and perhaps farther south. The song also describes a movement of forces from the south toward the north.

Nevertheless, the Song of Deborah mentions nothing about an exodus from Egypt. Nor does the text say anything concerning Moses, nor a war waged between YHWH and Pharaoh. In short, the song does not describe how Israel arrived inside the land of Canaan. Given no biblical account of an exodus, such an event could not be concluded, or even inferred, from the text in Judges.

Merneptah Stele

We may then take into account the evidence provided by the Merneptah Stele. Erected in the late 13th century B.C.E., the stele provides direct archaeological support for the early presence of Israelites in Canaan. It is also the earliest extrabiblical text to mention Israel. Pharaoh Merneptah was the son of Rameses II. Sometime during the last decade of the 13th century he led a military campaign into Canaan. In the stele that describes his activities there is a reference that claims the destruction of an unsettled people, Israel. The Israelites are depicted in the stele with the use of a determinative that identifies them as a people without any fortified city, living in open country. The implication is that they have only recently entered the land. The only indication that supports an Israelite "unsettled" period is that of the biblical description of the conquest and settlement under Joshua's leadership.

As suggested by G. A. Rendsburg, the stele provides a large part of the "sufficient evidence on the Egyptological side to substantiate the basic picture portrayed in the book of Exodus."[10] Quoting R. Giveon, Rendsburg states what has become a recurring litany: "We therefore believe that the Exodus was an historical event, although there is little to prove it outside the literary tradition of the Bible."[11]

The Egyptological evidence also provides support for A. Malamat in his acceptance of exodus historicity.[12] Although he recognizes the indirectness of the evidence ("...none of the Egyptian sources substantiate the story of the Exodus."),[13] there is sufficient evidence to support acceptance of the story. The presence of Hapiru slaves in Egypt, the building of Pi-Rameses (assumed to be the same as the store city of Exod 1:11), the Merneptah Stele and the presence of an Egyptian road along the northern coast of the Sinai Peninsula ("Way of Horus") are all accepted to prove historicity. There is adequate information to substantiate a kernel of historicity in the sojourn and enslavement in Egypt as well as the exodus flight and later conquest of Canaan.[14]

Critique. The evidence provided by the Merneptah Stele, as well as other Egyptian written sources mentioning Semitic slaves, may be countered in the same manner as with the Song of Deborah. First, Semitic slaves are known to have worked within Egypt. Some may even have escaped at some time. To claim the origin of the exodus tradition within this hypothetical situation is to jump to an unjustified conclusion.

Second, as the Merneptah Stele mentions Israel, it nevertheless does not mention how Israel arrived in Canaan. Admittedly, that is neither the intent nor the concern of the stele's author. At the same time, neither can the stele be utilized to conclude an exodus *from* Egypt. All that may be concluded from the Merneptah Stele is that Israel was present in Canaan at the end of the 13th century B.C.E.

Years of Slavery

Continuing with the blending of archaeology and the biblical account, the conversation has often turned to a discussion regarding the length of the slavery. The Hebrew Bible refers to this period in Exod 12:40–41:

ומושב בני ישראל אשר ישבו במצרים שלשים שנה וארבע מאות שנה ויהי מקץ שלשים שנה וארבע מאות שנה בעצם היום הזה...

[The amount of time that the children of Israel dwelled in Egypt was 430 years. And, at the end of 430 years, at the very day...]

Albright sees in this reference an accurate rendering of the years between the Hyksos era and an exodus that preceded the date of the Merneptah Stele. As this number is not rounded, it therefore is accurate.[15] It also represents an Egyptian era of some kind as the Hebrews did not keep accurate records. This, itself, was due to the fact that they were "most of the time in a condition of serfdom."[16] Albright understands the Hyksos era to be the source of the Bible's patriarchal stories.[17] Utilizing that period as the introduction of Israel's ancestors into Egypt, he calculates the beginning of the slavery. As discussed below, Albright dates the Hyksos from 1692–1580 B.C.E. Subtracting the 430 years of Exod 12:40–41 gives 1262 B.C.E. as a reasonable date for the exodus.

Critique. The number of years in Egypt, 430, is interesting. Albright is not concerned that the Hyksos left Egypt in 1580 B.C.E. If Albright is correct that the Hyksos represent the patriarchal stories of the book of Genesis, then the Israelite stay in Egypt had to have ended with the expulsion of the Hyksos. Thus, the date of the exodus can be no later than 1580 B.C.E.[18] The use of 430 is convenient, but perhaps the intent of the number is otherwise.

It has been observed that the biblical authors have, on occasion, made use of mathematics in seemingly unorthodox ways.[19] This is not a concern with *gematria* and its assigning of numerical value to letters in a particular word. It is rather the recognition of a possible familiarity with and use of mathematics in composing certain stories within the Hebrew Bible. It is not known whether the authors intend anything beyond mere punning (if even that). Perhaps they are only playing elaborate mathematical games within their writing. Then again, perhaps they are conveying some deeper connectedness that we no longer perceive. In any case, the phenomenon exists.

Is it possible that the same phenomenon is occurring with the 430 years of the Egyptian sojourn and slavery? S. Gevirtz notes the possible pattern involved with the number of Abraham's household retainers in Gen 14:14. The text claims a total of 318 accompanied Abraham as a rescue party. Gevirtz suggests that the origin of 318 was a manipulation of prime numbers. He suggests, specifically, the sum of the primes from 7 to 7^2 ($7+11+13+17+19+23+29+31+37+41+43+47=318$). Taking a clue from Gevirtz, I would suggest we add the next two primes, 53 and 59. The sum in this instance is 430. Where 318 is the sum of 12 primes between 7 and 7^2, 430 is the sum of the 14 (twice 7) primes counting from 7.

Now, this proposal may certainly be a misinterpretation of authorial intent, but the phenomenon does exist. Likewise, the 430 years of residence may be an accurate number, but the process of attaching it to the Hyksos era involves assumptions and conclusions about that era, and the era of Rameses II, which are tenuous and extremely difficult to support.

Moreover, it is worth noting that a careful reading of Exodus 1–2 reveals a slavery that lasted through two generations. There is no indication as to how long the family of Jacob resided in Egypt prior to the slavery. Nevertheless, the "Pharaoh who knew not Joseph" imposes the slavery. He also commands that the male babies be thrown into the Nile River. It is into this fearful setting that Moses is born and placed into a basket on the same threatening river. He flees from this same pharaoh who seeks his life, returning to free the Israelites only following this pharaoh's death. The exodus occurs within the second generation of slavery.

Song of the Sea

As discussed by F. M. Cross and Freedman,[20] the motifs present in this song are common for the Late Bronze Age. Cross counters the concerns of N. H. Snaith and Batto (presented below) that this song is heavily influenced by mythological images. In fact, he dates the poem utilizing a rather exhaustive method involving the following:

- typology of its language
- typology of its prosody
- orthographic analysis
- typology of the development of Israel's religion
- history of tradition
- historical allusions[21]

Through this analysis, he and Freedman date the poem to the 10th century B.C.E. at the latest.[22] They view the poem as a single, unified composition, into which "insertions and expansions would certainly mar the meter and strophic pattern."[23] In their opinion, this song is the oldest of the extant sources describing the exodus from Egypt. It is earlier than the surrounding parallel prose narrative.[24]

As one of the earliest biblical texts, it is based within historical events:

Behind the poem is the flight from Egypt, here barely touched on by the enemy in his speech in which he boasts that he will overtake, put to the sword, and plunder the people.[25]

With such a foundation forming its core, the Song of the Sea does not contain a mythologically derived conflict. It may utilize mythological concepts and images, but it is not an example of the historicizing of myth.[26] Therefore, the events it describes have their basis in a historical exodus from Egypt.

> According to the poet, the effect of the victory was not limited to Egypt, but extended to overwhelm the other neighboring and interested states: Philistia, Edom, Moab, and Canaan. Paralyzed by fear at the awesome display of Yahweh's power against the most powerful nation in that part of the world....[27]

Thus, even without direct archaeological evidence, the imagery and motifs of this text support a conflict with Egypt and flight from Pharaoh's oppression.

Critique. In keeping with the entire exodus narrative, the pharaoh is not named within the Song of the Sea. It is interesting, however, that within this song, Egypt is not named either. The nations of Philistia, Edom, Moab and Canaan are indeed prominently featured. It is curious that the leaders and inhabitants of these four countries are portrayed as cowering in fear while the country that has just been vanquished, Egypt, is not discussed. Although Egypt is mentioned more than one hundred times in the book of Exodus, the term never occurs in the Song of the Sea. It is true that Pharaoh is cursorily mentioned, but he is never identified in the Hebrew Bible as Egypt.[28] Egypt is not in this song because the focus of the author is not toward Egypt. The *locus* of the author appears to be closer to the four nations that *are* mentioned: the author's geographical perspective, and the story's location, is east of the Sinai Peninsula.

The presentations of Cross and Freedman depend heavily upon the historical allusions present in the song. They use these allusions to assist in deriving an appropriate date of composition. I would concur that the poem is to be dated with a *terminus ad quem* of the 10th century. There is, nevertheless, a cultural allusion noted by A. Bender that applies to Exod 15:4b:[29]

ומבחר שלשיו טבעו בים סוף

[...and the choice of his chariot riders sank in Yam Sûp.]

I accept that here, and in Exod 14:7, the correct translation of שׁלשׁ is as some reference to the soldiers riding the chariots. The context of each verse would appear to demand that understanding. Bender proposed that this designation, understood as the riders in Pharaoh's chariots, could not be a reference to Egyptian chariots, which carried two people. As evidenced in the Egyptian inscriptions portraying the battle of Kadesh (1286/1285 B.C.E.) the Levantine chariots carried three people.[30] Thus, the reference in this early poem to chariot riders does not refer to Egyptian chariots.

It is evident that the Song of the Sea refers to a flight from an agressive, pursuing enemy. It tells of a sea crossing at Yam Sûp (used interchangeably with ים סוף throughout this text), events strongly associated with the exodus from Egypt. Considered in isolation, however, it implies no more than a flight from "Pharaoh." Any battle could be described in the song. There is no evidence within the song that would support a flight from Egyptian slavery.

The Story Itself

With a recognition that direct archaeological evidence does not exist, supporters often turn to the exodus narrative itself for reinforcing its own historicity. Scholars such as Albright and R. Cohen have recounted the assumed scribal accuracy and pure conscientiousness in preserving this tale.

Albright maintains that there is an historical core present in the exodus story. Even with the tendency for myths to gather around every hero, this core is still visible.[31] In fact, this material would also have been passed on accurately, whether received in oral or written form. This conscientiousness was the result of a sacred fear that motivated the telling and retelling of the account:[32]

> Their undeveloped ideas of intellectual honesty were aided by an exaggerated notion of the sacredness of the material which they gathered and copied, and the fear of violating some tabu by inaccuracy. Being human they made mistakes and erroneous combinations, but we may safely credit them with a point of view similar to that exhibited by Egyptian and Mesopotamian scribes, whose praiseworthy respect for accuracy we are coming more and more to esteem.

This accurate accounting for history and conditions was so prevalent and strictly maintained that Cohen even proposes a 3rd millennium date for the exodus and settlement in Canaan. He bases his position on the settlement picture from the Central Negeb. As he states, the Central Negeb "offered striking parallels to the descriptions of the Israelite presence in this area as presented in the Old Testament tradition of the Exodus and Conquest."[33]

These comments, taken in consideration of the overall awe in which the story is held, lead to the impressions expressed by many scholars that the story is simply undoubtable. As stated by Albright, "...there *must* (italics mine) have been an early saga of the Exodus...."[34] And, reiterating the affirmation that there is no direct witness in Egyptian records regarding Israel's presence there, J. Bright comments nonetheless, "...the Biblical tradition *a priori* demands belief."[35] He refuses to accept any interpretation that the story could have been invented.

This level of acceptance has also been affirmed by N. Gottwald (as he is also quoted by Rendsburg): "There is an indeterminate measure of historical plausibility in the biblical report that Israelites migrated from Egypt to Canaan."[36]

Critique. No one can deny the importance of the exodus within the biblical text and traditions. The story permeates much of the later biblical events and its imagery is even read back into early narratives. Nevertheless, the Hebrew Bible also has a creation account in the first chapter of Genesis, the imagery of which permeates much in biblical poetry and ethics as well as defining the reasons for observing a day of rest. There is also a Genesis account of the Garden of Eden, the underlying interpretation of which permeates much in the Jewish and Christian conceptions of human life and behavior. And yet, it is very difficult to accept either story at face value just because the stories are so vitally impressive.

In any case, such interpretations of the exodus narrative cross over to the realm of belief. This belief may ultimately be supported and justified through textual and archaeological study. At the current time, however, and based as well on scholars' own admissions, there is no support for such an interpretation.

Nevertheless, the influence of this story in the biblical text does demand an explanation. As suggested previously, if we remove the exodus story, all references and allusions to it and all ethics and laws that derive from it, the Bible would indeed be a barren document. How do we explain its prominence in history and text, if indeed the events described never occurred? As is often believed, it simply *must* have evolved from an earlier saga. The clues to unravel this saga are to be found within the initial chapter of Exodus, in particular Exod 1:11:

וישימו עליו שרי מסים למען ענתו בסבלתם ויבן ערי מסכנות לפרעה את פתם ואת רעמסס

[So they placed over him corvée masters in order to oppress him with their slavery. And he built for Pharaoh store cities, Pithom and Rameses.]

Also related to the evidence for historicity are concerns about how the Israelites initially arrived in Egypt. Do these events have any basis in history? Second, can the cities the Bible claims the Israelites built, Pithom and Rameses, be identified archaeologically? Third, can any of the other "Egyptian" archaeological sites be identified?

Entry into Egypt

Aside from the known, frequent presence of Semitic slaves in Egypt, the Hyksos period (early 17th–early 16th centuries B.C.E.) provides scholars with a large Semitic population resident within Egypt. In the 3rd century B.C.E., Manetho described the occupation of Egypt by the Hyksos. In his ancient account, Manetho describes their entrance into Egypt as a fairly brutal invasion. Following their success, the Hyksos established a capital at Avaris, in the Nile Delta. Since Manetho was writing approximately thirteen centuries after the Hyksos invasion, it pays to be cautious concerning his own credibility. As discussed by I. Finkelstein and N. A. Silberman, the Hyksos take-over could have been much more gradual and peaceful.[37] In any case, under the leadership of Pharaoh Ahmose, the Egyptians forcibly drove the Hyksos back through Canaan in the mid-16th century B.C.E.

Albright strongly supports the notion that the biblical account in Num 13:22, which relates that Tanis was built seven years after Hebron, focuses attention on the patriarchal connection to the Hyksos invasion. He also suggests the notion that Avaris, Rameses and Tanis were successive names of the same city. This identification was also supported by Y. Aharoni.[38] Moreover, the identification of Semitic names among the Hyksos (*Ya'qob–har*, *Hur*) proves that Hebrews played an important role in Egypt during the Hyksos era.[39] In fact, Albright is so convinced of Hebrew participation in the Hyksos invasion that he claims that the children of Jacob even played an important role in the Hyksos confederation.[40]

Bright suggests that Exod 1:11 referred to the building of Avaris by the Hyksos.[41] The Israelites who built the city were slaves whose ancestors had come to Egypt with the Hyksos.[42] They were later joined by the remainder of the Israelite group and then enslaved.

Critique. Much is made of the identification of Tanis, Avaris and Rameses as the same site, changing its name through time. Biblical Zoan (Num 13:22; Isa 19:11, 13; 30:4; Ezek 30:14; Ps 78:12, 43) is understood as the Hebrew name of Dja'net, the Egyptian capital of the 21st and 22nd Dynasties (Gk. Tanis). The identification of Zoan (Num 13:22 and Ps 78:12, 43) with Goshen is an interesting pathway of identification and assumption. Assuming that Tanis=Avaris=Rameses, and that Rameses is the store city of Exod 1:11, then Zoan would be that particular store city. Since Ps 78:12, 43 identify the area (i.e., Zoan) where YHWH worked wonders against Egypt, it is also assumed therefore that Zoan is where the Israelites lived prior to the exodus (i.e., Goshen). This linkage is made in order to identify the city of Tanis/Avaris/Rameses with the region of Goshen. The Semitic presence in Goshen thus extends back to the Hyksos era. The Hyksos built Tanis as the original "Israelites." Rameses II followed suit by rebuilding it with Israelite slaves, the descendants of the Hyksos. Therefore, Zoan=Goshen.[43]

There is no identification of Zoan and Goshen in the Hebrew Bible, especially in Psalm 78. The identification of Zoan with Pi-Rameses and Avaris is not valid, as noted by D. B. Redford.[44] Thus, the identification breaks down. Zoan is not the same as Avaris, nor can a convincing argument be made that Zoan is Goshen.

The Hyksos presence in Egypt offers a tempting relationship between the biblical text and archaeological evidence. This attraction is even felt by those who oppose the historicity of the exodus. It is also strengthened through the existence of Semitic names within their population. Nevertheless, beyond these coincidences, there is no direct evidence that would warrant a leap to conclusions that the Semitic names and culture of the Hyksos represent the patriarchs of Israel. It is also an unwarranted assumption that permits the linkage of archaeological sites with the biblical record. Without more direct evidence it will not be possible to identify the Hyksos with an Israelite presence in Egypt, either through direct connection or historical memory.

Pithom and Rameses

It is admitted by those who support the historicity of the exodus that the identification of these two cities is tenuous.[45] Nevertheless, the knowledge of the building activities of the Hyksos, followed by those of Rameses II, led scholars to identify a number of locales for these store cities. G. I. Davies places Rameses at either Qantir or Tanis (San el-Hajar) and seems to identify Succoth and Pithom as both located at Tell el-Maskhuta in the Wadi Tumilat.[46]

C. Houtman, in his later extensive commentary on the book of Exodus, describes the several locations associated with Pithom. He identifies Tanis, Pi-hahiroth, Tell el-Maskhuta, Tell er-Retabe and Heliopolis as considered candidates.[47] In his discussion of Rameses he describes various sites offered as candidates.[48] They include Tell er-Retabe, ancient Pelusium, the Greek Tanis (again, biblical Zoan), the present San el-Hajar and Qantir.[49]

In addition, other sites have been suggested, at times with full awareness that there is no evidence. L. E. Axelsson identifies Shur as located in the Nile Delta, an identification made with no evidence.[50] E. Anati, on the other hand, draws upon the local evidence of drawn images to claim that Har Karkom (located 55 miles NNW of Elath and 25 miles SW of Kadesh-barnea) is indeed Mt. Sinai. In the process, the epigraphic evidence on the plateau forces him to date the exodus back into the 3rd millennium B.C.E., a claim that is resoundingly countered by Finkelstein as well as Davies.[51] Keeping within the Sinai Peninsula, D. Faiman locates Mt. Horeb at the Mitla Pass while W. Wifall identifies Yam Sûp as Shihor (which he translates directly as 'Lake of Horus').[52] Wifall does, however, admit that the identification of the primary sites, such as Baal-zephon, is difficult.[53]

In an early 20th century work, Snaith admitted that the archaeological identifications of Rameses, Succoth, Etham, Pi-hahiroth and Baal-zephon had not been firmly established.[54] Much later in the century, E. D. Oren and Redford were representative of the inability to localize the site identifications.[55] Redford's use of language is quite typical in revealing the tenuousness of this archaeological/biblical concern. He identifies sites for Pithom, Etham and Succoth, and through his use of specific vocabulary ("probably," "gives the appearance," "seems to indicate") reveals the weakness of the geographical connections.

Critique. It is tempting to link the various archaeological sites of the Nile Delta, as well as other locales, with the biblical locations mentioned in the exodus narrative. Those who support the historicity of the exodus do just that. They appear to approach the archaeological evidence with the biblical account presupposed. In other words, the Hebrew Bible tells the story of an enslavement in, and flight from, Egypt. Since the events described occurred in proximity to Egypt, the biblical sites will be found there. Thus, sites discovered primarily within the Nile Delta and the region between the Mediterranean Sea and Gulf of Suez are those that are considered candidates for the biblical sites.

As readily admitted by scholars, many of the sites described in the Hebrew Bible were not in existence during the Late Bronze Age dates traditionally ascribed to the exodus. This chronological conflict, plus the sheer inconclusiveness of site identification in the western Sinai region leads many to reserve judgement concerning the historicity of these events and locales during that era. In fact, "reserving judgement" would be an understatement. Many scholars are as determined in their opposition to exodus historicity as their counterparts discussed above are in their support.

OPPONENTS OF HISTORICITY

Those who oppose the historicity of the exodus do so from a wide range of opinions. From E. Meyer who denied the historicity of biblical texts altogether because of their intermingling of romantic and legendary material, to Finkelstein and Silberman who deny the historicity of the exodus but identify its historical memory during the Hyksos period, the focus tends to be on the lack of archaeological evidence.[56] Nevertheless, there appears to be an almost tacit recognition of the penetration of this story into the life of ancient Israel. In other words, even if it is not historically accurate, it had to originate somewhere.

The Hyksos and the Exile

The answer to that concern tends to focus on two historical poles, the Hyksos presence in Egypt and the exilic population that moved there from Judah following the events of 586 B.C.E. N. P. Lemche has, in fact, combined the two.[57] He recognizes that no historical kernel for the exodus can be placed within any specific period. Yet, at the same time, he identifies the extrabiblical parallels to the Joseph story evident within the Hyksos accounts. The Hyksos may serve as the source of much of the Egypt-related biblical material. Nevertheless, in reference to Manetho's account, "only a Hellenistic history of Egypt dating from the third century B.C.E. mentions such invasions."[58] Thus, the historical reliability of the Hyksos account is seriously questioned with a recognition that "certain elements in the Joseph saga cannot be proven to be older than the Persian period."[59]

Recognizing, once again, that there is no archaeological evidence to support a Late Bronze Age exodus, Redford and H. Cazelles draw upon the Hyksos memory as the source for the exodus narrative.[60] It is interesting that Cazelles recognizes the difficulty in portraying Yam Sûp strictly within the context of the Gulf of Suez. He proposes that there may have been a second slavery, this one located south of Canaan. This would take into consideration the divided understanding of the "Red Sea" introduced by the Septuagint (see Chapter Three, pp. 58–61).

Redford, in particular, identifies the post-exilic period as that time during which the story was composed. His archaeological analysis has indicated a common insecurity in identifying the initial exodus itinerary sites.[61] A number of the sites he identifies existed only as early as the 7th–5th centuries B.C.E. He believes the narrative points to the Saite or Persian period as the time of its origin. Therefore, the authors drew on the contemporary toponomy for their itinerary locations. In order not to identify the entire story as a fabrication, Redford proposes that a reminiscence of a "chain of historical events" formed the underlying narrative. That reminiscence was the vague recollection of "the Hyksos descent into and occupation of Egypt."[62]

Also relying heavily on the lack of archaeological evidence, scholars point to the inconclusiveness in the identification of Pithom and Rameses, as well as other locations. Although he identified Pithom as Tell Maskhuta, F. M.-J. Lagrange was able to situate neither Rameses nor Succoth.[63] A. Alt points to the weakness in the identification of Avaris with Tanis,[64] while A. Perevolotsky and Finkelstein note that all the archaeological activity in the Sinai Peninsula has contributed almost nothing to the understanding of the exodus.[65] J. Van Seters also adds to the discussion by noting that Pithom was not built in Egypt until around 600 B.C.E., which makes Exodus 1 an exilic text, at the earliest.[66] J. K. Hoffmeier also thoroughly details the difficulties inherent in identifying the sites of Rameses, Pithom and even Goshen.[67]

Critique. In many ways the objections to those who oppose exodus historicity are similar to the criticism of those who support historicity. To these opponents, the very same evidence from archaeology is held up to a more critical lens when compared to the biblical account. In their comparison of archaeological evidence as against the biblical text, the Bible occupies a lower level of priority vis à vis historicity. Nevertheless, even the opponents rely on the biblical account to a certain extent. They recognize the importance and centrality of the exodus narrative in ancient Israel's history. Thus they focus on the Egyptian motif of the story. As a result, they are locked in to determining some historical event that involves Egypt. Further, this precondition forces them to rationalize events to the post-exilic period (when Jews were returning from Egypt to Judah) or to some vague and nebulous recollection of an event that happened centuries before even the biblical tradition identified the exodus events. As with the supporters of historicity, there had to be some foundation, some kernel, to the entire story.

This "locked in" dilemma is clearly reflected by Finkelstein and Silberman. While hesitating to identify an exodus event, other than the historical memory of the Hyksos occupation, they support the notion that the Josianic history is to be considered the source for most of the layering onto an original narrative. Then they hesitate:

> The saga of Israel's Exodus from Egypt is neither historical truth nor literary fiction.
> It is a powerful expression of memory and hope born in a world in the midst of

change. The confrontation between Moses and pharaoh mirrored the momentous confrontation between the young King Josiah and the newly crowned Pharaoh Necho. To pin this biblical image down to a single date is to betray the story's deepest meaning. Passover proves to be not a single event but a continuing experience of national resistance against the powers that be.[68]

It may be noticed that there are two common threads that weave their way throughout the scholarship of both supporters and opponents of exodus historicity. These threads represent two geographical presuppositions. The first is that the exodus narrative has its origins in an event associated with Egypt, what I call the Egypt Presupposition. Regardless of the seeming absurdity in such a statement, the thread is present. The second thread I call the Red Sea Presupposition. This assumes that both the Gulfs of Elath and Suez are extensions, an eastern and western arm, respectively, of the Red Sea. Hence, Yam Sûp, as the Red Sea (from the Septuagint: see Chapter Three) may be understood as either gulf.[69] Both threads are evident and play a role in the conclusions drawn by scholars. Note also that the term "Gulf of Elath" is used throughout this text, rather than "Gulf of Aqaba." As will be evident from the geographical material presented in Chapter Two, the common, ancient name for this body of water was the "Aelanite(s) or Laeanites Gulf." This name was derived from the city of Elath, and is the identification used here (see Chapter Two, pp. 41, 240 n. 14).

These presuppositions are represented pictorially within Map 1. The exodus itinerary sites are situated in relationship to fixed locales (see Chapter Four, p. 81), compiled from various scholars.[70] The representation in Map 1 is that of the exodus sites as understood within the traditional perspective of an exodus from Egypt proper.

MYTHOLOGY AND ITINERARIES

Prior to indicating the examples of these presuppositions, it is importantto discuss the influential works of two scholars, B. F. Batto and G. I. Davies.[71]

B. F. Batto

In his work, *Slaying the Dragon*, Batto draws upon his own prior work as well as the earlier ideas of Snaith in reference to Yam Sûp.[72] In particular,

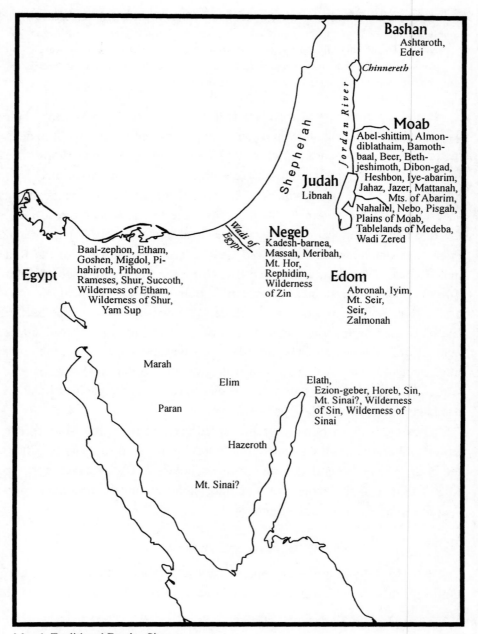

Bashan
Ashtaroth,
Edrei

Chinnereth

Moab
Abel-shittim, Almon-
diblathaim, Bamoth-
baal, Beer, Beth-
jeshimoth, Dibon-gad,
Heshbon, Iye-abarim,
Jahaz, Jazer, Mattanah,
Mts. of Abarim,
Nahaliel, Nebo, Pisgah,
Plains of Moab,
Tablelands of Medeba,
Wadi Zered

Shephelah

Jordan River

Judah
Libnah

Negeb
Kadesh-barnea,
Massah, Meribah,
Mt. Hor,
Rephidim,
Wilderness
of Zin

Wadi of Egypt

Baal-zephon, Etham,
Goshen, Migdol, Pi-
hahiroth, Pithom,
Rameses, Shur, Succoth,
Wilderness of Etham,
Wilderness of Shur,
Yam Sup

Egypt

Edom
Abronah, Iyim,
Mt. Seir,
Seir,
Zalmonah

Marah

Elim

Paran

Elath,
Ezion-geber, Horeb, Sin,
Mt. Sinai?, Wilderness
of Sin, Wilderness of
Sinai

Hazeroth

Mt. Sinai?

Map 1. Traditional Exodus Sites

his focus is on the Song of the Sea. As is the case with other scholars, Batto recognizes the fundamental importance and centrality of the exodus narrative. With M. Noth, he accepts the story as a "primary confession of Israel."[73] At the same time he also recognizes and details the mythic proportion that the story has achieved through time. Thus, he asks, "is the exodus narrative primarily historical memory or is it myth?"[74]

Batto also considers the possibility that the Song of the Sea may date from the 10th century B.C.E., suggesting that the reference to Zion as YHWH's mountain of abode would not be valid prior to the 10th century. His primary focus, however, is in the identification of Yam Sûp. He believes, as have others, that identifying it as "Reed Sea" is imaginative, but incorrect. Batto maintains that with "Yam Sûp" the Bible always refers to the Red Sea and/or one of its extensions to the Gulfs of Suez or Elath, or to the south and the waters that surround the Arabian Peninsula.[75]

Yam Sûp is described as the sea that the Israelites understood as that at the end of the world. Batto would read Yam Sôp instead of Yam Sûp, and thus "the sea of End/Extinction."[76] With the mythic imagery that is present within the Song of the Sea, he portrays the song as primarily a battle between YHWH and Pharaoh that is symbolic of the cosmic wars against chaos.[77] Essentially, no matter what the historical core may have been, the Priestly Writer has rewritten the story in mythic proportions, modeled it on the cosmic creation myths of Genesis and the ancient Near East, and presented a creation myth of the people Israel.[78]

Through this traditional mythical language the poet expressed the belief that the emergence of Israel as a people during the exodus was due to a creative act by YHWH equal to that of the original creation of the cosmos itself. The Egyptians, the evil force that threatens the existence of this new creation, are appropriately cast into the sea to perish. A more powerful symbol for Egypt/Pharaoh as the chaos dragon could scarcely be found than submergence into "the Sea of End/Extinction."[79]

Critique. Foreshadowing the next section, Batto provides evidence of both the Egypt and Red Sea Presuppositions. Even in moving the story to the world of mythos, there apparently still must be a geographical origin within

Egypt as well as the equating of the two gulfs.[80] For the most part, however, Batto removes himself from a decision as to where the historical core of the exodus is to be found. He focuses instead on the overall theme of mythological creation of the people Israel. By the time the later biblical authors receive the story they are in the process of historicizing mythology.[81]

He is not clear, however, why or how the later P author would re-create historical events from a mythological tale that the P author is also creating. It is also evident from the biblical references to seas outside the geographical boundaries of Israel that the ancient Israelite authors were indeed aware of other seas beyond Yam Sûp (see Chapter Four, under ים, pp. 111–12), including the Persian Gulf and the modern Red Sea (perhaps even the Indian Ocean). Thus, to claim that the reference to Yam Sûp could only mean, in the original story, a mythological Sea of Extinction, is reading geographical understandings and perceptions into ancient Israel that were not present.

On the other hand, the mythological images of creation and chaos are present in the Song of the Sea. YHWH does fight the enemy deity Pharaoh.[82] I disagree, however, with Batto's position that the origins of the exodus history are to be found only within the mythological images of the ancient Near East. The story exists as a historical awareness within all of the 8th century prophets, Israelite and Judean. These sources do not surround the story with any mythological images whatsoever. A reasonable conclusion might also be that the P source added the mythology to the history.

It is entirely possible that the historical kernel of the exodus may never be known. It is also possible that the author of the Song of the Sea spoke of a historical event, and then suffused it with mythological images. These images, rather than creating an entirely new story, would render the known story more meaningful and "confessional" to the people whose ancestors (or they, themselves) experienced the events.

G. I. Davies

Davies, on the other hand, as a historical geographer, details the exodus itinerary route. His work is therefore pertinent to the goals of this investigation. He structures his work within a thorough historical review of ancient Jewish, Christian and Arabic interpretations of the itinerary routes. As he states in reference to the Septuagint,

...renderings of itinerary-material which show an interest in geographical interpretations all relate to Egypt or its borders, and serve to locate the starting-point of the
journey, the encampment by 'the sea' and the actual sea that was crossed.[83]

This perception permeates all sources and forms the basis of Davies'
own geographical search. He does recognize, however, the lack of supportive
evidence from extrabiblical sources. He suggests that

...compilation of a continuous itinerary was a late and artificial phenomenon...the
Pentateuch might, and in fact does, contain divergent presentations of...parts of the
route....Moreover, the lack of precise and independent ancient references to most of
the places mentioned in the itineraries remains as much a problem today as it was
for older geographical studies.[84]

With this in mind, Davies approaches the itinerary using as a core the
narrative in Num 33:1–49. He assumes the exodus began in Egypt, somewhere in the eastern Nile Delta.[85] As noted above, he acknowledges the difficulties inherent in physically identifying the earliest sites, such as Rameses,
Succoth, Migdol, etc. In keeping with other scholars as well, he identifies
Yam Sûp as referring to either the Gulf of Suez or to the Gulf of Elath. In
this instance, however, in reference to the sea of the crossing, he identifies
the Gulf of Suez as the likely candidate.[86]

Critique. Davies presents a very thorough review and analysis of the
historical-geography regarding the exodus itineraries. All the same, the
assumption that "all roads lead to Egypt" is not necessarily a path with a
resolution at the end. He readily admits that the archaeological data provide
unsure links with the biblical sites. He notes that, "...a century and more of
exploration has been unable to discover more than a handful of plausible
equivalents for names in the itineraries...."[87]

Thus, my critique of Davies' work is similar to those I have made of the
previous scholars. In consideration of the inadequacies inherent in the results
of archaeological discoveries, the textual mosaic of different sources con-
tributing material at different eras, the dependence upon a geographical perspective created by the Septuagint and later texts, how can a scholar hope to
determine a route and direction of the exodus? Again, the assumption that

the origins of the exodus *must* be in Egypt invariably locks one into a presupposition that the sea crossing also *must* have taken place at or near the Gulf of Suez. This reflects an accepted, received (and canonical) understanding that is not supportable within the Hebrew Bible (see Chapter Four, under ים סוף, pp. 98–106).

PRESUPPOSITIONS

As revealed in his work, Davies manifests the Egypt and Red Sea Presuppositions.[88] Is concern about these presuppositions warranted? Is the exodus tradition so foundational within ancient Israel that consideration of a flight from anywhere *other* than Egypt is inconceivable? Before proceeding to these questions it is worthwhile to describe the existence of these presuppositions within scholarship. It matters not whether a scholar is aligned as a conservative or liberal, a maximalist or minimalist. All relevant scholars studied for this investigation assume the exodus (or its tradition or source) to have its origin within Egypt.[89] Those concerned with the identity of Yam Sûp locate the sea in the western Sinai peninsula.

The evidence crosses time boundaries as well. The presuppositions exist within the most recent literature, e.g., Finkelstein and Silberman, who, though denying the historicity of the exodus, still agree with Redford that a memory of the Hyksos occupation of Egypt serves as the geographical source for the narrative.[90] Egypt and the Red Sea are presupposed within earlier literature of the 20th century as well. Albright suggests that not only did the Hyksos provide the memory for the exodus, but their occupation provided the specific population that would be enslaved and later flee. The Egypt Presupposition may even be found in one of the earliest references studied, that of Strabo (early 1st century C.E.). In his Geography (16.2.35) he identifies Moses as an Egyptian priest holding part of Lower Egypt. As a result of his dissatisfaction with theological expressions there, Moses led a flight from Egypt.

οὕτω δ' ὄντων μιγάδων, ἡ κρατοῦσα μάλιστα φήμη τῶν περὶ τὸ ἱερὸν τὸ ἐν τοῖς Ἱεροσολύμοις πιστευομένων Αἰγυπτίους ἀποφαίνει τοὺς προγόνους τῶν νῦν Ἰουδαίων λεγομένων.

[But though the inhabitants are mixed up thus, the most prevalent of the accredited reports in regard to the temple at Jerusalem represents the ancestors of the present Judaeans, as they are called, as Aegyptians.] Geography 16.2.34

Μωσῆς γάρ τις τῶν Αἰγυπτίων ἱερέων, ἔχων τι μέρος τῆςκάτω καλουμένης χώρας, ἀπῆρεν ἐκεῖσε ἐνθένδε, δυσχεράνας τὰ καθεστῶτα, καὶ συνεξῆραν αὐτῷ πολλοὶ τιμῶντες τὸ θεῖον. ἔφη γὰρ ἐκεῖνος καὶ ἐδίδασκεν, ὡς οὐκ ὀρθῶς φρονοῖεν οἱ Αἰγύπτιοι θηρίοις εἰκάζοντες καὶ βοσκήμασι τὸ θεῖον, οὐδ' οἱ Λίβυες· οὐκ εὖ δὲ οὐδ' οἱ Ἕλληνες, ἀνθρωπομόρφους τυποῦντες· εἴη γὰρ ἓν τοῦτο μόνον θεὸς τὸ περιέχον ἡμᾶς ἅπαντας καὶ γῆν καὶ θάλατταν, ὃ καλοῦμεν οὐρανὸν καὶ κόσμον καὶ τὴν τῶν ὄντων φύσιν.

[Moses, namely, was one of the Aegyptian priests, and held a part of Lower Aegypt, as it is called, but he went away from there to Judaea, since he was displeased with the state of affairs there, and was accompanied by many people who worshipped the Divine Being. For he said, and taught, that the Aegyptians were mistaken in representing the Divine Being by the images of beasts and cattle, as were also the Libyans; and that the Greeks were also wrong in modelling gods in human form; for, according to him, God is this one thing alone that encompasses us all and encompasses land and sea—the thing which we call heaven, or universe, or the nature of all that exists.] Geography 16.2.35

Ἐκεῖνος μὲν οὖν τοιαῦτα λέγων ἔπεισεν εὐγνώμονας ἄνδρας οὐκ ὀλίγους καὶ ἀπήγαγεν ἐπὶ τὸν τόπον τοῦτον, ὅπου νῦν ἐστι τὸ ἐν τοῖς Ἱεροσολύμοις κτίσμα.
[Now Moses, saying things of this kind, persuaded not a few thoughtful men and led them away (from Egypt) to this place where the settlement of Jerusalem now is.] Geography 16.2.36

As noted above, both Cazelles and Noth comment on the possibility of two exodus traditions. They recognize the differences between the textual location of Yam Sûp and the traditional sea of crossing, located near the Gulf of Suez or the bodies of water to the north.[91] In addition, researchers have long been aware that the Septuagint is to be held responsible for identifying the Gulf of Suez as Yam Sûp. That may well be the case, but the question arises, what was the general geographical perspective of the people living in the ancient Near East, prior to, during and following the completion of the Septuagint translation?

METHODS AND APPROACH

It is worth investigating the perceived geography of the biblical era. How far back in time is it possible to identify the same two presuppositions? We have seen the evidence of the Exodus Presupposition in the work of Strabo. Is his an isolated case? Can the presuppositions be identified even within the Hebrew Bible, itself? In order to accomplish this, a control of some sort would be most useful. This term is not often applied to biblical studies, but perhaps one can be derived.

First, the Egypt and Red Sea Presuppositions must be eliminated as presuppositions. It is possible that the biblical presentation of the exodus will be determined to have proceeded out of Egypt. It may well be that Yam Sûp is to be identified as one of the bodies of water located in the western Sinai Peninsula or in the region between the Gulf of Suez and the Mediterranean. But neither conclusion may be assumed from the beginning of the investigation.

Second, the exodus narrative does indeed permeate the biblical text. The original form may even be much narrower in scope than the received story. Nevertheless, the *creating* authors either originally perceived a flight from Egypt or from some other place. In addition, later generations of editors and/or redactors maintained and preserved the received tradition of a flight from Egypt.

In any case, it is the initial assumption of this work that the physical geography of the region did not change. It *is* possible that names designating locations of human origin (such as towns) may have changed through time, either due to the relocation of a site or the simple changing of its name. It is also possible that any particular geographical location may be identified by different names during different eras. This investigation will reveal any evidence that such changes have occurred. Nevertheless, the overall physical geography will have remained unaltered.

Third, there is no archaeological support for the exodus outside of the most meager circumstantial evidence. Thus, any attempt to fit biblical itinerary sites into a weak archaeological matrix has been resisted.

Fourth, and finally, the geographical knowledge, presentation and consistency of the biblical authors will be shown. *Their* description of the physical location of what they and we refer to as exodus itinerary sites, as suggested within the Hebrew Bible itself, will be the basis for locating where *the authors* thought these places were located. This is not a study of direction and movement of wandering Israelites under the leadership of Moses. This is, on the other hand, an attempt to situate physically, within the geographical perspective of Hebrew Bible sources, the relative location of particular sites.

The controls offered will be several. First, the geographical framework as described by the region's historians/geographers is detailed. Second, I present the non-geographical texts that originate within the region's religious documents. Third, the attempt is made to neutralize the cultural, religious and political influence of the various biblical sources. Thus, all itinerary site references have been divided into their various sources, according to the models of S. R. Driver, M. Noth and R. Friedman. In this way, any influence is visible, any differences in site location readily apparent. With no variation across the sources in terms of site placement, the hypothesis will be supported (see p. 1).

CHAPTER TWO

THE MORE THINGS CHANGE...: ANCIENT GEOGRAPHERS AND HISTORIANS—NON-SCRIPTURAL SOURCES

As discussed, there is one primary presupposition with which nearly all scholars, commentators and/or translators have approached the topic of the exodus geography. No matter the era, the exodus narrative is consistently described as a movement of a group of people out of the Nile Delta region of Egypt, or, more generally, from the far western region of what we today call the Sinai Peninsula. This pattern may be noted within the ancient sources as well, the earliest investigated being the Septuagint.

Related to the presupposition of Egyptian origins of the exodus is the derived modern interpretation that, in antiquity, the Red Sea was understood as including both the present day gulfs of Suez and Elath (the "western and eastern branches" of the Red Sea): the term ים סוף applies to either gulf. This opinion is exemplified by B. A. Levine in his commentary on Numbers:

> To the authors of the accounts in Exodus 14–17, and to the author/compiler of Numbers 33, it (ים סוף) applied both to the sea of the Gulf of Aqaba, and to the sea lying between east Africa and the Sinai Peninsula, in the Gulf of Suez, and this is its intended location here. (Num 33:10–12)[1]

Both the primary presupposition as well as its derived Red Sea Presupposition must be questioned and ultimately discarded, as the ancient evidence indicates otherwise. The Egypt Presupposition constitutes the bulk of this investigation and is discussed in Chapter One (pp. 28–30). It is vital, however, to understand the geographical context pertaining to the seas/waters of the ancient Near East. For it is through this secondary investigation that the Egypt Presupposition of the Septuagint is also revealed.

The Masoretic Text states that the Israelites encountered יָם סוּף, while the Septuagint places the encounter at Ἐρυθρά θάλασσα, the Red Sea. Are these two bodies of water the same? Was the Gulf of Suez, to the ancient writers, the same as the Red Sea? What was the Red Sea? Was the Gulf of Elath part of the Red Sea? Are we justified in our modern interpretations that the Gulf of Suez can be the referent mentioned as יָם סוּף in the Hebrew text? To these questions, and more, this investigation now turns.

There are five bodies of water that are the focus of concern. Given the presuppositions that exist within our contemporary perceptions of ancient Near Eastern geography, it is important to acknowledge their modern identifying names. The names by which we recognize these waters are names that often derive from ancient times. Nevertheless, a particular ocean, sea or gulf may today bear a name that identified a different body of water in antiquity.

Two examples of this will clarify. First, the "Red Sea" of antiquity described the waters from the northwestern end of the Persian Gulf around the Arabian Peninsula to the northwestern tip of the Gulf of Suez. Within this investigation, the term "Today's Red Sea" designates the sea from the southern tip of the Sinai Peninsula ending at the Bab el Mandeb Straits. Second, the term "Arabian Gulf" is today applied to the Persian Gulf. Ancient authors never identified the Persian Gulf in that manner. Instead, they used "Arabian Gulf" to designate the Gulf of Suez and Today's Red Sea.

Thus, modern terminology describes the five bodies of water as follows:

- Gulf of Elath
- Gulf of Suez
- Today's Red Sea
- Indian Ocean
- Persian Gulf

I now turn to the investigation of the primary sources, from Homer to Ammianus Marcellinus. They will reveal the identifications and locations of the ancient waters, the context within which the exodus narrative was told.

HOMER AND THE BABYLONIANS

These bodies of water were discussed in numerous ancient sources. The earliest sources investigated were the writings of Homer (mid–late 8th century B.C.E.), as well as the Babylonian geographical texts (mid 8th–6th B.C.E.). Although Homer indicates no awareness of the waters south of the Mediterranean Sea,[2] the Babylonian texts view the Lower Sea (*tâmtu šaplītu*) as identical to the Persian Gulf, and the Upper Sea (*tâmtu elītu*) as the Mediterranean.[3]

AESCHYLUS, PINDAR AND ARISTOPHANES

It is evident that Greek oral tradition knows of a Red Sea, perhaps as early as Aeschylus (mid 6th–5th B.C.E.), as a reference is mentioned by Strabo (first half of 1st B.C.E.).[4]

> ὅ τε γὰρ Αἰσχύλος ἐν Προμηθεῖ τῷ λυομένῳ φησὶν οὕτω·
> φοινικόπεδόν τ'ἐρυθρᾶς ἱερὸν χεῦμα θαλάσσης...
> [Aeschylus, in his Prometheus Unbound, speaks thus:
> "The sacred flood of the Red Sea..."] (Geography 1.2.27)

Moreover, within the plays of Pindar[5] (5th B.C.E.) and Aristophanes[6] (late 5th B.C.E.) there exists clear evidence that these authors portrayed knowledge of the Red Sea.

> ἔν τ' Ὠκεανοῦ πελάγεσσι μίγεν πόντῳ τ' ἐρυθρῷ...
> [They came to the expanses of Okeanos, to the Red Sea...]
> (Pindar, Pythian Ode 4 — 251)

> Τη. ὦ δειλακρίων σύ, τῶν κακῶν οἵων ἐρᾷς.
> ἀτὰρ ἔστι γ' ὁποίαν λέγετον εὐδαίμων πόλις
> παρὰ τὴν ἐρυθρὰν θάλατταν.
> [Tereus: You poor little thing, what troubles you yearn for!
>   Well, there is a happy city of the sort you're talking
>   about, beside the Red Sea.]
> (Aristophanes, The Birds — line 145)

HERODOTUS

Herodotus (mid 5th B.C.E.) presents the earliest written description of ancient Near Eastern geography.[7] He describes the Persian Gulf, Indian Ocean, Today's Red Sea and the Gulf of Suez.

Identifying the Persian Gulf

τὸ γὰρ μέσον αὐτῆς ποταμὸς διέργει, τῷ οὔνομα ἐστὶ Εὐφρήτης· ῥέει δὲ ἐξ Ἀρμενίων, ἐὼν μέγας καὶ βαθὺς καὶ ταχύς· ἐξιεῖ δὲ οὗτος ἐς τὴν Ἐρυθρὴν θάλασσαν.

[...for it is cut in half by a river named Euphrates, a wide, deep and swift river, flowing from Armenia and issuing into the Red Sea.] (Book I.180)

Τίγρην, ὃ δὲ παρὰ Ὦπιν πόλιν ῥέων ἐς τὴν Ἐρυθρὴν θάλασσαν ἐκδιδοῖ...
[...the Tigris, which again passes the city of Opis and issues into the Red Sea...] (Book I. 189)

ὃ δὲ ἀναβὰς ἐς Σοῦσα ἀπέκτεινε Σμέρδιν, οἳ μὲν λέγουσι ἐπ' ἄγρην ἐξαγαγόντα, οἳ δὲ ἐς τὴν Ἐρυθρὴν θάλασσαν προαγαγόντα καταποντῶσαι.
[Prexaspes went up to Susa and so did (killed Smerdis); some say that he took Smerdis out a–hunting, others that he brought him to the Red Sea and there drowned him.] (Book III. 30)

Πέρσαι οἰκέουσι κατήκοντες ἐπὶ τὴν νοτίην θάλασσαν τὴν Ἐρυθρὴν καλεομένην...
[The land where the Persians dwell reaches to the southern sea, that sea which is called Red...] (Book IV. 37)

Identifying the Indian Ocean

Αὕτη μέν νυν ἡ ἑτέρη τῶν ἀκτέων, ἡ δὲ δὴ ἑτέρη ἀπὸ Περσέων ἀρξαμένη παρατέταται ἐς τὴν Ἐρυθρὴν θάλασσαν, ἥ τε Περσικὴ καὶ ἀπὸ ταύτης ἐκδεκομένη ἡ Ἀσσυρίη καὶ ἀπὸ Ἀσσυρίης ἡ Ἀραβίη· λήγει δὲ αὕτη, οὐ λήγουσα εἰ μὴ νόμῳ, ἐς τὸν κόλπον τὸν Ἀράβιον, ἐς τὸν Δαρεῖος ἐκ τοῦ Νείλου διώρυχα ἐσήγαγε.
[This is the first peninsula. But the second, beginning with Persia, stretches to the Red Sea, being the Persian land, and next the neighbouring country of Assyria, and after Assyria, Arabia; this peninsula ends (yet not truly but only by common consent) at the Arabian Gulf, whereunto Darius brought a canal from the Nile.] (Book IV. 39)

...τὰ πρὸς ἠῶ τε καὶ ἥλιον ἀνατέλλοντα, ἔνθεν μὲν ἡ Ἐρυθρὴ παρήκει θάλασσα, πρὸς βορέω δὲ ἡ Κασπίη τε θάλασσα...
[...eastward and toward the rising sun, this is bounded on the one hand by the Red Sea, and to the north by the Caspian Sea...] (Book IV. 40)

ὁρμηθέντες ὧν οἱ Φοίνικες ἐκ τῆς Ἐρυθρῆς θαλάσσης ἔπλεον τὴν νοτίην θάλασσαν...
[So the Phoenicians set out from the Red Sea and sailed the southern sea...] (Book IV. 42)

Identifying Today's Red Sea

...αἳ δ' ἐν τῷ Ἀραβίῳ κόλπῳ ἐπὶ τῇ Ἐρυθρῇ θαλάσσῃ...
[...and some in the Arabian Gulf, by the Red Sea coast...] (Book II. 159)

...τοῦ Ἀραβίου κόλπου τοὺς παρὰ τὴν Ἐρυθρὴν θάλασσαν...
[...from the Arabian Gulf and subdued all the dwellers by the Red Sea...] (Book II. 102)

Ἔστι δὲ τῆς Ἀραβίης χώρης, Αἰγύπτου δὲ οὐ πρόσω, κόλπος θαλάσσης ἐσέχων ἐκ τῆς Ἐρυθρῆς καλεομένης θαλάσσης...
[Now in Arabia, not far from Egypt, there is a gulf of the sea entering in from the sea called Red...] (Book II. 11)

Αὕτη μέν νυν ἡ ἑτέρη τῶν ἀκτέων, ἡ δὲ δὴ ἑτέρη ἀπὸ Περσέων ἀρξαμένη παρατέταται ἐς τὴν Ἐρυθρὴν θάλασσαν, ἥ τε Περσικὴ καὶ ἀπὸ ταύτης ἐκδεκομένη ἡ Ἀσσυρίη καὶ ἀπὸ Ἀσσυρίης ἡ Ἀραβίη· λήγει δὲ αὕτη, οὐ λήγουσα εἰ μὴ νόμῳ, ἐς τὸν κόλπον τὸν Ἀράβιον, ἐς τὸν Δαρεῖος ἐκ τοῦ Νείλου διώρυχα ἐσήγαγε.
[This is the first peninsula. But the second, beginning with Persia, stretches to the Red Sea, being the Persian land, and next the neighbouring country of Assyria, and after Assyria, Arabia; this peninsula ends (yet not truly but only by common consent) at the Arabian Gulf, whereunto Darius brought a canal from the Nile.] (Book IV. 39)

Identifying the Gulf of Suez

ὃς τῇ διώρυχι ἐπεχείρησε πρῶτος τῇ ἐς τὴν Ἐρυθρὴν θάλασσαν φερούσῃ...
[It was he who began the making of the canal into the Red Sea...] (Book II. 158)

τῇ δὲ ἐλάχιστον ἐστὶ καὶ συντομώτατον ἐκ τῆς βορηίης θαλάσσης ὑπερβῆναι ἐς τὴν νοτίην καὶ Ἐρυθρὴν τὴν αὐτὴν ταύτην καλεομένην, ἀπὸ τοῦ Κασίου ὄρεος τοῦ οὐρίζοντος Αἴγυπτόν τε καὶ Συρίην, ἀπὸ τούτου εἰσὶ στάδιοι ἀπαρτὶ χίλιοι ἐς τὸν Ἀράβιον κόλπον.
[Now the shortest and most direct passage from the northern to the southern sea or Red Sea is from the Casian promontory, which is the boundary between Egypt and Syria, to the Arabian Gulf, and this is a distance of one thousand furlongs, neither more nor less.] (Book II. 158)

...τὸν δὲ Ἀράβιον, τὸν ἔρχομαι λέξων...εἰ ὧν ἐθελήσει ἐκτρέψαι τὸ ῥέεθρον ὁ
Νεῖλος ἐς τοῦτον τὸν Ἀράβιον κόλπον...
[...and the other, the Arabian Gulf of which I will speak...Now if Nile choose to
turn his waters into this Arabian Gulf...] (Book II. 11)

ὃς ἐπείτε τὴν διώρυχα ἐπαύσατο ὀρύσσων τὴν ἐκ τοῦ Νείλου διέχουσαν ἐς τὸν
Ἀράβιον κόλπον...
[He, when he had made an end of digging the canal which leads from the Nile to the
Arabian Gulf...] (Book IV. 42)

XENOPHON

Xenophon (5th/4th B.C.E.), in his discussion of the reign of Cyrus,[8]
describes the eastern border of his empire and thus the Indian Ocean.

Καὶ ἐκ τούτου τὴν ἀρχὴν ὥριζεν αὐτῷ πρὸς ἕω μὲν ἡ Ἐρυθρὰ θάλαττα...
[From that time on his empire was bounded on the east by the Red Sea...]
(Cyropaedia VIII. vii. 21)

AGATHARCHIDES

Agatharchides (215–145 B.C.E.) is the first source to mention the Gulf of
Elath, identifying it as the Laeanites Gulf.[9] He preserves the identification of
Arabian Gulf for the Gulf of Suez and Today's Red Sea.

Identifying the Indian Ocean

...ἀπὸ γὰρ Αὐταίων, οἳ τὸν ἔσχατον μυχὸν κατοικοῦσιν, ὃν τῇ μεγάλῃ συμβέβηκε
συγκλείεσθαι θαλάττῃ, μέχρι τῆς Ἰνδικῆς...
[...from the Autaei, who inhabit the innermost recesses of the gulf, which ends at
the Great Sea, as far as India...] (Book 5. 31a, *On the Erythraean Sea*)

Identifying Today's Red Sea

Περὶ δὲ τῶν ἐθνῶν τῶν κατοικούντων τήν τε παράλιον τοῦ Ἀραβίου κόλπου καὶ
Τρωγλοδυτικὴν, ἔτι δ' Αἰθιοπίαν τὴν πρὸς μεσημβρίαν καὶ νότον πειρασόμεθα
διεξιέναι.
[But as for the tribes that inhabit the coast of the Arabian Gulf and Troglodytice
and, in addition, that part of Aithiopia that faces south and the south-wind, we shall
try to give an account of them.] (Book 5. 30b)

Περὶ πρώτων δὲ τῶν Ἰχθυοφάγων ἐροῦμεν τῶν κατοικούντων τὴν παράλιον τὴν ἀπὸ
Καρμανίας καὶ Γεδρωσίας ἕως τῶν ἐσχάτων τοῦ μυχοῦ τοῦ κατὰ τὸν Ἀράβιον

κόλπον ἱδρυμένου, ὃς εἰς τὴν μεσόγειον ἀνήκων ἄπιστον διάστημα δυσὶν ἠπείροις περικλείεται πρὸς τὸν ἔκπλουν, τῇ μὲν ὑπὸ τῆς εὐδαίμονος Ἀραβίας, τῇ δ'ὑπὸ τῆς Τρωγλοδυτικῆς.

[We shall speak first about the Fisheaters who inhabit the coast from Carmania and Gedrosia as far as the innermost recess of the Arabian Gulf, which extends into the interior for an unbelievable distance and is enclosed by two continents at its exit, on the one side by Arabia Felix and on the other by Troglodytice.] (Book 5. 31b)

Ὁ δὲ προσαγορευόμενος Ἀράβιος κόλπος ἀνεστόμωται μὲν εἰς τὸν κατὰ μεσημβρίαν κείμενον Ὠκεανόν, τῷ μήκει δ' ἐπὶ πολλοὺς πάνυ παρήκων σταδίους, τὸν μυχὸν ἔχει περιοριζόμενον ταῖς ἐσχατιαῖς τῆς Ἀραβίας καὶ Τρωγλοδυτικῆς.

[The Arabian Gulf, as it is called, opens into the ocean that lies in the south. In length the gulf extends for very many stades and its innermost recess is bounded by the furthest regions of Arabia and Troglodytice.] (Book 5. 81)

Identifying the Gulf of Suez

Ἡ μὲν οὖν καφαλαιώδης τοῦ κόλπου τούτου θέσις ὑπάρχει τοιαύτη. Ἡμεῖς δ' ἀπὸ τῶν ἐσχάτων τοῦ μυχοῦ τόπων ἀρξάμενοι τὸν ἐφ' ἑκάτερα τὰ μέρη παράπλουν τῶν ἠπείρων καὶ τὰς ἀξιολογωτάτας κατ' αὐτὰς ἰδιότητας διέξιμεν· πρῶτον δὲ ληψόμεθα τὸ δεξιὸν μέρος, οὗ τὴν παραλίαν τῶν Τρωγλοδυτῶν ἔθνη νέμεται μέχρι τῆς ἐρήμου. Ἀπὸ πόλεως τοίνυν Ἀρσινόης κομιζομένοις παρὰ τὴν δεξιὰν ἤπειρον ἐκπίπτει κατὰ πολλοὺς τόπους ἐκ πέτρας εἰς θάλατταν ὕδατα πολλά, πικρᾶς ἁλμυρίδος ἔχοντα γεῦσιν.

[Such is the general character of the gulf. Beginning from the furthest points of the innermost recess, we shall describe the voyage along the coasts of both mainlands and the most noteworthy peculiarities of each. We shall treat first the right side, the coast of which Troglodyte tribes inhabit as far as the desert. Now, people who sail from Arsinoe with the mainland on the right, encounter numerous streams which fall in many places from the cliffs into the sea and have a bitter brackish taste.] (Book 5. 82b)

Identifying the Gulf of Elath

Τὸ δ' ἄλλο μέρος τῆς ἀντιπέραν παραλίου τὸ προσκεκλιμένον Ἀραβίᾳ πάλιν ἀναλαβόντες ἀπὸ τοῦ μυχοῦ διέξιμεν.

[But we shall take up the remaining portion, the opposite shore which joins Arabia, and describe it, beginning again from the innermost recess.] (Book 5. 87a)

Παραπλεύσαντι δὲ ταύτην τὴν χώραν ἐκδέχεται κόλπος Λαιανίτης, περιοικούμενος πολλαῖς κώμαις Ἀράβων τῶν προσαγορευομένων Ναβαταίων.

[After sailing past this country, one encounters the Laeanites Gulf around which there are many villages of the so-called Nabataean Arabs.] (Book 5. 90a)

῎Οτι μετὰ καλούμενον Λαιανίτην κόλπον, ὃν ῎Αραβες περιοικοῦσιν...
[After what is called the Laeanites Gulf, around which Arabs live...] (Book 5. 91a)

The name, Laeanites, is possibly derived from Liḥyan, a people and state within early Arabia. They are believed to have populated the region to the east of the Gulf of Elath, flourishing between the 6th and 3rd centuries B.C.E.[10]

ARTEMIDORUS

It is to be noted that Pliny the Elder mentions the possibility of this derivation. He also notes two others, Artemidorus and Juba, who describe the Aelanite Gulf. In fact, from the end of the 2nd century B.C.E. until the end of the 1st century C.E. we find at least nine individuals who write about and detail this geography. Beginning with Pliny's comments noted above, they may be listed as well.[11]

In Discussing Today's Red Sea, He Mentions the Gulf of Elath

sinus intimus in quo Laeanitae, qui nomen ei dedere. regia eorum Agra et in sinu Laeana vel, ut alii, Aelana; nam et ipsum sinum nostri Laeaniticum scripsere, alii Aelaniticum, Artemidorus Alaeniticum, Iuba Leaniticum.
[Then a bay running far inland on which live the Laeanitae, who have given it their name. Their capital is Agra, and on the bay is Laeana, or as others call it Aelana; for the name of the bay itself has been written by our people 'Laeanitic', and by others 'Aelanitic', while Artemidorus gives it as 'Alaenitic' and Juba as 'Laenitic'.] (Book VI. xxxii. 156)

Strabo, on the Work of Artemidorus (Late 2ndCentury B.C.E.).[12]

Ταῦτ' εἰπὼν περὶ τῶν Τρωγλοδυτῶν καὶ τῶν προσχώρων Αἰθιόπων ἐπάνεισιν ἐπὶ τοὺς ῎Αραβας· καὶ πρώτους ἔπεισι τοὺς τὸν Ἀράβιον κόλπον ἀφορίζοντας καὶ ἀντικειμένους τοῖς Τρωγλοδύταις, ἀρξάμενος ἀπὸ τοῦ Ποσειδίου. φησὶ δὲ ἐνδοτέρω κεῖσθαι τοῦτο τοῦ Αἰλανίτου μυχοῦ...
[After saying all this about the Troglodytes and the neighbouring Aethiopians, Artemidorus returns to the Arabians; and first, beginning at Poseidium, he describes the Arabians who border on the Arabian Gulf and live opposite the Troglodytes. He says that Poseidium lies farther in than the Aelanites Gulf...] (Geography 16. 4. 18)

Artemidorus may in fact be responsible for changing the name Laeanites to Aelanites. As noted by S. M. Burstein,[13] this could indicate the absence of the Lihyānite kingdom by the end of the 2nd century B.C.E. Artemidorus would then be naming the gulf after the ancient city of Elath (Ailana) at the gulf's northern tip. Contrary to some opinions, Ailana should not be considered as a Greek rendition of 'Aqaba, but rather Elath.[14]

AGATHEMERUS

Agathemerus (1st B.C.E.)[15] discusses Today's Red Sea in relation to Arabia.

Ὁ δὲ Ἀράβιος κόλπος, στενὸς ὢν καὶ προμήκης, ἄρχεται ἀπὸ Ἡρώων πόλεως, παρὰ τὴν Τρωγλοδυτικὴν ἕως τῆς Πτολεμαΐδος τῆς ἐπὶ θήρας, σταδίων...τὸ μῆκος· ... πλοῦς σταδίων...· τὰ δὲ κατὰ Δειρὴν στενὰ σταδίων...· ἔνθεν ἑξῆς πλοῦς παρὰ τὴν Ἐρυθρὰν θάλασσαν ἕως ὠκεανοῦ σταδίων...τὸ δὲ λοιπὸν οὐ πλεῖται. Τὸ δὲ παρὰ τὴν Ἀραβίαν πλευρὰν ἀπ' Αἰλανίτου μυχοῦ...
[The Arabian Gulf, narrow and elongated, originates at the city of Heroom, next to the Troglodytes and reaches until Ptolemaios...stade....From thence it is one continuous sailing via the Red Sea until the ocean...stade further more. There is also, next to the side of Arabia, the Aelanites Gulf...] (GGM II, p. 476. 16)

DIODORUS

Diodorus (c. 60 B.C.E.) identifies the Red Sea as bordering Babylonia and Arabia,[16] which would thus identify the Persian Gulf, Indian Ocean and Today's Red Sea. He discusses the geography of the Arabian Gulf in greater detail, noting that it begins at Arsinoe (at the northern end of the Gulf of Suez)[17] and empties into the Red Sea. This occurs at either Today's Red Sea or the Gulf of Aden.

The Promontory of Alanites, which may be a description of the southern Sinai Peninsula, is at the end of the other initial body of water (the Gulf of Elath) that empties into the Arabian Gulf.[18] Diodorus describes this gulf as separate from the Arabian Gulf (Today's Red Sea). He is clearly describing the Gulf of Elath.

JUBA

Juba (late 1st B.C.E–early 1st C.E.), quoted by Pliny and Aelian (late 2nd C.E.), identifies the Gulf of Elath as the Laeanites Gulf. He also presents the

Red Sea as bordering both Arabia and India.[19]

STRABO

The most extensive geography following Herodotus belongs to Strabo.[20] Writing in the first half of the 1st century C.E., he perceived the world as surrounded by the Exterior Sea, from which water enters the inhabited world along many gulfs. The four largest gulfs are the Northern (which apparently is the Caspian Sea), the Interior Sea (the Mediterranean Sea, also the largest), the Persian Gulf and the Arabian Gulf (Today's Red Sea), both filled by the Southern Sea (which includes the Red Sea). He describes the pertinent bodies of water.

Indicating the Persian Gulf, Indian Ocean and Arabian Gulf

ὧν ὁ μὲν βόρειος Κασπία καλεῖται θάλαττα, οἱ δ' Ὑρκανίαν προσαγορεύουσιν· ὁ δὲ Περσικὸς καὶ Ἀράβιος ἀπὸ τῆς νοτίας ἀναχέονται θαλάττης, ὁ μὲν τῆς Κασπίας κατ' ἀντικρὺ μάλιστα, ὁ δὲ τῆς Ποντικῆς·
[Of these four gulfs the northern one is called the Caspian Sea (though some call it the Hyrcanian Sea); the Persian Gulf and the Arabian Gulf pour inland from the Southern Sea, the one opposite the Caspian Sea and the other about opposite the Pontus...] (Geography 2. 5. 18)

ταύτης δὲ τὸ μὲν προσάρκτιον πλευρὸν ἡ λεχθεῖσά ἐστιν ἔρημος, τὸ δ' ἐῷον ὁ Περσικὸς κόλπος, τὸ δὲ ἑσπέριον ὁ Ἀράβιος, τὸ δὲ νότιον ἡ μεγάλη θάλαττα ἡ ἔξω τῶν κόλπων ἀμφοῖν, ἣν ἅπασαν Ἐρυθρὰν καλοῦσιν. Ὁ μὲν οὖν Περσικὸς κόλπος λέγεται κεὶ ἡ κατὰ Πέρσας θάλαττα·
[The northern side of Arabia Felix is formed by the above-mentioned desert, the eastern by the Persian Gulf, the western by the Arabian Gulf, and the southern by the great sea that lies outside both gulfs, which as a whole is called Erythra. Now the Persian Gulf is also called the Persian Sea.] (Geography 16. 3. 1–2)

...καὶ τὸν Ἀράβιον κόλπον στενὸν ὄντα τελέως τὸν διείργοντα ἀπὸ τῶν Τρωγλοδυτῶν τοὺς Ἄραβας...
[...and also that the Arabian Gulf, which separates the Arabians from the Troglodytes, is extremely narrow.] (Geography 16. 4. 22)

Indicating the Gulf of Suez (in Speaking of the Arabian Gulf)

πῶς οὖν ἡγνόει τὸν ἰσθμόν, ὃν οὗτος ποιεῖ πρὸς τὸ Αἰγύπτιον πέλαγος.
[How then, can the poet have been ignorant of the isthmus which the gulf forms with the Egyptian Sea?] (Geography 1. 2. 28)

Ἄλλη δ' ἐστὶν ἐκδιδοῦσα εἰς τὴν Ἐρυθρὰν καὶ τὸν Ἀράβιον κόλπον κατὰ πόλιν Ἀρσινόην, ἣν ἔνιοι Κλεοπατρίδα καλοῦσι.
[There is another canal which empties into the Red Sea and the Arabian Gulf near the city Arsinoe, a city which some call Cleopatris.] (Geography 17. 1. 25)

Indicating the Gulf of Elath

ἔστι δ' ἡ Αἴλανα πόλις ἐν θατέρῳ μυχῷ τοῦ Ἀραβίου κόλπου, τῷ κατὰ Γάζαν τῷ Αἰλανίτῃ καλουμένῳ...τοῦ δ' Ἀραβίου κόλπου τὸ μὲν παρὰ τὴν Ἀραβίαν πλευρὸν...
[Aelana is a city on the recess of the Arabian Gulf, the recess near Gaza called Aelanites, as I have said before.... The part of the Arabian Gulf along the side of Arabia, beginning at the Aelanites recess...] (Geography 16. 4. 4)

Αἴλαν πόλιν ἐπὶ τῷ μυχῷ τοῦ Αραβίου κόλπου κειμένην· διττὸς δ' ἐστίν· ὁ μὲν ἔχων εἰς τὸ πρὸς τῇ Ἀραβίᾳ καὶ τῇ Γάζῃ μέρος, ὃν Αἰλανίτην προσαγορεύουσιν ἀπὸ τῆς ἐν αὐτῷ πόλεως...
[...to Aela, a city situated near the recess of the Arabian Gulf. This consists of two recesses: one extending into the region near Arabia and Gaza, which is called Aelanites, after the city situated on it...] (Geography 16. 2. 30)

These comments by Strabo may indicate the first instance in which the Gulf of Elath is linked, in some way, to Today's Red Sea, but only within the context of the "Arabian Gulf." It is also to be seen below that this linkage is not carried further in other sources through the end of the first century. Thus it is also possible that Strabo recognized the Aelanite Gulf as extending north from the head of the Arabian Gulf, but not sharing its name.

ARRIAN

Arrian (early–mid 1st C.E.), in his "Anabasis Alexandi," does find occasion to discuss a number of these geographical concerns.[21] While the majority of his pertinent comments are directed toward the Indian Ocean and Persian Gulf, he does indeed mention Today's Red Sea and the Gulf of Suez.

Indicating the Indian Ocean and Persian Gulf

Ἀπείργεσθαι δὲ τὴν Ἰνδῶν χώραν πρὸς μὲν ἔω τε καὶ ἀπηλιώτην ἄνεμον ἔστε ἐπὶ μεσημβρίαν τῇ μεγάλῃ θαλάσσῃ·
[India itself both east and west right down to the south, is bounded by the Great Sea...] (Anabasis V. 6. 3)

Ἀλλὰ ὑπέρ Ἰνδῶν ἰδίᾳ μοι γεγράψεται ὅσα πιστότατα ἐς ἀφήγησιν οἵ τε ξὺν Ἀλεξάνδρῳ στρατεύσαντες καὶ ὁ ἐκπεριπλεύσας τῆς μεγάλης θαλάσσης τὸ κατ' Ἰνδοὺς Νέαρχος, ἐπὶ δὲ ὅσα Μεγασθένης τε καὶ Ἐρατοσθένης, δοκίμω ἄνδρε, ξυνεγραψάτην, καὶ νόμιμα ἄττα Ἰνδοῖς ἐστὶ καὶ εἰ δή τινα ἄτοπα ζῷα αὐτόθι φύεται καὶ τὸν παράπλουν αὐτὸν τῆς ἔξω θαλάσσης.

[However, about India I shall write a special monograph based on all the most reliable facts from Alexander's fellow-campaigners and Nearchus, who coasted along the part of the Great Sea which lies towards India, adding besides all that Megasthenes and Eratosthenes, who are both men of repute, have written; the customs of India, any strange beasts which live there, and the voyage round it by the Outer Sea.] (Anabasis V. 5. 1)

...ἀπὸ τῆς ἑῴας τῆς κατ' Ἰνδοὺς ἐκπεριερχομένη ἡ μεγάλη θάλασσα ἀνακεῖται εἰς κόλπον τὸν Ὑρκάνιον, καθάπερ οὖν καὶ τὸν Περσικὸν ἐξεῦρε, τὴν Ἐρυθρὰν δὴ καλουμένην θάλασσαν, κόλπον οὖσαν τῆς μεγάλης θαλάσσης.

[...or whether on the east side towards India the great sea circling round pours into a gulf, the Hyrcanian, just as he had discovered the Persian Gulf or, to use its actual name, the Red Sea, to be only a gulf of the ocean.] (Anabasis VII. 16. 2)

...τὸ μὲν κατὰ τὸν Εὐφράτην ποταμὸν ἀναπεπλευκὸς ἀπὸ θαλάσσης τῆς Περσικῆς, ὅ τι περ σὺν Νεάρχῳ ἦν...

[...the part which was with Nearchus had sailed up the Euphrates from the Persian Sea...] (Anabasis VII. 19. 3)

...ἐπὶ τὸν κόλπον τὸν Περσικὸν καὶ τὰς ἐκβολὰς τοῦ τε Εὐφράτου καὶ τοῦ Τίγρητος.

[...towards the Persian Gulf and the mouths of the Euphrates and Tigris.] (Anabasis VI. 19. 5)

...ἐπὶ τὴν θάλασσαν τὴν Περσικὴν καὶ τὸ στόμα τοῦ Τίγρητος...

[...to the Persian Sea and the mouth of the Tigris...] (Anabasis VI. 28. 6)

Indicating Today's Red Sea and the Gulf of Suez

ἦν μὲν γὰρ αὐτῷ προστεταγμένον περιπλεῦσαι τὴν χερρόνησον τὴν Ἀράβων πᾶσαν ἔστε ἐπὶ τὸν κόλπον τὸν πρὸς Αἰγύπτῳ τὸν Ἀράβιον τὸν καθ' Ἡρώων πόλιν·

[...though his sailing orders were to coast round the whole Arabian peninsula till he reached the Arabian Gulf on the Egyptian side at Heroonpolis...] (Anabasis VII. 20. 8)

POMPONIUS MELA

The next thorough geographical presentation is that of Pomponius Mela

THE MORE THINGS CHANGE

(43 C.E.).[22] His geography, while not mentioning the Gulf of Elath, does clearly detail the other areas.

Indicating the Persian Gulf

Rursus ex iis: quæ meridiem spectant: eædemque gentes interiora littora usque ad sinum persicum. Sup hunc sunt Parthi & Assyrii. Super illum alterum Babylonii.
[Turning from these toward the south—these being considered as one nation—they occupy the interior even to the shore of the Persian Gulf. Here exist the Parthians and the Assyrians. Upon the other shore, are the Babylonians.] (Book I, p. 4)

Indicating the Indian Ocean (Context is the Ganges and Indus Rivers)

Inde ad prícipia rubri maris...
[From here to the beginning of the Red Sea...] (Book III, p. 16)

Indian Ocean (Continuing in a Southeastern Direction)

Arabia hinc ad rubrum mare ptinet...
[Arabia, from this point, extends to the Red Sea...] (Book I, p. 14)

Indicating the Persian Gulf and Today's Red Sea

Sed quas ripas inflexerat bis irrumpit: duosque iterum sinus aperit persicus uocatur dictis regionibus propior: Arabicus ulterior. Persicus qua mare accipit utrinque rectis lateribus grande ostium quasi ceruice complectitur. Deinde terris in omnem partem uaste & æqua portione cædentibus magno littorum orbe pelagus incingens reddit formam capitis humani. Arabici & osarctius & latitudo minor est. Maior ali-quáto recessus: & multo magis longa latera init penitus. Introrsusque dum ægyptum pene & monté arabiæ Casium attingit: quodam fastigio minus: ac minus latus. Et quo magis penetrat angustior.
[However, the waterway breaks out into two channels; the nearer of the two touches the regions of the Persian Gulf, and the further touches those of the Arabian Gulf. The Persian Gulf, at the place where it meets the ocean, spreads wide in a large inlet with curving, neck-like sides. Thereafter, the landmass, stretching all around, draws ever more narrowly toward the waters, and, at last, encompasses it in a shape that would resemble a human head. The Arabian Gulf, however, is smaller and more restricted, but the depth of its recess is somewhat greater and its interior more extended. It advances by Egypt nearly as far as Mount Casius in Arabia, at which point its breadth becomes less and less.] (Book III, p. 17)

Indicating Today's Red Sea, Continuing to the Tip of the Gulf of Suez

Alterum sinum undiq arabes incin gunt ab ea parte: quæ introeuntibus dextra est. Vrbes sunt Carrë & arabia & gadamus. In altera ab intimo angulo. Prima beronice

inter hyeroopoliticum: & scrobilum. De inde inter promontoria moronenon: & colloca Philoteris & ptolemais ultra arsinoe: & alia beronice. Tú sylua q̃ hebenú
odoresque generat:& manu factus amnis. Ideoq referendus: q ex nili alueo dioryge
adductus extra sinú ue rú inflexú & non rubri maris...
[The other gulf lies around Arabia, and, on entering the waterway, Arabia is to the
right. Its cities are: Carra, Arabia and Gadamus. At the upper inlet is the city of
Beronice, set between the areas of Hyeropolicus and Scrobilum. Thereafter, between
the promontories Moronenon and Colloca, are the cities, Philoteris and Ptolemais.
Beyond is Arsinoe and the other city, Beronice. The forests of ebony trees and
spices are nearby. Here is that river, made by hands, and it must be described. From
the Nile, the canal was dug entirely around the Red Sea...] (Book III, p. 18)

PLINY THE ELDER

An approximate contemporary of Mela is Pliny the Elder, writing in the
mid 1st century C.E.[23] Within his Natural History, Pliny presents us with a
geography from India around the entire Arabian Peninsula, extending to the
Gulfs of Suez and Elath.

Indicating the Persian Gulf

Persae Rubrum mare semper accoluere, propter quod is sinus Persicus vocatur.
[The Persians have always lived on the shore of the Red Sea, which is the reason
why it is called the Persian Gulf.] (Book VI. xxix. 115)

Indicating the Indian Ocean

navigant autem ex India vento Volturno et, cum intravere Rubrum Mare, Africo vel
Austro.
[They set sail from India with a south-east wind, and after entering the Red Sea,
continue the voyage with a south-west or south wind.] (Book VI. xxvi. 106)

Indicating Today's Red Sea

ipsa vero paeninsula Arabia inter duo maria Rubrum Persicumque procurrens...
[Arabia itself however is a peninsula projecting between two seas, the Red Sea and
the Persian Gulf...] (Book VI. xxxii. 143)

Indicating Today's Red Sea (Plus the Persian Gulf)

sed in duos dividitur sinus. is qui ab oriente est Persicus appellatur, xxv circuitu, ut
Eratosthenes tradit. ex adverso est Arabia, cuius xv longitudo; rursus altero ambitur
sinu Arabico nominato, oceanum qui influit Azanium appellant.
[However, this sea is divided into two bays. The one to the east is called the Persian
Gulf, and according to the report of Eratosthenes measures 2500 miles round. Oppo-

site is Arabia, with a coastline 1500 miles in length, and on its other side Arabia is encompassed by the second bay, named the Arabian Gulf; the ocean flowing into this is called the Azanian Sea.] (Book VI. xxviii. 108)

Indicating the Gulf of Suez

gens Tyro, Daneon Portus, ex quo navigabilem alveum perducere in Nilum qua parte ad Delta dictum decurrit, LXII D intervallo, quod inter flumen et Rubrum Mare interest...

[Then come the Tyro tribe and the Harbour of the Daneoi, from which there was a project to carry a ship-canal through to the Nile at the place where it flows into what is called the Delta, over a space of 62½ miles, which is the distance between the river and the Red Sea...] (Book VI. xxxiii. 165)

Indicating the Gulf of Elath (the Arabian Shore of Today's Red Sea)

sinus intimus in quo Laeanitae, qui nomen ei dedere. regia eorum Agra et in sinu Laeana vel, ut alii, Aelana; nam et ipsum sinum nostri Laeaniticum scripsere, alii Aelaniticum, Artemidorus Alaeniticum, Iuba Leaniticum.

[Then a bay running far inland on which live the Laeanitae, who have given it their name. Their capital is Agra, and on the bay is Laeana, or as others call it Aelana; for the name of the bay itself has been written by our people 'Laeanitic', and by others 'Aelanitic', while Artemidorus gives it as 'Alaenitic' and Juba as 'Leanitic'.] (Book VI. xxxii. 156)

Situs autem ita se habet: a sinu Laeanitico alter sinus quem Arabes Aean vocant...

[The lie of the land is as follows: on leaving the Laeanitic Gulf there is another gulf the Arabic name of which is Aeas...] (Book VI. xxxiii. 165)[24]

CLAUDIUS PTOLEMY

Perhaps the most extensive ancient geography is that of Claudius Ptolemy, writing in the late 1st century C.E.[25] For our purposes Ptolemy describes the regions from the Persian Gulf around the Arabian Peninsula extending to both gulfs, Suez and Elath. His coordinate system is helpful in that it allows us the opportunity to place sites relative to each other.

Concerning the Lands in Proximity to Egypt

ἀπὸ δὲ ἀνατολῶν τῆς τε Ἰουδαίας μέρει τῷ ἀπὸ Ἀνθηδόνος πόλεως μέχρι πέρατος, οὗ θέσις 64° 15   30° 40 καὶ τῇ ἐντεῦθεν Ἀραβίᾳ Πετραίᾳ μέχρι τοῦ καθ᾽ Ἡρώων πόλιν μυχοῦ τοῦ Ἀραβίου κόλπου, οὗ θέσις 63° 30   29° 50 καὶ μέρει τοῦ Ἀραβίου κόλπου, κατὰ περιγραφὴν τῆς παραλίου τοιαύτην· μετὰ τὸν μυχὸν τοῦ κόλπου τὸν εἰρημένον, ὃς ἐπέχει μοίρας 63° 30   29° 50   Ἀρσινόη 63° 20   29° 10...

[It is terminated on the east by a part of Judaea which runs from the city Anthedon to the terminus which is in 64 15   30 40 and then by Arabia Petraea as far as the recess in the Arabian Bay near the city Heroum which is located in 63 30   29 50 and by a part of the Arabian Bay. The coast is thus described: Next to the turn of the Bay which we have said is located in 63 30   29 50 is Arsinoe 63 20   29 10...] (Book 4, Chapter V)

Concerning the Region in Proximity to Ethiopia

ἀπὸ δὲ ἀνατολῶν τῷ τε λοιπῷ μέρει τοῦ Ἀραβίου κόλπου καὶ τῇ ἐφεξῆς Ἐρυθρᾷ θαλάσσῃ καὶ τῷ Βαρβαρικῷ πελάγει...

[It is terminated on the east by a part of the Bay of Arabia and the Red Sea, and the Barbaricus Sea...] (Book 4, Chapter VII)[26]

Concerning the Region in Proximity to Arabia Petraea

ἡ Πετραία Ἀραβία περιορίζεται ἀπὸ μὲν δύσεως τῷ ἐκτεθειμένῳ τῆς Αἰγύπτου μέρει; ἀπὸ δὲ ἄρκτων τῇ τε Παλαιστίνῃ ἢ Ἰουδαίᾳ καὶ τῷ μέρει τῆς Συρίας κατὰ τὰς διωρισμένας αὐτῶν γραμμάς; ἀπὸ δὲ μεσημβρίας τῷ μυχῷ τοῦ Ἀραβίου κόλπου τῷ κατὰ τὸν Ἡρωοπολίτην κόλπον ἀπὸ τοῦ ἐκτεθειμένου πρὸς τῇ Αἰγύπτῳ πέρατος μέχρι τοῦ κατὰ Φαρὰν ἀκρωτηρίου, ὃ ἐπέχει μοίρας 65°   28° 30 καὶ τῷ ἐντεῦθεν Αἰλανίτῃ κόλπῳ μέχρι τῆς ἐπιστροφῆς αὐτοῦ, ἣ ἐπέχει μοίρας 66° 29°...

[Arabia Petraea is terminated on the west by that part of Egypt to which we have referred; on the north by Palestina or Judaea and the part of Syria along the line which we have indicated as its southern border; on the south by the bend of the Arabian Bay and by the Heroopolites bay to the terminus as indicated on the confines of Egypt near the Pharan Promontory, which is located in 65   28 30 and by the bay, which is the Elanite, to its turn which is in 66   29...] (Book 5, Chapter XVI)[27]

Concerning the Location of Arabia Deserta

ἡ Ἔρημος Ἀραβία περιορίζεται ἀπὸ μὲν ἄρκτων Μεσοποταμίας μέρει κατὰ τὸ ἐκτεθειμένον μέρος τοῦ Εὐφράτου ποταμοῦ; ἀπὸ δὲ δυσμῶν τοῖς διωρισμένος μέρεσι τῆς τε Συρίας καὶ τῆς Πετραίας Ἀραβίας; ἀπὸ δὲ ἀνατολῶν τῇ τε Βαβυλωνίᾳ διὰ τῆς ὀρεινῆς τῆς ἀπὸ τοῦ εἰρημένου πρὸς τῷ Εὐφράτῃ ποταμῷ πέρατος μέχρι τοῦ μυχοῦ τοῦ Περσικοῦ κόλπου, ἧς τὸ πρὸς τῷ κόλπῳ πέρας ἐπέχει μοίρας 79°   30° 10 καὶ τῷ ἐντεῦθεν μέρει τοῦ Περσικοῦ κόλπου μέχρι πέρατος, οὗ ἡ θέσις ἐπέχει μοίρας 79°   29°; ἀπὸ δὲ μεσημβρίας τῇ Εὐδαίμονι Ἀραβίᾳ διὰ τῆς ὀρεινῆς τῆς ἀπὸ τοῦ ἐκτεθειμένου πρὸς τῇ Πετραίᾳ Ἀραβίᾳ πέρατος ἐπὶ τὸ κατὰ τὸν Περσικὸν κόλπον διωρισμένον πέρας.

[Arabia Deserta is terminated on the north by that part of Mesopotamia which borders on the Euphrates River as we have noted; on the west by a part of Syria and of Arabia Petraea; on the east by Babylonia separated by those mountains which begin at the terminus as we have indicated, near the Euphrates River extending to the interior bend of the Persian Gulf near the bay, the location of which terminus is in 79 30 10 and that part of the Persian Gulf to a terminus, the location of which is 79 29; on the south moreover by Arabia Felix terminating in the confines of Arabia Petraea which we have indicated as being near the Persian Gulf.] (Book 5, Chapter XVIII)

Concerning the Location of Babylonia

ἡ Βαβυλωνία περιορίζεται ἀπὸ μὲν ἄρκτων Μεσοποταμίᾳ κατὰ τὸ ἐκτεθειμένον τοῦ Εὐφράτου μέρος; ἀπὸ δὲ δύσεως τῇ Ἐρήμῳ Ἀραβίᾳ κατὰ τὴν εἰρημένην ὀρεινήν; ἀπὸ δὲ ἀνατολῶν Σουσιανῇ παρὰ τὸ λοιπὸν τοῦ Τίγριδος μέρος μέχρι [τοῦ ἀνατολικοῦ στόματος] τῶν εἰς τὸν Περσικὸν κόλπον ἐκβολῶν, ὃ ἐπέχει μοίρας 80° 30 31°.

[Babylonia is terminated on the north by Mesopotamia along the parts of the Euphrates River we have described; on the west by Arabia Deserta, next to which are the mountains which we have described; on the east by Susiana along the remaining parts of the of the Tigris River as far as its eastern mouth which opens into the Persian Gulf in 80 30 31.] (Book 5, Chapter XIX)

Concerning the Region in Proximity to Arabia Felix

ἡ Εὐδαίμων Ἀραβία περιορίζεται ἀπὸ μὲν ἄρκτων ταῖς ἐκτεθειμέναις μεσημβριναῖς πλευραῖς τῆς τε Πετραίας καὶ τῆς Ἐρήμου Ἀραβίας καὶ τῷ νοτίῳ μέρει τοῦ Περσικοῦ κόλπου; ἀπὸ δὲ δύσεως τῷ Ἀραβίῳ κόλπῳ; ἀπὸ δὲ μεσημβρίας τῇ Ἐρυθρᾷ θαλάσσῃ; ἀπὸ δὲ ἀνατολῶν μέρει τε τοῦ Περσικοῦ κόλπου καὶ τῇ ἀπὸ τοῦ στόματος αὐτοῦ μέχρι τοῦ Συάγρου ἀκρωτηρίου θαλάσσῃ. ἡ μὲν οὖν παράλιος αὐτῆς περιγραφὴν ἔχει τοιαύτην· μετὰ τὰ ἐν τῷ Ἐλανίτῃ μυχῷ ὅριον Ἀραβίου κόλπου.

[Arabia Felix is terminated on the north by the designated border of Arabia Petraea and of Arabia Deserta; on the northeast by a part of the Persian Gulf; on the west by the Arabian Gulf; on the south by the Red Sea; on the east by that part of the Persian Gulf and the sea, which extends from the entrance to this gulf as far as the Syagros promontory. The maritime coast of this region is thus described: from the terminus of the Arabian Gulf near the Elanite Bay...] (Book 6, Chapter VII)

THE PERIPLUS OF THE ERYTHRAEAN SEA

An anonymous author wrote *The Periplus of the Erythraean Sea* in the early 2nd century C.E.[28] This description begins at the northern end of

Today's Red Sea and proceeds to the Indian Ocean.

Indicating the Starting Point of the description

Τῶν ἀποδεδειγμένων ὅρμων τῆς Ἐρυθρᾶς θαλάσσης καὶ τῶν περὶ αὐτὴν ἐμπορίων πρῶτός ἐστι λιμὴν τῆς Αἰγύπτου Μυὸς ὅρμος. Μετὰ δὲ αὐτὸν εἰσπλεόντων ἀπὸ χιλίων ὀκτακοσίων σταδίων ἐν δεξιᾷ ἡ Βερνίκη. Ἀμφοτέρων [δὲ] οἱ λιμένες ἐν τῷ ἐσχάτῳ τῆς Αἰγύπτου κόλποι τῆς Ἐρυθρᾶς θαλάσσης κεῖνται.

[Among the established harbours of the Erythraean Sea and the marts round it, the first is the Egyptian harbour of Muos Hormos. Those who sail from here come, after 1800 stades, to Bernikē on the right hand. The harbours of both are on the edge of Egypt and lie in bays of the Erythraean Sea.] (Chapter 1)

Indicating the Southeastern Terminus of Today's Red Sea

Ἤδη [δὲ] ἐπ' ἀνατολὴν ὁ Ἀραβικὸς κόλπος διατείνει καὶ κατὰ τὸν Αὐαλίτην μάλιστα στενοῦται.

[From here the Arabian Gulf stretches eastward, and near Aualitēs becomes narrowest.] (Chapter 7)

Indicating the Coastal Journey around Arabia to the Persian Gulf

Περικολπίζοντι δὲ τὴν ἐχομένην ἤπειρον εἰς αὐτὴν τὴν ἄρκτον ἤδη περὶ τὴν εἰσβολὴν τῆς Περσικῆς θαλάσσης...

[Sailing round the bay along the neighbouring mainland, now going northwards towards the entrance of the Persian Sea...] (Chapter 34)

Indicating the Coastline near the Mouth of the Indus River [29]

Μετὰ δὲ ταύτην τὴν χώραν, ἤδη τῆς ἠπείρου διὰ τὸ βάθος τῶν κόλπων ἐκ τῆς ἀνατολῆς ὑπερκερώσης, ἐκδέχεται [τὰ] παραθαλάσσια μέρη τῆς Σκυθίας παρ' αὐτὸν κειμένης τὸν βορέαν, ταπεινὰ λίαν, ἐξ ὧν ποταμὸς Σίνθος, μέγιστος τῶν κατὰ τὴν Ἐρυθρὰν θάλασσαν...

[After this region the mainland disappears into the distance eastwards owing to the depth of the bays, and there succeed the coast parts of Skuthia, which stretch towards the north and are very low-lying. From them comes the river Sinthos, the greatest of the rivers which flow into the Erythraean Sea...] (Chapter 38)

CAIUS JULIUS SOLINUS

Two final sources may be briefly mentioned. In the 3rd century C.E. Caius Julius Solinus preserved the same identifications that are now familiar.[30] The Red Sea (Erythraeum) borders Egypt, Arabia and India. It divides into two gulfs bordering the Arabian Peninsula: the Persian and Arabian Gulfs.

Arabia, itself, stretches from the Pelusium Nile to the Red Sea. As with the other sources, the Sinai Peninsula, although not named as such, is not part of Egypt proper. The city of Arsinoe is also identified as located at the tip of the Red Sea. Solinus does not mention the Gulf of Elath.

AMMIANUS MARCELLINUS

Ammianus Marcellinus (end 4th C.E.) perpetuates the same geographical perceptions.[31] The Persian Gulf, as part of the Red Sea, empties into the Indian Ocean, itself being located at the southern end of the Arabian Peninsula. This peninsula is surrounded on the "left" by the Persian Gulf and on the "right" by the Arabian Gulf. The Arabian Gulf/Red Sea borders Egypt on its entire eastern side. Again, the Sinai Peninsula is described as part of Asia and Syria. He also does not mention the Gulf of Elath.

SYNOPSIS, TABLE AND MAPS

As summarized in Tables 1a, b and Maps 2 and 3, it is possible to formulate clear conclusions concerning the ancient view of these particular ancient Near Eastern waters. To the ancients, from at least the mid 5th century B.C.E., the term "Red Sea" described the ocean that surrounded the Arabian Peninsula, except for the Gulf of Elath. Although the Persian Gulf and Indian Ocean were known by these specific designations, they were considered part of the Red Sea. Today's Red Sea was also known as the Arabian Gulf, as was the Gulf of Suez. Both were also considered part of the Red Sea and were so designated.

Only the Gulf of Elath was known and designated by a different name, generally referred to as the Aelanite Gulf. The ancient geographers drew a distinction between the eastern and western arms of Today's Red Sea. These two bodies of water were not the same. When and why were the Suez and Elath Gulfs viewed in a collective sense? This question is addressed and answered in the next chapter, through the investigation of scriptural texts and their composition within the clarified framework of ancient geography.

NAME/SOURCE	DATE/BCE	COMMENTS	GULF OF ELATH	GULF OF SUEZ
Sargon Geography	mid 8th–6th			
Aeschylus	mid 6th–5th	Red Sea (Oral)		
Herodotus	mid 5th			Arabian Gulf Red Sea
Pindar	5th	Red Sea (Oral)		
Aristophanes	late 5th	Red Sea (Oral)		
Xenophon	5th–4th			
Agatharchides	c. 215–145		Laeanites Gulf	Arabian Gulf
Artemidorus	late 2nd		Aelanite Gulf	
Agathemerus	1st century		Aelanite Gulf	
Diodorus	c. 60		perhaps identified as Aelanite Gulf	Arabian Gulf
Juba	late 1st		Laenites Gulf	
	DATE/CE			
Strabo	early 1st		Aelanites Gulf	Arabian Gulf
Arrian	early–mid 1st			Arabian Gulf
Pomponius Mela	c. 43			Arabian Gulf
Pliny the Elder	mid 1st		Aelanite Gulf Laenites Gulf	Red Sea
Claudius Ptolemy	late 1st		Elanite Gulf	Arabian Bay
Periplus	early 2nd			
Solinus	3rd			Red Sea
Ammianus Marcellinus	4th			Red Sea Arabian Gulf

Table 1a—**ANCIENT GEOGRAPHERS**

NAME/SOURCE	DATE/BCE	TODAY'S RED SEA	INDIAN OCEAN	PERSIAN GULF
Sargon Geography	mid 8th–6th		Lower Sea	Lower Sea
Aeschylus	mid 6th–5th			
Herodotus	mid 5th	Arabian Gulf Red Sea	Southern Sea Red Sea	Red Sea
Pindar	5th			
Aristophanes	late 5th			
Xenophon	5th–4th		Red Sea	Red Sea
Agatharchides	c. 215–145	Arabian Gulf	Great Sea	
Artemidorus	late 2nd			
Agathemerus	1st century	Red Sea Arabian Gulf	Ocean	
Diodorus	c. 60	Red Sea Arabian Gulf	Southern Sea Red Sea	Red Sea
Juba	late 1st	Red Sea	Red Sea	Red Sea
	DATE/CE			
Strabo	early 1st	Arabian Gulf Red Sea	Red Sea	Persian Sea
Arrian	early–mid 1st	Arabian Gulf	Great Sea Outer Sea Red Sea	Great Sea Persian Gulf/Sea Red Sea
Pomponius Mela	c. 43	Arabian Gulf	South Sea Indian Ocean Red Sea	Persian Gulf
Pliny the Elder	mid 1st	Arabian Gulf Azanian Sea	Red Sea	Persian Gulf Red Sea
Claudius Ptolemy	late 1st	Arabian Gulf	Red Sea	Persian Gulf
Periplus	early 2nd	Red Sea	Red Sea	Persian Gulf Red Sea
Solinus	3rd	Red Sea	Red Sea	Persian Gulf Red Sea
Ammianus Marcellinus	4th	Red Sea Arabian Gulf	Indian Ocean Red Sea	Persian Gulf Red Sea

Table 1b—**ANCIENT GEOGRAPHERS**

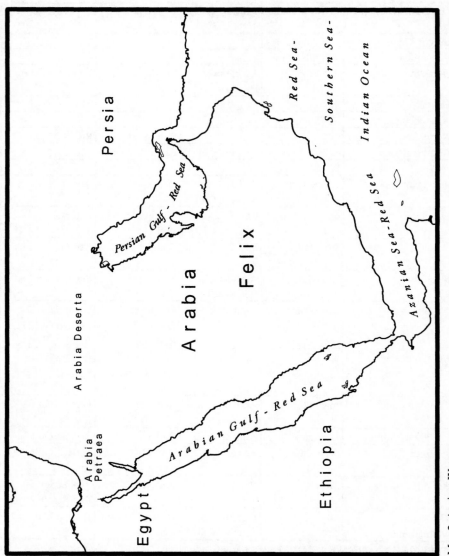

Map 2. Ancient Waters

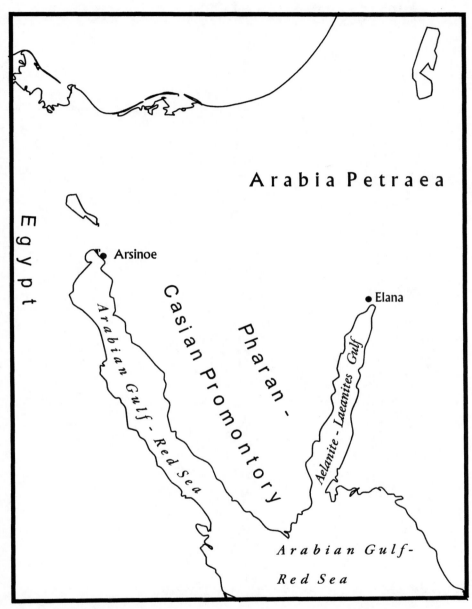

Map 3. Sinai Waterways

CHAPTER THREE

...THE MORE THEY REMAIN THE SAME: ANCIENT GEOGRAPHY—SCRIPTURE OUTSIDE THE HEBREW BIBLE

The geographical context within which the post-exilic scriptural texts were composed was examined in the last chapter. It is reasonable, however, to expect a dilemma inherent in the scriptural presentations of these same sites. Because the authors were not only dealing with an accepted geographical perspective, they may also have had to reconcile a canonical perspective as contrasted with the known contemporary geography. In addition, they may have harbored certain presuppositions.

The texts investigated in this chapter are composed in Hebrew, Aramaic, Syriac, Greek, Latin and Ethiopic and are drawn from the following sources:

- Septuagint
- Pseudepigrapha
  - Artapanus
  - Jubilees
  - Enoch
  - Assumption of Moses
  - Testament of Solomon
- Apocrypha—1 Maccabees
- Dead Sea Scrolls
- Targumim
  - Jonathan
  - Pseudo-Jonathan
  - Onkelos

- ◦ Neophyti
- ◦ Various fragments
- Josephus
- New Testament
- Vulgate
- Rabbinic Literature
  - ◦ Mishnah
  - ◦ Talmud
  - ◦ Commentaries

Within these texts the investigation will focus primarily on the previously observed distinction between the Gulf of Suez and the Gulf of Elath. Within that context, two sources are critical: the Septuagint (3ʳᵈ–1ˢᵗ B.C.E.) and the Dead Sea Scrolls (1ˢᵗ B.C.E.–1ˢᵗ C.E.).

SEPTUAGINT

The term "Red Sea" never occurs within the Hebrew Bible. It would appear that the Septuagint translators were the first to introduce Ἐρυθρά θάλασσα to the biblical text.[1] On all occasions when ים סוף is mentioned, except two, the Septuagint translates as "Red Sea."[2] The two specific exceptions are as follows:

Judg 11:16

כי בעלותם ממצרים וילך ישראל במדבר עד ים סוף ויבא קדשה
[...but when they came up from Egypt, Israel walked in the wilderness of Yam Sûp and they came toward Kadesh.]

ὅτι ἐν τῷ ἀναβαίνειν αὐτοὺς ἐξ Αἰγύπτου ἐπορεύθη Ἰσραὴλ ἐν τῇ ἐρήμῳ ἕως θαλάσσης Σίφ, καὶ ἦλθεν εἰς Κάδης.
[...for in their going up out of Egypt Israel went in the wilderness as far as the sea of Siph, and came to Cades.]

1 Kgs 9:26

ואני עשה המלך שלמה בעציון גבר אשר את אלות על שפת ים סוף בארץ אדום
[King Solomon built a (fleet of ships) ship at Ezion-geber, which is near Elath on the shore of Yam Sûp, in the land of Edom.]

Καὶ ναῦν ὑπὲρ οὗ ἐποίησεν ὁ βασιλεὺς Σαλωμὼν ἐν Γασίων Γαβὲρ τὴν οὖσαν ἐχομένην Αἰλὰθ ἐπὶ τοῦ χείλους τῆς ἐσχάτης θαλάσσης ἐν γῇ Ἐδώμ.
[...even that for which king Solomon built a ship in Gasion Gaber near Elath on the shore of the extremity of the sea in the land of Edom.]

Why would the translators have chosen to render these two verses differently? More specifically, what can be learned from the different translations, in particular that of 1 Kgs 9:26?

In the other 22 instances it is possible, from the Egyptian geographical perspective of the Septuagint translators, to interpret ים סוף as the Gulf of Suez. After all, to these translators, the biblical exodus tradition was clear. The Israelites fled Egypt and crossed a "sea." The closest sea, revealed to us by the translation Ἐρυθρά θάλασσα must be the Gulf of Suez.

If ים סוף is therefore Ἐρυθρά θάλασσα, why was it not translated in 1 Kgs 9:26 as Ἐρυθρά θάλασσα? Although modern translations of the Septuagint render the verse as quoted above, nevertheless it remains a controversial passage. As noted by J. A. Montgomery, the different Greek versions "have unanimously ἡ ἐσχάτη θάλασσα, i.e., vocalizing as sôp instead of sûp. This gives a novel but admirable name for that Sea, which as an arm of the Indian Ocean is *ultimum mare*."[3]

Montgomery does not accept the translation of ים סוף as, in his words, "Sea of Sledge." He would rather read it as does the Septuagint in 1 Kgs 9:26. In other words, ים סוף is the sea "at the end" of the Indian Ocean. His rendering is not much different from that proposed by J. K. Hoffmeier, who understands that ים סוף refers both to the sea that was crossed as well as to the Gulf of Elath.[4] Hoffmeier translates v. 26 as "...on the shore of the extremity of the sea in the land of Edom." He suggests that the Septuagint, in the other 22 instances, translated ἐρυθρά because of two possibilities. Either the translators perceived that the crossing took place in the Gulf of Suez (Red Sea) or they believed that ים סוף actually meant Ἐρυθρά θάλασσα. Hoffmeier thus implies that the translators perceived the Gulf of Elath to be as much a part of the Red Sea as is the Gulf of Suez.

B. Moritz was perhaps the first to suggest that 1 Kgs 9:26 in the Septuagint is translated with the intention of indicating relative distance rather than vegetation.[5] He proposes that "τῆς ἐσχάτης θαλάσσης" refers to this particular sea as the most distant. It is stated as a contrast to the Gulf of Suez, which is both the nearest sea as well as the actual "Reed Sea." This proposal reflects the reality of the above mentioned geographical perspective and location of the Septuagint translators, i.e., they are situated in Egypt. In addition (and as with Hoffmeier, Montgomery and the others noted above),[6] the Red Sea Presupposition discussed in Chapter Two is clearly evident.

Closer examination of the Greek text is warranted. The relevant clause reads, ...ἐπὶ τοῦ χείλους τῆς ἐσχάτης θαλάσσης ἐν γῇ Ἐδώμ. This is a clarification of the location of Ezion-geber and/or Elath, being situated on the shore of "X" in the land of Edom. "X" represents the genetive phrase τῆς ἐσχάτης θαλάσσης. If translated as "...extremity of the sea..." the text would require an additional definite article prior to θαλάσσης, thus reading τῆς ἐσχάτης as a noun. Within its present context the clause must be read as definite article–attributive adjective–noun. Thus the correct translation is "...of the end sea...." Given that interpretation the relevant clause is translated "...on the shore of the End Sea in the land of Edom."

Why translate יָם סוּף in this way? Moritz and Montgomery are partially correct; the Septuagint translators were reading the Hebrew as sôp. They are incorrect, however, in that the Septuagint is not portraying this sea as an "end sea of the Red Sea (Indian Ocean)." The answer is derived from the geographical (both real and canonical) perspective of the translators. They were writing in Egypt with a perspective that the Israelites came forth from Egypt itself. To them, the Gulf of Suez was the Red Sea, while the Gulf of Elath was the Aelanite Gulf. As the Israelites fled Egypt, the sea they crossed had to be associated with the Gulf of Suez.[7] Hence, יָם סוּף must be Ἐρυθρά θάλασσα.

Given these perceptions, and the strength of canonical presuppositions, it is a simple matter to interpret nearly every occurrence of יָם סוּף in the Hebrew Bible as "Red Sea." On two occasions, however, it is not possible. Both Judg 11:16 and 1 Kgs 9:26 are quite specific in their localization of יָם סוּף. It is not located off the western Sinai Peninsula, but rather must be identified as the Aelanite Gulf (see discussion in Chapter Four, pp. 98–106).

The Septuagint version of Judg 11:16 renders the sea as σιφ. Why the translators apparently chose to transliterate, and not translate, the Hebrew is unclear. Hoffmeier discusses various possibilities but there may be others as well.[8] Perhaps the Hebrew text they viewed actually read "סיף." They would have little choice other than a simple transliteration. Perhaps, based on the specificity of the text, the translators could not identify the sea as the Red Sea. Locating the Red Sea in close proximity to Kadesh would be geographically meaningless. Then again, they may have been hesitant to identify it as the "End Sea" because of the text's seeming lack of clarity regarding the sea's exact location: thus they transliterate.

In any case, the critical verse is 1 Kgs 9:26. It is in this verse that the Hebrew Bible unequivocally identifies ים סוף as the Gulf of Elath. The Septuagint translators knew this. They knew as well that the Aelanite Gulf was not part of the Red Sea. They were not yet tempted to violate known geographical customs and link these two gulfs. To them, the Aelanite Gulf was not the extremity of the Indian Ocean. Their translation reflects their geographical reality. They did read the text as *sôp* and simply translated it into Greek—hence, the "End Sea." By re-reading the unvocalized Hebrew they maintained the integrity of both their canonical and geographical views. The "Red Sea" was the sea the Israelites crossed (*sûp*), while the End Sea/Aelanite Gulf (*sôp*) is something entirely different.

This interpretation also reveals a great deal of important information concerning the Septuagint. As will be seen below and in Chapter Four, ים סוף in the Hebrew Bible is indeed to be identified as the Aelanite/Elath Gulf. Consider, as well, the differentiation between the Gulfs of Suez and Elath. It is thus evident that the Septuagint identification of ים סוף as Red Sea is a canonical interpretation. In other words, "ים סוף must be the Red Sea/Gulf of Suez because our ancestors came out of Egypt and this is the closest sea...it must therefore be ים סוף."

DEAD SEA SCROLLS

Support for this interpretation is also found in the Dead Sea Scrolls. The most telling evidence is within the Genesis Apocryphon.[9] On two occasions specific geographical references are made.

In Describing the Land Apportioned to Shem's sons

...ליד מי הדקל נהרא עד דדבק לימא ש[מו]קא..

[…by the waters of the river Tigris, until it reaches the R[e]d Sea…][10] 1QapGen ar
XVII:7

In Describing Abram's Journey around the Arabian Peninsula

...ואזלת אנה אברם למסחר ולמחזה ארעא ושרית למסחר מן גיחון נהרא ואתית ליד ימא עד די דבקת
לטור תורא וסחרת מן לי[ד]ימא רבא דן די מלחא ואזלת ליד טור תורא למדנחא לפותי ארעא עד די
דבקת לפורת נהרא וסחרת ליד פורת עד די דבקת לימא שמוקא למדנחא והוית אתה לי ליד ימא שמוקא
עד די דבקת ללשן ים סוף די נפק מן ימא שמוקא וסחרת לדרומא עד די דבקת גחון נהרא

[I, Abram, went out to traverse and see the land. I began the traverse at the River
Gihon. I went along the shore of the sea until I reached the mountain of the Bull. I
walked from the sh[ore] of this Great Sea of Salt, skirting the mountain of the Bull
towards the East, through the breadth of the land, until I reached the River
Euphrates. I proceeded towards the East along the bank of the Euphrates, until
reaching the Red Sea. I continued walking along the shore of the Red Sea until
arriving at the branch of the Sea of Reeds that issues from the Red Sea, and continued towards the South until I reached the River Gihon.] 1QapGen ar XXI:15–19

Although there is some question concerning the location of Gihon,[11]
Abram clearly departs from, and returns to that place. And whether one
translates לדרומא וסחרת as "and I turned southward" or "I went around the
southern region,"[12] Abram's journey is revealing in and of itself. In keeping
with the contemporary geographical perspective, and following Abram on
his journey, the Red Sea (שמוקא ימא) begins at the Persian Gulf, continues
into the Indian Ocean and extends up through Today's Red Sea. As Abram is
journeying along the coast of the Arabian Peninsula, the next body of water
he would have encountered would be the Gulf of Elath, not the Gulf of Suez.
The text identifies this body of water as סוף ים לשן, "the tongue of ים סוף,"
which extends off the Red Sea.

It is not altogether clear whether the author has identified ים סוף as a part,
or just an extension, of the Red Sea. Nevertheless, there is a definite identification of ים סוף as the Gulf of Elath/Aelanite Gulf. This is the only extant
instance in the Dead Sea Scrolls in which these bodies of water are identified
in this manner. There do exist, however, other examples in which שמוקא ימא
as well as ים סוף may be found.[13]

Identification of סמוקא ימא—Moving East from an Unknown Location

6 [...תא]פא [מדנ]ח[...] 5 [...ל[מדנ]ח[...] 4 [...באת]ר אזלת[...] 3 [...] חד[...] 2–1
16 [...ניא]באיל ו.[...] 15 [...לאין]מ דב[ה...] 14 [...] 13–7 [...ן]מע[מד...]

[ריח כדי]מדקק קלפוהי א[נון...] מן 17 [טוריא] אלן כלצפון מדנחהון [אחז]ית טורין אחרנין

18 [מלאין נ]רד טב וצפר וקרדמן [ופ]לפלין 19 [למד]נה כל טוריא אלן ומן תמן הובלת

רחוק מנהון למדנח ארעא ואחלפ[ת] 20 [על]א מן י[מא] [על]א מן י[מא] שמוקא וארחקת שגיא מנה

[1–2 […] 3 […] one [… that flowed towards the North-east, taking the water and
the dew to every section.] 4 [From there] I went to [another] pla[ce in the desert and
I moved away] 5 [a great deal] to the [Ea]st [of this] locat[ion. There I saw
uncultivated trees that] 6 gave off [an aroma of incense and myrrh …] 7–13 […] 14
[… in] it, f[ull of resin and it is like the bark] 15 [of the almond tree. When] their
bark is ground i[t is superior to any fragrance. Beyo]nd 17 these [mountains]
towards the North-east of them, I was [sho]wn (still) other mountains 18 [full of]
choice [na]rd, mastic, cardamum [and pe]pper. *blank* From there I went on 19 [to
the Ea]st of all those mountains, far from them, to the East of the land; [I] passed on
20 [above] the Red S[ea] and I moved very far from it…] 4QEnoch^e ar Frag. 3(=1
Enoch 28:3–29:2 + 31:2–32:3)

Identification and Naming of ים סוף

...ותעש להמה כפרעוה וכשלישי מרכבותיו בים סו[ף]...

[You shall treat them like Pharaoh, like the officers of his chariots in Yam Sûp.]
1QWar Scroll XI:9–10

As Represented within Biblical Texts, Targumim and Phylacteries

[לס]וסו ולרכבו ולפרש[ו א]שר ה[צ]יף את ה[ ]מי ים סוף על פני[המה...

[…to his horses and chariots and horsemen, how he made the water of the Yam Sûp
flow over them…] 4QPhylA and K (Deut 11:4)

The Same Verse in Greek

[ιππον αυτω]ν ως επε [λυσεν το υδωρ] [της θαλασς]ης ερυθρας…4QSeptuagintDeut

[אלה הדברים אשר דבר מושה אל כול ישראל בעבר הירדן במדבר בערבה] מול סוף בי[ן פרן...]
[These are the words that Moses spoke to all Israel beyond the Jordan in the wilderness, in the arabah near Sûp, between…] 4QDeut^h (Deut 1:1–6)

[ ]סוף כאשר דבר יהוה אלי ונסב את הר שעיר...]
[{ } Sûp, as YHWH told me and we skirted Mt. Seir…] 4QDeut^h (Deut 2:1)

It is likely that the Dead Sea Scrolls references to ים סוף require a canonical understanding. In other words, the biblical tradition is that the Israelites
crossed ים סוף. Thus, any reference to that sea is carried over into any
reference to it being represented in the Dead Sea Scrolls liturgical and

canonical texts. Even the War Scroll text quoted above identifies the sea of
the exodus crossing as יָם סוּף. The underlying principle would be that the
integrity of the biblical canon must be maintained. Nonetheless, it is interesting that the Septuagint tradition of a "Red Sea" crossing is not maintained
within the Dead Sea Scrolls tradition, except in the Greek texts. Nevertheless, the Red Sea (יַמָּא שְׂמוּקָא) is apparently known to the Dead Sea Scrolls
authors. Even with the canonical intent described above, it is reasonable to
suggest that these authors (outside of the Septuagint tradition) maintained
the distinction between the Red Sea and יָם סוּף. This would further suggest
some level of understanding that the sea of the exodus crossing was indeed
the Gulf of Elath.

Taking this data into consideration along with the Septuagint material,
we may derive the following conclusions:

• The presupposition that the Israelite exodus proceeded from
Egypt is discerned as early as at least the 3rd century B.C.E.; and,

• Textual evidence would indicate that within Hebrew/Aramaic traditions (and supported by the Greek Septuagint) יָם סוּף is to be identified as
the Gulf of Elath, reaffirming what is evident from the Greek and Latin
geographies.

ARTAPANUS

The text of Artapanus (3rd–2nd B.C.E.) returns the investigation to a
chronological order.[14] His text on Moses (27:34) contains this description of
the exodus:

...διαβάντας τοὺς κατὰ τὴν Ἀραβίαν ποταμοὺς, καὶ διαβάντας ἱκανὸν τόπον, ἐπὶ τὴν
Ἐρυθρὰν τριταίους ἐλθεῖν θάλασσαν.
[...they crossed the rivers on the Arabian side and passed through a broad area to
come to the Red Sea on the third day.]

As the crossing takes place on the third day, it is likely that Artapanus is
referring here to the Gulf of Suez, or waters nearby.

JUBILEES

The Book of Jubilees (2nd century B.C.E.) is also found in the pseudepigrapha.[15] Within the descriptions of land assigned to Shem and Ham, the region's seas are mentioned.

And the lot of Shem was assigned...as the middle of the earth...from the midst of the Rafa Mountains, from the mouth of the water of the river Tina. And his portion goes toward the west through the midst of this river, and it goes on until it draws near to the water of the abysses from which this river goes forth. And its waters pour forth into the Me'at Sea. And this river goes on into the Great Sea. And everything which is toward the north belongs to Japheth, and everything which is toward the south belongs to Shem. And (his portion) goes on until it draws near Karaso, which is in the bosom of the tongue which looks toward the south. And his portion goes on toward the Great Sea. And it goes straight until it draws near to the west of the tongue which looks toward the south because the name of this sea is the tongue of the Sea of Egypt. And it is turned from there toward the south, toward the mouth of the Great Sea on the shore of the waters. And it goes on toward the west of Åfra. And it goes on until it draws near...the river Gihon, and toward the south of...Gihon, toward the shore of that river. And it goes on toward the east until it draws near...to the south and east of all the land of Eden, and to all of the east. And it turns in the east...until it draws near toward the last of the mountain whose name is Rafa. 8:12–16

And he knew that a blessed portion...had reached Shem...all the land of Eden, all of the land of the Red Sea, all of the land of the East, India, along the Red Sea... 8:21

1 And Ham divided...among his sons. ...to Cush toward the east, and west of him for Mizraim. And west of him for Put. And west of him for Canaan. And toward his west was the sea. 2 And Shem also divided among his sons. ...to Elam and his sons toward the east of the Tigris River until it approaches toward the east...of India, along the Red Sea on its shore, the waters of Dedan, and all of the mountains of Mebri and Elam all of the land of Susa, and everything which is beside Pharnak as far as the Red Sea and up to the Tina River. 3 ...to Asshur...all of the land of Asshur and Nineveh and Shinar and as far as the vicinity of India. And then it goes up and skirts the river. 4 And to Arpachshad...the region of Chaldea toward the east of the Euphrates, which is near the Red Sea, and all of the waters of the desert as far as the vicinity of the tongue of the sea which faces toward Egypt... 9:1–4

These passages are revealing. They indicate the expected identification of the Persian Gulf and Indian Ocean with the Red Sea. As Jubilees precedes the Dead Sea Scrolls, there is also an initial reference to a "tongue of the sea of X." It is difficult to determine the referent of the pronouns in 9:1. Nevertheless, by following the description of the portions given to Shem's sons, it is possible to suggest that the "tongue of the sea which faces toward Egypt" is either Today's Red Sea or the Gulf of Suez, or perhaps a combined identification of the two. With the preceding comment that Arpachshad was assigned the "waters of the desert *as far* (italics mine) as the vicinity of the tongue..." (italics mine) it is likely that the Gulf of Suez is intended.

The description of Shem's portion in 8:12–16 appears to begin at verse 12 with a river (Tina) that empties into the Mediterranean. South of this river is the territory of Shem. His territory extends to the south and west toward the Mediterranean and what appears to be the Nile Delta ("the mouth of the Great Sea on the shore of the waters") and the "tongue which looks toward the south...." As this feature is identified as the "tongue of the Sea of Egypt," the only geographical feature in that region that would fit this description is the Gulf of Suez.

This phrase ("tongue of the Sea of 'X'") also occurs within the Hebrew Bible on several occasions: Josh 15:2, 5; 18:19 and Isa 11:15. It is worth considering these verses at this juncture.

Josh 15:2—Describing the Border of Judah

ויהי להם גבול נגב מקצה ים המלח מן הלשן הפנה נגבה

[And this is their southern border: from the end of the Dead Sea, from "the tongue that faces southward..."]

In keeping with the suggestion by R. G. Boling (who suggests "the turning tongue"), הפנה is to be read as a qal active participle meaning "the one who faces/is turning."[16] In keeping with the tenor of his comment on v. 5, however, the Lisan opposite Masada does not turn toward the south, but rather faces west.[17] In a sense, the Lisan divides the Dead Sea in two. Thus הלשן הפנה נגבה is to be understood as the southern, southerly pointing, "tongue-shaped" portion of the Dead Sea.

Josh 15:5—Continuing the Border of Judah

וגבול קדמה ים המלח עד קצה הירדן וגבול לפאת צפונה מלשון הים מקצה הירדן

[And the eastern border is the Dead Sea until the end of the Jordan. And the north-side boundary is from the tongue of the sea, from the end of the Jordan.]

There is no reason to translate לשון הים as does Boling ("western tongue").[18] He correctly states that there is no geographical feature that would fit this description. If, as with v. 2, לשון is understood as a tongue-shaped body of water, the border description is quite clear. The text is referring to the northern-pointing portion of the Dead Sea.

Josh 18:19—Describing the Border of Benjamin

...והיה תצאותיו הגבול אל לשון ים המלח צפונה אל קצה הירדן נגבה זה גבול נגב

[...and the extremity of the boundary is at the tongue of the Dead Sea, at end of the Jordan, toward the south. This is the southern boundary...]

There is textual concern about the feminine noun תצאותיו, which should perhaps be read with the *qere* as תצאות (as in Josh 15:4). Although the non-suffixed reading is present in multiple manuscripts (q.v., BHS note to 18:19), the proper reading is not relevant to this boundary concern. Boling translates אל לשון ים המלח as, "at the northern side of the Tongue." He also comments, "The latter is apparently the distinctive geological terrace jutting into the Dead Sea from Transjordan. There is no bay or 'inlet' (NEB) on the north or northwest shoreline to match this description which is extremely odd as a point of reference for the border."[19] Again, as suggested by the NRSV translation "...northern bay of the Dead Sea...," it is credible to understand the northern "tongue of the Dead Sea" as that extension of the sea pointing northward from the Lisan. This tongue meets the Jordan River, as it ends at the Dead Sea.

Isa 11:15—Describing Divine Revenge against Egypt

והחרים יהוה את לשון ים מצרים

[...and YHWH will make desolate the tongue of the Sea of Egypt...]

Regarding והחרים, the Septuagint reads καὶ ἐρημώσει (supported by the Syriac, Targumim and Vulgate), implying the Hebrew root ח–ר–ב rather than the Hebrew Bible ח–ר–ם. These roots both occur in hiphil in the Hebrew Bible. ח–ר–ם appears 49 times, on two other occasions with YHWH as the subject, while ח–ר–ב appears 7 times, also on two other occasions with YHWH as the subject. While YHWH may be able to destroy a body of water just as easily as making it desolate, it would appear contextually that the root

ח–ר–ב may be more appropriately applied here.[20] In any case, the subtleties of that particular translation play no role in the meaning of the phrase לשון ים מצרים.

Isa 11:15 is the only occurrence of this phrase in the Hebrew Bible.[21] Nevertheless, there are only two possibilities that present themselves for the identification of the "tongue of the Sea of Egypt." It is either the Nile Delta at the Mediterranean Sea or the Gulf of Suez.[22] In light of the previous data gathered from the Dead Sea Scrolls, Pseudepigrapha and Hebrew Bible, it is likely that the phrase "tongue of the Sea of 'X'" refers to a body of water and not a peninsula-like body of land. Thus the "tongue" in this instance is not the projection of land extending into the Mediterranean at the Nile Delta. It is rather to be understood as the Gulf of Suez, the only other body of water that could possibly qualify.

1 MACCABEES

Within the Apocryphal literature, 1 Maccabees (2nd–1st B.C.E.) also mentions the exodus.[23] As noted above, this Greek text also appears to follow the Septuagint canonical tradition in that the sea of the crossing is identified as the Red Sea, and thus the Gulf of Suez.

μνήσθητε ὡς ἐσώθησαν οἱ πατέρες ἡμῶν ἐν θαλάσσῃ ἐρυθρᾷ, ὅτε ἐδίωκεν αὐτοὺς Φαραω ἐν δυνάμει·
[Remember how our fathers were saved at the Red Sea, when Pharaoh pursued them with a host.] 1 Macc 4:9

ENOCH

The Book of Enoch (2nd B.C.E.–1st C.E.), quoted above from its Dead Sea Scrolls manuscript, contains references to ימא שמוקא.[24] These comments serve to corroborate the Greek and Latin geographies in locating the Red Sea to the east (as opposed to the Great Sea, i.e., the Mediterranean, in the west), likely intending the Persian Gulf and perhaps the Indian Ocean.

I saw seven rivers on the earth, greater than all other rivers; one of them, coming from the west, sheds its waters into the Great Sea. And two come from the north to the sea and shed their waters into the Erythrean Sea in the east. And the remaining four come from the northern side toward the sea, two to the Erythrean Sea, and two empty into the Great Sea...[25]

TARGUM JONATHAN

The first of the Aramaic Targumim to be investigated is Targum Jonathan (1st B.C.E.–1st C.E.).[26] A representative and relevant verse to consider is 1 Kgs 9:26.

וספינתא עבד מלכא שלמה בעציון גבר דעם אילות על כיף ימא דסוף בארעא דאדום:

[King Solomon built a fleet of ships at Ezion-geber, which is near Elath, on the shore of Yam Sûp, in the land of Edom.]

Once again, Elath is identified as being on the shore of ים סוף in the land of Edom. In fact, all references to ים סוף that are found within Targum Jonathan are translated directly into the Aramaic as ימא דסוף (Josh 2:10; 4:23; 24:6; Judg 11:16; Jer 49:21; Pss 106:7, 9, 22; 136:13, 15). Even in a time when the Red Sea (ימא שמוקא) was a known entity, the sea of the exodus crossing is never translated as Red Sea. This may reflect the contemporary geographical reality or the strength of the canonical perspective, or a combination of the two.

ASSUMPTION OF MOSES

The next pseudepigraphical text to investigate is the Assumption of Moses (early 1st C.E.).[27] Written in Latin, it also appears to reflect the Septuagint tradition relative to the sea of the exodus crossing.

Nonne hoc est quod testabatur nobis tum Moyses in profetis, qui multa passus est in Aegypto et in Mari Rubro et in heremo annis XL
[Is it not this, the things which Moses formerly testified to us in his prophecies? Moses, who suffered many things in Egypt, and in the Red Sea, and in the desert, during 40 years.] 3:11

FLAVIUS JOSEPHUS

Flavius Josephus (late 1st C.E.) is investigated here due to his dependence on the biblical text for his history. He thus is not so much a geographer as he is a re-teller of biblical narrative. On two occasions Josephus mentions the waters with which this investigation is concerned.[28]

Concerning the Persian Gulf

...Εὐφράτης δὲ καὶ Τίγρις ἐπὶ τὴν Ἐρυθρὰν ἀπίασι θάλασσαν·
[Euphrates also, as well as Tigris, goes down into the Red Sea.] Ant. I:I, 3

Concerning the Sea of the Exodus Crossing

συντόμως δὲ ποιούμενοι τὴν ἄφοδον εἰς Βεελσεφῶντα χωρίον τριταῖοι παραγίνονται τῆς Ἐρυθρᾶς θαλάσσης.
[Quitting the country by the shortest route they arrived on the third day at Beel-sephon, a place beside the Red Sea.] Ant. II:XV, 1

Identifying the Gulf of Suez as the Arabian Gulf (Quail Miracle Story)

καὶ μετ' ὀλίγον ὀρτύγων πλῆθος, τρέφει δὲ τοῦτο τὸ ὄρνεον ὡς οὐδὲν ἕτερον ὁ Ἀράβιος κόλπος, ἐφίπταται τὴν μεταξὺ θάλατταν ὑπερελθὸν...
[And, not long after, a flock of quails—a species of bird abundant, above all others, in the Arabian Gulf—came flying over this stretch of sea...] Ant. III:I, 5

Concerning Solomon's Port at Elath

Ἐναυπηγήσατο δὲ ὁ βασιλεὺς ἐν τῷ Αἰγυπτιακῷ κόλπῳ σκάφη πολλὰ τῆς Ἐρυθρᾶς θαλάσσης ἔν τινι τόπῳ λεγομένῳ Γασιωνγάβελ οὐ πόρρω Αἰλανῆς πόλεως, ἢ νῦν Βερενίκη καλεῖται·
[The king also built many ships in the Egyptian gulf of the Red Sea at a certain place called Gasiōn-gabel not far from the city of Ailanē, which is now called Berenikē.] Ant. VIII:VI, 4

This is an extremely problematic statement. "Egyptian gulf" occurs in no other place and would imply that Josephus is referring to the Gulf of Suez. At the same time, this text is reproducing the story found in 1 Kgs 9:26 and would imply that Josephus considers the Gulf of Elath to be the "Egyptian gulf of the Red Sea." In keeping with the contemporary geographies as well as the Septuagint the Gulf of Elath is not an Egyptian gulf of the Red Sea. Further, although Ailane (Elath) and Gasion-gabel (Ezion-geber) are in close proximity to one another, Berenike (in the geographers studied) is never located at the Gulf of Elath. It is only here identified as Elath.

Josephus' presentation of the geography in and around the Sinai Peninsula seems faulty. On the other hand, if Josephus is accurate, this would be the earliest reference to the Gulf of Elath being a part of the Red Sea. Nevertheless, his placement of sites is still inconsistent with both the biblical accounts (Hebrew Bible and Septuagint) as well as known geographical identifications. There is little room other than to conclude that he is inaccurate in his geographical knowledge and representation. Perhaps he is attempting to blend his canonical perspective with the known regional sites. Perhaps he has misread Pomponius Mela, as Mela also describes the location of Berenike, but only locating it on Today's Red Sea.[29]

NEW TESTAMENT

The New Testament text (1st–2nd C.E.) refers to the Red Sea on two occasions: Acts 7:36 and Heb 11:29. In both instances the Greek reads ἡ ἐρυθρὰ θάλασσα in reference to the Israelite crossing of the sea. Once again, a canonical perspective is reflected stemming from the original Septuagint translation.

PSEUDO-JONATHAN

Returning to a consideration of Targumic literature, the Targum of Pseudo-Jonathan of the Pentateuch (1st–2nd C.E.) continues the pattern observed in Targum Jonathan.[30] The root ס–מ–ק ("red", "tanned") is extensively utilized within the text, but never in reference to the exodus or ים סוף (Gen 25:25, 30; Exod 26:14; 39:34; Lev 13:19, 42, 49; Num 19:2 +). As with Targum Jonathan, all the Hebrew references to ים סוף are translated directly into the Aramaic as ימא דסוף (Exod 10:19; 13:18; 15:4, 22; 23:31; Num 14:25; 21:4; 33:10, 11; Deut 1:40; 2:1; 11:4 plus other instances where the translator adds in the name of the sea, e.g., Exod 2:21; 14:13; 18:8; Deut 28:68).

ONKELOS

Onkelos, writing in the 2nd century C.E., maintains the observed pattern within the Targumim.[31] He also makes use of the root ס–מ–ק, as in Gen 25:25, 30 and Num 19:2. Nevertheless, Onkelos is also consistent when translating Hebrew ים סוף. On all occasions he renders the Aramaic as ימא

סוף (Exod 13:18; 15:4, 22; 23:31; Num 14:25; 21:4; 33:10, 11; Deut 1:40; 2:1; 11:4).

TESTAMENT OF SOLOMON

The final pseudepigraphical text is the Testament of Solomon (2nd–5th C.E.).[32] The Red Sea is mentioned several times within this text (6:3, 5, 6; 12:4; 23:2; 24:1), but it is within 25:5–6 that a clear identification is made. The author perceives the Red Sea as that of the exodus crossing, reflecting, I suggest again, the Septuagint perspective identifying the Gulf of Suez.

> εἶπον οὖν αὐτῷ πῶς οὖν εὑρέθης ἐν τῇ Ἐρυθρᾷ θαλάσσῃ; ὁ δὲ ἔφη· ἐν τῇ ἐξόδου τῶυ υἱῶν Ἰσραὴλ ἐγὼ ἐσκλήρυνα τὴν καρδίαν Φαραὼ καὶ ἀνεπτέρωσα αὐτοῦ τὴν καρδίαν καὶ τῶν θεραπόντων αὐτοῦ. καὶ ἐποίησα αὐτοὺς ἵνα καταδιώξωσιν ὀπίσω τῶν υἱῶν Ἰσραὴλ, καὶ συνηκολούθησε Φαραὼ καὶ πάντες οἱ Αἰγύπτιοι. τότε ἐγὼ παρήμην ἐκεῖ καὶ συνηκολουθήσαμεν, καὶ ἀνήλθομεν ἅπαντες ἐν τῇ Ἐρυθρᾷ θαλάσσῃ.
>
> [I therefore said to him, "How is it that you are found in the Red Sea?" He responded, "During the time of the Exodus of the sons of Israel, I gave Pharaoh pangs of anxiety and hardened the heart of him, as well as of his subordinates. I caused them to pursue closely after the sons of Israel, and Pharaoh followed with (me) and (so did) all the Egyptians. I was there at that time and we followed together. We all approached the Red Sea.] 25:5–6

And Perhaps Identifying Today's Red Sea (Gulf of Elath?)

> ὅτε δὲ ἤκουσα ἐγὼ Σολομῶν τὸ ὄνομα τοῦ ἀρχαγγέλου ηὐξάμην καὶ ἐδόξασα τὸν θεὸν τοῦ οὐρανοῦ καὶ τῆς γῆς, καὶ σφραγίσας αὐτὸν ἔταξα εἰς τὴν ἐργασίαν τῆς λιθοτομίας, τοῦ τέμνειν λίθους τοῦ ναοῦ ἀρθέντας διὰ θαλάσσης Ἀραβίας τοὺς κειμένους παρὰ αἰγιαλόν.
>
> [When I, Solomon, heard the archangel's name mentioned, I honored and glorified the God of heaven and earth. After I sealed (the demon) with my seal, I ordered him into the stone quarry to cut for the Temple stones which had been transported by way of the Arabian Sea and dumped along the seashore.] 2:5

VULGATE

In comparison to the Septuagint version of 1 Kgs 9:26, in which the Gulf of Elath and the Gulf of Suez are clearly distinguished from each other, the Vulgate translation (4th–5th C.E.) removes the distinction.[33]

...quae est iuxta Ahilam in litore maris Rubri in terra Idumea.
[...it is near Elath on the shore of the Red Sea in the land of Edom.]

From the material investigated it appears that the Vulgate is the first instance in which the Gulfs of Elath and Suez are portrayed as gulfs of the Red Sea. It is this linkage that is carried forward to modern scholarship, as discussed in Chapters One and Two (pp. 28–30, 33–34). Furthermore, within Jewish tradition in the centuries to follow, the examples seen so far in the Targumim are also carried forward.

SYRIAC PESHITTA, TARGUM NEOPHYTI, SAMARITAN TARGUM, FRAGMENTS

The Syriac Peshitta Version of the Old Testament (5th–6th C.E.), in all instances of the Hebrew ים סוף, represents the sea as ימא דסוף.[34] The same is true for Targum Neophyti (6th C.E.),[35] the Samaritan Targum of the Pentateuch (12th–16th C.E.)[36] and various Fragment Targumim (various eras).[37]

RABBINIC LITERATURE

Interestingly, within Rabbinic literature (Mishnah, Talmud and Commentaries) the Aramaic term ימא סמוקא does not appear. Whenever the sea of the exodus crossing is discussed the Rabbis consistently make use of ים סוף (e.g., Soṭah 12a; Zebaḥ. 116a; Pesaḥ. 118a; Ta'an. 16b). Finally, Ibn Ezra (11th C.E.) makes a fascinating comment in his discussion of Exod 13:18.[38]

סוף – הוא שם מקום וי"א שהוא מגזרת סוף דבר כי הוא סוף העולם והוא ים אוקינוס כאשר כבר זכרתי
וזאת טעות גדולה כי הוא ים מזרחי כנגד מצרימים ספרדי גדול ממנו

[Red Sea—Suf is the name of a place. Others say that suf comes from the same root as sôp in *the end of the matter* (Eccl 12:13). It is so called because it lies at the end of the world. The reference is to the Atlantic, which I have already mentioned. However, this is a major blunder, because it (ים סוף) lies in the east opposite Egypt, while the Atlantic (perhaps Mediterranean?) is larger than it is.]

This passage will be discussed further in Chapter Four (pp. 102–3) as it pertains directly to the discussion concerning Deut 1:1 and a proposed identification of סוף.

SYNOPSIS, TABLE AND MAP

A summary of this data is presented in Table 2 and Map 4. As reflected in the Vulgate translation, by the 5th century C.E. the tradition exists that the Gulf of Elath is as much a part of the Red Sea as is the Gulf of Suez. It is also quite difficult to determine within Aramaic, Syriac and Hebrew litera- ture just when ים סוף was perceived in a more canonical context as opposed to the context of contemporary geography. It may be as late as the Vulgate or perhaps as early as Josephus.

In any case, it is apparent from the Septuagint and Dead Sea Scrolls materials that a change occurred. From these texts we learn that a distinction between the Gulfs of Elath and Suez was drawn as early as the 3rd century B.C.E.. This is not altogether unexpected, as the same distinction is found within the Greek and Latin geographies of the time. Most importantly for this study, the Gulf of Elath is identified as ים סוף. The issues that remain involve whether or not this distinction is evident in the Hebrew Bible. Is the distinction one carried forward in Israel's tradition from earlier times, or is it a later phenomenon strongly influenced by the Greek tradition? Chapter Four continues specifically with the investigation of the exodus itinerary sites as described throughout the Hebrew Bible. The study of the location of ים סוף will be critical, given the centrality of this sea in the exodus narrative.

NAME/SOURCE	DATE/BCE	GULF OF ELATH	SEA OF EXODUS	GULF OF SUEZ	TODAY'S RED SEA	INDIAN OCEAN	PERSIAN GULF
Masoretic Text		(in Chapter 4)	Yam Sûp	Tongue of the Sea of Egypt			
Septuagint	3rd–1st	Yam Sôp	Red Sea	Red Sea			
Artapanus	3rd–2nd		Red Sea	Red Sea			
Jubilees	2nd			Tongue of the Sea of Egypt	Red Sea	Red Sea	Red Sea
1 Maccabees	2nd–1st		Red Sea			Red Sea	Red Sea
Enoch	2nd–1st					Red Sea	Red Sea
Dead Sea Scrolls	1st BCE–1st CE	Yam Sûp, Tongue of Yam Sûp	Yam Sûp		Red Sea		
Targum Jonathan	1st BCE–1st CE	Yam Sûp	Yam Sûp				
	DATE/CE						
Assumption of Moses	1st		Red Sea	Red Sea			
Josephus	1st	?	Red Sea	?, Arabian Gulf			Red Sea
New Testament	1st–2nd		Red Sea				
Targum Pseudo-Jonathan	1st–2nd		Yam Sûp				
Onkelos	2nd		Yam Sûp				
Testament of Solomon	2nd–5th	Arabian Sea?	Red Sea	Red Sea	Arabian Sea?		
Vulgate	5th	Red Sea		Red Sea			
Syriac Peshitta	5th–6th	Yam Sûp	Yam Sûp				
Targum Neophyti	6th		Yam Sûp				
Samaritan Targum	12th–16th		Yam Sûp				
Fragment Targumim	various		Yam Sûp				

Table 2—ANCIENT SCRIPTURES

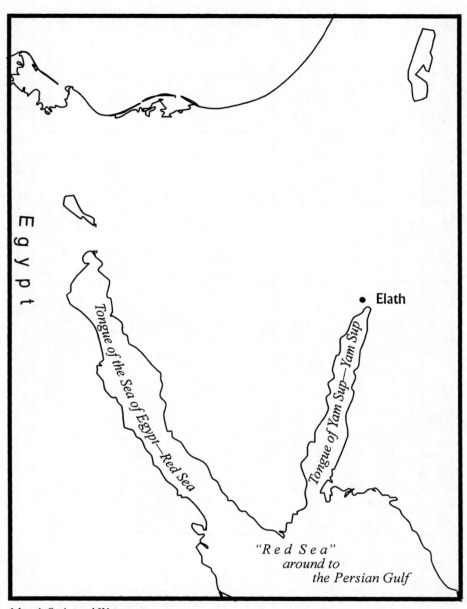

Map 4. Scriptural Waterways

CHAPTER FOUR

THE JOURNEY: THE EXODUS ITINERARY SITES LOCATED BY THE BIBLICAL SOURCES

The authors of the biblical text described, represented, created, inherited and transmitted a tradition of an Israelite flight from Egypt: the exodus. This story was passed down within many contexts. It was transmitted across time, from century to century. It was also absorbed and re-created across national and religious boundaries. According to these authors (ultimately redacted into the text we have received) the ancient Israelites traveled great distances and visited numerous sites during their journey.

The itinerary of their encampments between Egypt and the Jordan River is mentioned on numerous occasions within the Pentateuch. It is most concisely described in essentially two texts, within the narrative of Exod 12:37–19:25 and in Num 33:1–49 (plus chapter 21). The book of Deuteronomy provides several sites as well. A listing of these sites, plus important and related nearby locales, is found in Tables 3a and b along with their pertinent itinerary text references.

A point of re-clarification is vital at this juncture. This study is not an attempt to link archaeological sites with their supposed matches in the Bible. The concern of this investigation is not to judge or determine whether or not the itinerary from Yam Sûp to Kadesh-barnea is so extensive that it implies a journey across the Sinai Peninsula to the north, south, directly east or a variety of combinations, alternatives or permutations of these. The sole purpose of this investigation is to determine the geographical perspective of the authors regarding the locations they describe as exodus itinerary sites. When these sites are described within the Hebrew Bible, where are they? Where did the authors situate them, if so designated within the biblical corpus? Are they consistent in their localizations, or are they "all over the map" in their descriptions? Each site is detailed in the order delineated in Tables 3a and b.

In order to divide the textual material into sources the works of S. R. Driver, M. Noth and R. E. Friedman have been consulted.[1] Their categorizations of the pentateuchal sources J, E, P and D (Genesis through 2 Kings) is compared to determine any source-based geographical differences. The remainder of the Hebrew sources (Isaiah through 2 Chronicles) is also studied to compare their perspectives. In order to fix more easily the location of the exodus sites, a number of "fixed locales" are established (see Map 5). These include the following:

- Egypt
- Edom
- Negeb
- Judah
- Shephelah
- Moab
- Jordan River Valley
- Chinnereth
- Bashan

If the textual sources describe the itinerary sites in relationship to these fixed locales, this investigation will be able to determine the consistency of the biblical geographical perspective vis à vis the exodus journey. The geographical perspective of the biblical authors is now presented, from the border with Egypt to Abel-shittim.

THE BORDER WITH EGYPT

Having risen in power within Egypt, Joseph brings his entire family to live in Goshen. Nearly always identified as located near the Nile Delta, or in locales that would be amenable to pasturing and shepherding, Goshen is perceived as located within Egypt proper. But just where does Egypt share its border with Canaan? This must be considered at the outset. As stated by N. Na'aman:

Goshen	Related site
Rameses	Exod 12:37; Num 33:3, 5
Succoth	Exod 12:37; 13:20; Num 33:5–6
Derech Yam Sûp	Exod 13:18
Yam Sûp	Exod 13:18; 15:4, 22; Num 33:10–11; Deut 2:1
Etham	Exod 13:20; Num 33:6–7
Pi-hahiroth	Exod 14:2, 9; Num 33:7–8
Baal-zephon	Exod 14:2, 9; Num 33:7
Migdol	Exod 14:2; Num 33:7
The Sea	Exod 14:2, 21–29; 15:4, 10, 19; Num 33:8
Wilderness of Etham	Num 33:8
Shur/Wilderness of Shur	Exod 15:22
Marah	Exod 15:23; Num 33:8–9
Elim	Exod 15:27; 16:1; Num 33:9–10
Wilderness of Sin	Exod 16:1; 17:1; Num 33:11–12
Dophkah	Num 33:12–13
Alush	Num 33:13–14
Rephidim	Exod 17:1, 8; 19:2; Num 33:14–15
Massah	Exod 17:7
Meribah	Exod 17:7
Wilderness of Sinai	Exod 19:1–2; Num 33:15–16
Mt. Sinai	Exod 19
Mt. Horeb	Exod 17:6; Deut 1:2, 19
Mt. Seir/Seir	Deut 2:1, 5, 8, 29
Kibroth-hattaavah	Num 33:16–17
Hazeroth	Num 33:17–18
Rithmah	Num 33:18–19
Rimmon-perez	Num 33:19–20
Libnah	Num 33:20–21
Rissah	Num 33:21–22
Kehelathah	Num 33:22–23
Mt. Shepher	Num 33:23–24
Haradah	Num 33:24–25
Makheloth	Num 33:25–26
Tahath	Num 33:26–27
Terah	Num 33:27–28

Table 3—**EXODUS ITINERARY SITES (continued on p. 80)**

Mithkah	Num 33:28–29
Hashmonah	Num 33:29–30
Moseroth	Num 33:30–31
Bene-jaakan	Num 33:31–32
Hor-haggidgad	Num 33:32–33
Jotbathah	Num 33:33–34
Abronah	Num 33:34–35
Ezion-geber	Num 33:35–36; Deut 2:8
Elath	Related site
Wilderness of Zin	Num 33:36
Paran/Wilderness of Paran	Related site
Kadesh-barnea	Num 20:1, 22; 33:36–37; Deut 1:19
Mt. Hor	Num 20:22–23, 25, 27; 21:4; 33:37, 38, 41
Zalmonah	Num 33:41–42
Punon	Num 33:42–43
Oboth	Num 21:10–11; 33:43–44
Iye-abarim	Num 21:11; 33:44
Dibon-gad/Dibon	Num 33:45–46
Almon-diblathaim	Num 33:46–47
Wadi Zered	Num 21:12; Deut 2:13
Beer	Num 21:16
Mattanah	Num 21:18–19
Nahaliel	Num 21:19
Bamoth/Bamoth-baal	Num 21:19–20
Pisgah	Num 21:20
Jahaz	Num 21:23
Heshbon	Num 21:26; Deut 1:4; 2:24
Jazer	Num 21:32
Edrei	Num 21:33; Deut 1:4
Ashtaroth	Deut 1:4
Tablelands of Medeba	Num 21:30
Mts. of Abarim	Num 33:47–48
Mt. Nebo	Num 33:47
Plains of Moab	Num 33:48–49
Beth-jeshimoth	Num 33:49
Abel-shittim	Num 33:49

Table 3—**EXODUS ITINERARY SITES (continued)**

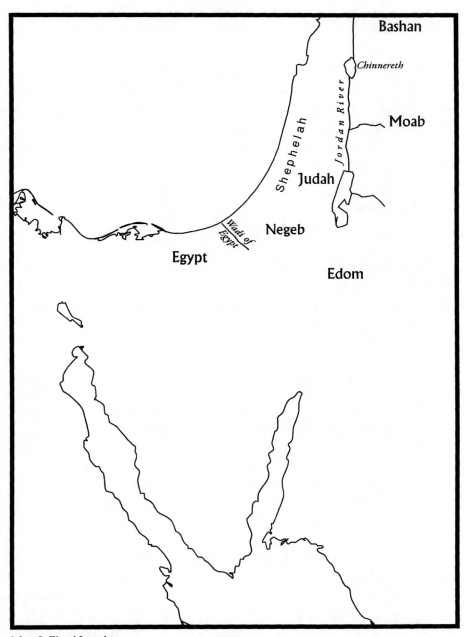

Map 5. Fixed Locales

It is perhaps of interest that in the description of the Exodus, the perspective and the terms used are those of people coming out of Egypt, towards the Land of Canaan.[2]

The question remains, is the perspective that of an author writing in Egypt or in Canaan? The eastward reach of the Egyptian border appears to be an issue of geographical perspective. As determined from the Greek and Latin geographies the Sinai Peninsula was known to those authors as Arabia Petraea. It was not included within the territory of Egypt. This appears to reflect a perspective that was strongly influenced by Egyptian tradition.

Much has been written concerning the Egyptian border with Canaan.[3] Focus has concentrated on two sites, Shihor and the Wadi of Egypt.

Shihor—שחור

Occurring 5 times in the Hebrew Bible, Shihor is often identified as the Nile River. It has also been suggested by T. O. Lambdin that it is located in and around the Bubastite or Pelusiac arm of the Nile.[4] It is interesting to compare the Hebrew Bible with the Septuagint translation:

Josh 13:3

מן השיחור אשר על פני מצרים ועד גבול עקרון צפונה לכנעני תחשב חמשת סרני פלשתים העזתי והאשדודי...

[...from the Shihor, which is next to Egypt, northward as far as the border of Ekron (considered Canaanite). There are five Philistine rulers: of Gaza, Ashdod...]

...ἀπὸ τῆς ἀοικήτου τῆς κατὰ πρόσωπον Αἰγύπτου ἕως τῶν ὁρίωνἈκκαρὼν ἐξ εὐωνύμων τῶν Χαναναίων προσλογίζεται ταῖς πέντε σατραπείαις τῶν Φυλιστιεὶμ...

[...from the wilderness before Egypt, as far as the borders of Accaron on the left of the Chananites the land is reckoned to the five principalities of the Phylistines...]

The Hebrew text is describing unconquered lands associated with the Philistine nation (Josh 13:2). Verse 3 clarifies the extent of that land. As Philistia extends from Egyptian territory north, it is important to understand the meaning of על פני in its context here. It occurs no fewer than 130 times in the Hebrew Bible. On most occasions it carries the meaning "on the surface of" (Gen 1:2, 20, 29; 7:18, 23; 11:8–9; Exod 16:14; 32:20; Num 11:31; Deut 7:6; 2 Sam 11:11; Isa 23:17; Jer 25:26, 33; Ezek 32:4; Amos 9:6; Job 5:10).

Prominent as well is the meaning "next to" or "toward" (as
50:13; Num 21:11; 33:7; Josh 15:8; 18:14; 19:11; 1 Sam 26:1, 3; 1 ᴋᵦ
2 Kgs 23:13; Ezek 42:8). Within a geographical context, a related directional
translation would be appropriate, in this case, "east." This meaning is evident in the Hebrew Bible as well (as in 1 Kgs 17:3, 5). To be located at the
Nile Delta the expected intent of the author would be to situate the Shihor *in*
Egypt. Thus, the Hebrew indicates that the Shihor is located to the east of
Egypt, at the southern extent of Philistia.

Josh 19:26

ואלמלך ועמעד ומשאל ופגע בכרמל הימה ובשיחור לבנת

[...and Alammelech, Amad and Mishal. And on the west it touches Carmel and
Shihor-libnath.]

...καὶ Ἐλιμελὲχ, καὶ Ἀμιὴλ, καὶ Μαασά καὶ συνάψει τῷ Καρμήλῳ κατὰ θάλασσαν,
καὶ τῷ Σιὼν, καὶ Λαβανάθ

[...and Elimelech, and Amiel, and Maasa, and the lot will border on Carmel
westward, and on Sion, and Labanath.]

Josh 19:26 pertains to the border of Asher, located in the north. It would
thus appear that this Shihor is another site of similar name, and not relevant
to the discussion here.

Isa 23:2, 3

דמו ישבי אי סחר צידון
עבר ים מלאוך ובמים רבים
זרע שחר קציר יאור תבואתה ותהי סחר גוים

[Be still, O inhabitants of the coast, O merchants of Sidon,
your messengers crossed over the sea and were on the mighty waters;
your revenue was the grain of Shihor, the harvest of the Nile; you
were the merchant of the nations.][5]

Τίνι ὅμοιοι γεγόνασιν οἱ ἐνοικοῦντες ἐν τῇ νήσῳ, μετάβολοι Φοινίκης, διαπερῶντες
τὴν θάλασσαν ἐν ὕδατι πολλῷ σπέρμα μεταβόλων; ὡς ἀμητοῦ εἰσφερομένου, οἱ
μετάβολοι τῶν ἐθνῶν.

[To whom are the dwellers in the island become like, the merchants of Phoenicia,
passing over the sea in great waters, a generation of merchants? as when the harvest
is gathered in, so are these traders with the nations.]

Jer 2:18

ועתה מה לך לדרך מצרים לשתות מי שחור ומה לך לדרך אשור לשתות מי נהר

[What value is it to you to travel to Egypt to drink the waters of Shihor? And what
value is it to you to travel to Assyria to drink the waters of the Euphrates?]

Καὶ νῦν τί σοι καὶ τῇ ὁδῷ Αἰγύπτου πιεῖν ὕδωρ Γηῶν;
καὶ τί σοι καὶ τῇ ὁδῷ Ἀσσυρίων τοῦ πιεῖν ὕδωρ ποταμῶν;

[And now what hast thou to do with the way of Egypt, to drink the water of Geon?
and what hast thou to do with the way of the Assyrians, to drink the water of rivers?]

It is possible to understand לדרך as either an infinitive construct ("to
travel") or as a masculine noun in construct with מצרים and אשור. In either
case, the meaning does not alter the obvious parallelism, מצרים//אשור and
שחור//נהר. Jeremiah would seem to be identifying Shihor as the Nile River, if
נהר is translated as Euphrates (as is recognized in translations and commentaries).[6] It is possible, on the other hand, to understand the Euphrates as
designating the general area or even border of the Assyrians.[7] In this case,
the parallelism would still be valid and the implied identification of Shihor
with Egypt would be consistent with the previously clearly stated identification as noted in Josh 13:3.

1 Chr 13:5

ויקהל דויד את כל ישראל מן שיחור מצרים ועד לבוא חמת להביא את ארון האלהים...

[David assembled all Israel from the Shihor of Egypt to as far as Lebo-hamath to
bring the ark of God...]

Καὶ ἐξεκκλησίασε Δαυὶδ τὸν πάντα Ἰσραὴλ ἀπὸ ὁρίων Αἰγύπτου καὶ ἕως ιἐσόδου
Ἡμάθ τοῦ εἰενέγκαι τὴν κιβωτὸν τοῦ Θεοῦ...

[So David assembled all Israel, from the borders of Egypt even to the entering in of
Hemath, to bring in the ark of God...]

This verse renders no clear understanding as to the location of Shihor.
Only with a presupposition derived from Isaiah and/or Jeremiah can Shihor
be identified as the Nile. The Chronicler gives us no true indication.

Except for Josh 19:26, the Septuagint does not retain the Hebrew name
of Shihor. Nevertheless, the parallelism in Jer 2:18 would suggest שחור be

understood as the Nile, at least perhaps to Jeremiah. It is interesting that the
Septuagint translates it as *Γηῶν*, as in Gen 2:13, in reference to גיחון. The
Septuagint translations are problematic, to say the least.

If שחור is to be discussed as a specific geographic site, attention must be
directed to the Hebrew Bible. The sole text that identifies שחור as a border of
Israel is 1 Chr 13:5. Nevertheless, even the Chronicler does not present a
clear identification as to its specific location. If the Nile is intended it is
likely an anachronistic reading of the idealized borders of David's kingdom.
Even within that scenario, the idealized borders may be due to a poorly inter-
preted Jeremiah text. Should the Chronicler, on the other hand, be presenting
a view more in keeping with the text of Josh 13:3, then a border closer to
Philistia would be implied. As stated above, a reading in concert with the
border described in Joshua 13 can be applied to each of these pertinent texts.

The Wadi of Egypt—נחל מצרים

The textual references to the Wadi of Egypt may be classified as follows:

VERSE	Driver	Noth	Friedman
Num 34:5	P	Other	P
Josh 15:4	P	D	—
Josh 15:47	P	D	—
1 Kgs 8:65	D	D	—
2 Kgs 24:7	D	D	—
Isa 27:12	—	—	—
2 Chr 7:8	—	—	—

Num 34:5

ונסב הגבול מעצמון נחלה מצרים והיו תוצאתיו הימה

[The boundary will turn from Azmon toward the Wadi of Egypt, and it will go out
toward the sea.]

The context of this verse is a description of the southern boundary of the
Israelites. This boundary extends from the Dead Sea south to Kadesh-barnea
(location discussed below) and around to the Mediterranean. Although the

Samaritan translation reads נחל מצרים, the Hebrew Bible also represents a grammatically correct reading with the directional ה, hence "toward the Wadi of Egypt."[8]

Josh 15:4

ועבר עצמונה ויצא נחל מצרים והיה תצאות הגבול ימה זה יהיה לכם גבול נגב

[It (the boundary) crosses to Azmon, and goes out along the Wadi of Egypt. The border will go out toward the Sea. This will be your southern border.]

Again, as with Num 34:5, the context is the southern boundary. Here, however, the boundary is that of Judah, not the entire Israelite nation. In any case, although והיה is vocalized to be read as third person plural, the meaning is not altered. The border extends in a line from the Dead Sea around Kadesh-barnea and proceeding to the Mediterranean.

Josh 15:47

אשדוד בנותיה וחצריה עזה בנותיה וחצריה עד נחל מצרים והים הגבול וגבול

[Ashdod, its villages and its settlements; Gaza, its villages and its settlements; until the Wadi of Egypt and the Great Sea and border.]

It is correct to alter, along with many manuscripts as well as the *qere*, the adjective גבול to be read as גדול. Thus, the text's "border sea" is to be understood as "great sea," hence the Mediterranean. The importance of this text is that it locates the Wadi of Egypt in the approximate locale of Gaza and the region of Philistia. This follows the pattern observed in the previous verses that the Wadi of Egypt was perceived by these authors as located somewhere on the Mediterranean coast, south of Gaza.

1 Kgs 8:65

ויעש שלמה בעת ההיא את החג וכל ישראל עמו קהל גדול מלבוא חמת עד נחל מצרים...

[Solomon established the festival at that time. And all Israel was with him, a great gathering from Lebo-hamath until the Wadi of Egypt.]

Although this verse does not contain a fixable geographic reference to the Wadi of Egypt, it represents the author's perception of the extent of the

borders of Solomon's Israel. If the other references are consistent throughout, this again implies that the Israel of Solomon's day extended to the south
until just beyond the region of Philistia.

2 Kgs 24:7

ולא הסיף עוד מלך מצרים לצאת מארצו כי לקח מלך מלך בבל מנחל מצרים עד נהר פרת כל אשר היתה
למלך מצרים

[The king of Egypt did not come out again from his land because the king of
Babylon took, from the Wadi of Egypt until the Euphrates River, all that belonged
to the king of Egypt.]

As with 1 Kgs 8:65, this verse is not geographically specific. Nevertheless, from the literature noted below, it is known that the nations of Asia
(those located to the northeast of Egypt) considered the Sinai Peninsula to be
part of Egypt. This seems to be the case in Israel as well. Thus, the
Babylonians have succeeded in pushing Egypt back behind Egypt's old
northeastern border with "Asia."

Isa 27:12

...והיה ביום ההוא יחבט יהוה משבלת הנהר עד נחל מצרים

[On that day, YHWH will beat out from the stream of the Euphrates to the Wadi of
Egypt...]

Again, נחל מצרים is used in the context of the southern border of perhaps
the Assyrian empire. Only within the context of the passages from the books
of Numbers and Joshua can we identify the wadi as located in a line between
Kadesh-barnea and the Mediterranean coast south of Gaza.

2 Chr 7:8

ויעש שלמה את החג בעת ההיא שבעת ימים וכל ישראל עמו קהל גדול מאד מלבוא חמת עד נחל מצרים
[Solomon established the festival at that time for seven days. All Israel was with
him, a great gathering from Lebo-hamath until the Wadi of Egypt.]

This passage is essentially the same as 1 Kgs 8:65, reflecting the
southern boundary of Solomon's Israel, as reproduced by the Chronicler.

As with Shihor, the Wadi of Egypt has been discussed in the literature. It has been identified as either Wadi Besor or Wadi el-'Arish.[9] The actual physical location is not as important for this study as is its placement by the biblical authors. It is evident from the textual material that the authors considered נחל מצרים to be part of the southern border of Canaan/Israel, extending to the Mediterranean Sea. It is located near Philistia and represents the consistent biblical view that the southwestern border with Egypt was at the eastern side of the Sinai Peninsula. It is not to be located at or near the Nile Delta.

This perspective is also consistent with the information presented in the previously noted literature. In other words, to those outside of Egypt to the east, the Sinai Peninsula was considered part of Egypt. To the Egyptians, their eastern border was just east of the Nile River. The Sinai Peninsula formed a buffer zone between Egypt and Asia.

This Israelite geographical perspective presents an interesting dilemma. If the biblical authors identify a site as located in Egypt, we are offered a wide-ranging geographical region in which to place the site. Without a specific statement such as, "site X is located next to the Nile," site X could be placed anywhere from the Nile River eastward to the Negeb. Without additional clarifying statements, this may limit our placement of certain sites.

GOSHEN—גשן

This dilemma may be the case regarding Goshen, which is localized in 12 verses. They are divided into sources as follows:

VERSE	Driver	Noth	Friedman
Gen 45:10	J	E	J
Gen 46:28	J	J	J
Gen 46:29	J	J	J
Gen 46:34	J	J	J
Gen 47:1	J	J	J
Gen 47:4	J	J	J
Gen 47:6	J	J	J

VERSE	Driver	Noth	Friedman
Gen 47:27	J	P	J
Josh 10:41	D^2	D	D
Josh 11:16	D^2	D	D
Josh 15:51	P	D	D

Gen 45:10

וישבת בארץ גשן והיית קרוב אלי אתה ובניך ובני בניך וצאנך ובקרך וכל אשר לך

[You will settle in the land of Goshen and will be *close* to me, you, your children, your children's children, your sheep, your cattle and all that is yours.]

Joseph is here speaking to his family, instructing that they will settle in Goshen. In Joseph's words, they are located קרוב אלי, normally understood as in close geographic proximity to Joseph, who lives in Egypt, in the region of the Nile with Pharaoh. קרוב is used over 30 times in the Hebrew Bible, only twice as here in Genesis. Often it means "near" in physical proximity to the subject (Exod 13:17; Num 24:17; 1 Kgs 21:2), more frequently in a temporal sense (Deut 32:35; Ezek 7:7; 30:3; Zeph 1:7, 14), and often in a sense of personal intimacy or closeness (Deut 22:2; 2 Sam 19:42; Jer 12:2; Pss 34:19; 85:10; Ruth 2:20; 3:12). With the physical sense, we have no direct indication as to where exactly Goshen is located. Since it is not clear where Joseph actually resides, there is thus no hint where "near to me" would be.

It is the third meaning that may provide the clue to its usage in Gen 45:10. The only other instance of קרוב אל is found in Deut 30:14, in speaking of the intimate closeness of God's word to the people. Reading Joseph's comment within the context of his family relationship, I suggest that קרוב אל should be understood in the sense of the return of intimacy with his family. In other words, they now have the opportunity to be emotionally close and reconnected as a family, that which has been missing for years. And thus, this verse offers no indication as to the physical location of Goshen.

An interesting alternative is presented in the Septuagint. Here, as well as in Gen 46:34, Goshen is translated as γῆ Γεσὲμ Ἀραβίας, "the land of Gesem the Arabian." The Septuagint is not consistent in its translation of Goshen. It twice renders Ἡρώων πόλιν, "city of Heroes," (otherwise unknown) in Gen 46:28, 29, and most often translates as just "land of Gesem." It is interesting

that its meaning in 45:10 and 46:34 could indicate a further Septuagint
awareness of the predominant Greek geographical model. In other words,
Arabia is the name given to the Sinai Peninsula by the Septuagint translators.
If the Septuagint here identifies Goshen as being located in Arabia, perhaps
it is preserving a tradition that locates Goshen outside of Egypt, somewhere
in or near the Sinai Peninsula.

The next seven references to Goshen (Gen 46:28, 29, 34; 47:1, 4, 6, 27)
will be considered together as they are, contextually, within the same story
and assigned to the same textual source (J) by all three scholars, with the
exception of 47:27, assigned by Noth as a P text.

46:28

ואת יהודה שלח לפניו אל יוסף להורת לפניו גשנה ויבאו ארתה גשן

[He sent Judah before him to Joseph to lead before him to Goshen, and they came
toward the land of Goshen.]

46:29

ויאסר יוסף מרכבתו ויעל לקראת ישראל אביו גשנה וירא אליו ויפל על צואריו ויבך על צואריו עוד

[Joseph prepared his chariot and he went up toward Goshen to meet Israel, his
father. He looked upon him and fell upon his neck and cried again upon his neck.]

46:34

ואמרתם אנשי מקנה היו עבדיך מנעורינו ועד עתה גם אנחנו גם אבתינו בעבור תשבו בארץ גשן כי
תועבת מצרים כל רעה צאן

[You will say, "Your servants have been keepers of cattle from our youth until now,
both we and our ancestors." This is in order that you may dwell in the land of
Goshen, because shepherds are the abomination of Egypt.]

47:1

ויבא יוסף ויגד לפרעה ויאמר אבי ואחי וצאנם ובקרם וכל אשר להם באו מארץ כנען והנם בארץ גשן

[Then Joseph came and spoke to Pharaoh and said, "My brothers and my father,
their flocks, cattle and all they have have come from the land of Canaan. And now
they are in the land of Goshen."]

47:4

ויאמרו אל פרעה לגור בארץ באנו כי אין מרעה לצאן אשר לעבדיך כי כבד הרעב בארץ כנען ועתה
ישבו נא עבדיך בארץ גשן

[They said, "We have come into the land to sojourn because there is no shepherding for your servants due to the heaviness of the famine in the land. Now, may your servants dwell in the land of Goshen."]

47:6

ארץ מצרים לפניך הוא במיטב הארץ הושב את אביך ואת אחיך ישבו בארץ גשן

[The land of Egypt is in front of you. It is the best of the earth. Settle your father and your brothers. They will dwell in the land of Goshen.]

or

[The land of Egypt, it is in front of you. In the best of the land settle your father and your brothers. They will dwell in the land of Goshen.]

47:27

וישב ישראל בארץ מצרים בארץ גשן...

[Israel settled in the land of Egypt, in the land of Goshen...]

Even though 47:11 (not quoted here) appears to identify Goshen with the land of Rameses, the context of these two chapters may lead to the conclusion that Goshen is a region located within the greater territory of Egypt. If that is indeed the case, then perhaps a clear understanding of the context of chapters 46 and 47 will allow us to place Rameses in the same general vicinity as Goshen. This is often assumed to be the case, locating the two within Egypt proper, within the region of the Nile Delta. It is not clear, however, whether it is at all possible to identify the land of Rameses with the store city Rameses of Exod 1:11. Goshen is definitely outside of Canaan. The question remains, where within Egypt is it to be located? The only perspectives we have are two. First, there is an apparent Egyptian concern to isolate shepherds, as seen in 46:34. Second, the story is told from an Israelite perspective, for an Israelite audience.

Goshen may be a district of Egypt, as evidenced in 47:27. Nevertheless, this information also indicates nothing about the exact location. I believe that 47:6 offers a possible clarification. If this verse is translated with the understanding that Goshen is the lesser of the two lands (Egypt vs. Goshen) then Pharaoh is opting to isolate the Israelites in a separate district, whereabouts unknown. If he is offering Joseph the choice of a parcel out of the best of Pharaoh's own country, then there appears to be no concern for the abomination of shepherding. For that reason, it would seem that the first option is more reasonable. This also would be consistent with the context of these chapters.

Thus, according to the author(s) of Genesis 46–47, Goshen would be perhaps a district of Egypt, located somewhere to the south and west of the Wadi of Egypt. A feasible solution is offered as a result of the investigation of the next three verses in which Goshen is identified.

Josh 10:41

ויכם יהושע מקדש ברנע ועד עזה ואת כל ארץ גשן ועד גבעון

[Joshua struck them from Kadesh-barnea to Gaza, and all the land of Goshen to Gibeon.]

All three scholars identify this text as from the Deuteronomist. The geographical context of this verse is the region from Kadesh-barnea to the coast at Gaza, then up to Gibeon. Gibeon is consistently identified as near Jerusalem within the tribe of Benjamin (Josh 18:25; 21:17; 2 Sam 20:8; 1 Chr 8:29, 32; 9:35, 38). Thus, this description does not include any portion of the Sinai Peninsula or, needless to say, the Nile Delta.

Josh 11:16

ויקח יהושע את כל הארץ הזאת ההר ואת כל הנגב ואת כל ארץ הגשן ואת השפלה ואת הערבה ואת הר
ישראל ושפלתה

[Joshua took all of this land: the mountains and all of the Negeb; all of the land of Goshen and the Shephelah and the Arabah and the mountains of Israel and its Shephelah.]

This verse is also identified as from the Deuteronomist. It is interesting to note that without considering Goshen, the geographical region described essentially extends from the mountains and coastal plain of Samaria southward to the Negeb and from the coastal plain eastward to the Jordan River Valley. It must be emphasized at this point that the Arabah has been correctly described by M. Haran as essentially the Jordan River Valley.[10]

In separately confirming his work, I have isolated those texts that indicate the location of the Arabah.[11] In no instance is the Arabah ever described as extending between the Dead Sea and the Gulf of Elath to the south. In the more than 30 instances when it is described, one conclusion is warranted. The Arabah, to the biblical authors, extends from Chinnereth south to (and perhaps including) the Dead Sea.

Thus, when Goshen is placed back into the context of 11:16, the Deuteronomist apparently perceives its location as near the Negeb.

Josh 15:51

וגשן וחלן וגלה ערים אחת עשרה וחצריהן

[And Goshen and Holon and Giloh: eleven cities and their villages.]

In a description of the cities and villages located within the hill country of Judah, the Deuteronomist (according to Noth and Friedman) or P (according to Driver) has located a town of Goshen within Judah. It is possible that the land of Goshen had a city within it of the same name. This also seems to be the case with sites such as Etham and the Wilderness of Etham, Paran and the Wilderness of Paran, plus others. Although there is no exact necessary correlation between Goshen and the land of Goshen, it is obvious that this city is not located in Egypt.

Summary and Analysis

A question arises from the above material. There is no indication in the Hebrew text that ארץ גשן mentioned in Joshua differs from that of the book of Genesis. Thus, why would the Deuteronomist and Priestly sources place the land of Goshen in an area that is clearly associated with the region of the Negeb? By the time they had received the Egyptian slavery tradition it would have been clear to them that the Israelites had been enslaved in Egypt. A concern arises, however, about the dating and provenance of the later sources, especially P. An exilic or post-exilic P source would be writing from a perspective of an accepted exodus tradition.[12] This perspective may be observed through the filling of geographical gaps in the itinerary narrative, and through the elaboration and embellishment of the original exodus narrative (a topic for future research).

Much discussion has ensued, on the other hand, concerning a pre-exilic dating for the Priestly source.[13] In his dissertation, T. J. King has detailed the evidence that suggests the existence of an Israelite (Northern Kingdom) Priestly source, P^N, writing from the latter part of the 8th century, B.C.E.[14] I would suggest, though, that a pre-exilic (even Israelite) P^N source would approach the exodus narrative with a similar temporal perspective as a later author. It is clear from the evidence within the 8th century prophets, both Israelite and Judean, that the exodus tradition is to be found originally within the national story of the Northern Kingdom. Only much later (late 7th–mid 6th centuries) do the Judean prophetic materials indicate an acquisition of this, and other, Israelite traditions into the culture of Judah.[15] Therefore, even P^N would be receiving and elaborating upon a local and established exodus tradition.

Still, these sources locate Goshen in or near the Negeb. Considering the Egyptian border with Canaan this would locate Goshen outside Canaan, but near this eastern border of Egypt. The book of Genesis portrays Goshen as a land in which the Israelites were shepherds. Other than the anachronistic nature of this image, it is still quite true that the Negeb was utilized as pasturage during the Bronze and Iron Ages.[16]

I return to a consideration of D and P in these verses and their localization of Goshen vis à vis their perspective of the Egyptian slavery. The implications of this identification are important for an underlying theme of this investigation; that of presuppositions within a given author's writing. It would be my contention that the geographical realities of the day underlie the Joshua texts. Both D and P know where Goshen is located and do not change its placement in these verses to fit a preconceived ideological understanding of their ancestors' history.[17] And yet, in other verses that relate to the exodus itinerary (discussed further on in this chapter), they attempt to locate sites closer to, or within, the Egypt of their days.

There is no indication in the Hebrew Bible that the Israelites moved from the Negeb westward toward Egypt and then returned back to the east. What is evident in the identification of Goshen by D and P is the same presupposition detailed as present in the writing of modern scholars as well as in the Septuagint. In other words, we can identify a presupposition within the biblical authors that the Israelites must have come forth from Egypt, no matter what the geography indicated.

RAMESES—רעמסס

VERSE	Driver	Noth	Friedman
Exod 1:11	J	J	E
Exod 12:37	P	J	R
Num 33:5	P	Other	R

Exod 1:11

וישימו עליו שרי מסים למען ענתו בסבלתם ויבן ערי מסכנות לפרעה את פתם ואת רעמסס

[They placed over him corvee masters to oppress him with their forced labor. And he built store cities Pithom and Rameses for Pharaoh]

Exod 12:37

...ויסעו בני ישראל מרעמסס סכתה

[And the Israelites journeyed from Rameses toward Succoth...]

Num 33:5

ויסעו בני ישראל מרעמסס ויחנו בסכת

[And the Israelites journeyed from Rameses, and camped at Succoth.]

Summary and Analysis

The location of Rameses is unresolved in the biblical text. Although it has been variously identified in historical-geographies (see Chapter One, pp. 17–22, 27), its exact placement is unknown. The association in the book of Numbers, placing it in proximity to Succoth only exists within the exodus narrative. If Succoth were a fixed and recognized locale, this could indicate a relative placement for Rameses. On the other hand, perhaps it is to be located in Goshen, a possibility suggested by the context of Gen 47:11.

If, to the contrary, my prior analysis is correct, then Rameses is to be understood in an allegorical sense, representing Jerusalem.[18] This interpretation may be derived from careful analysis of Exodus 1 and linked closely to the location of Succoth (see below). In any case, there is nothing within the biblical references that would locate Rameses in proximity to any specific Egyptian site other than a general "default" location near the eastern border with Canaan, near the Negeb, if anywhere at all. I would conclude that Rameses, outside of an allegorical identification, is not placeable within the literature of the Hebrew Bible.

SUCCOTH—סכות

The following texts locate Succoth in relationship to other sites:

VERSE	Driver	Noth	Friedman
Gen 33:17	J	J	E
Exod 13:20	P	J	R
Num 33:6	P	Other	R
Josh 13:27	P	D	–
Judg 8:4–9	pre-D	D	–
Judg 8:14–16	pre-D	D	–
1 Kgs 7:46	D	pre-D	–
Ps 60:8	–	–	–
Ps 108:8	–	–	–
2 Chr 4:17	–	–	–

Gen 33:17

ויעקב נסע סכתה ויבן לו בית ולמקנהו עשה סכתעל כן קרא שם המקום סכות

[Jacob journeyed toward Succoth and built for himself a house. And for his cattle he built booths. Thus he named the place Succoth.]

The context of this verse is the journey Jacob is making back to Canaan following his many years of work with Laban. He has crossed the Jabbok River and is somewhere between the river and Shechem.

Exod 13:20

ויסעו מסכת ויחנו באתם בקצה המדבר

[Then they journeyed from Succoth and camped at Etham at the edge of the wilderness.]

Within this short verse is described the movement from Rameses to Etham. The only indication as to the whereabouts of Succoth is the "edge of the wilderness." Nevertheless, even this portion of the wilderness is undefined. Thus, this verse is not helpful in locating Succoth. Num 33:6 is the exact comment as here, offering no clarity.

Josh 13:27

ובעמק בית הרם ובית נמרה וסכות וצפון יתר ממלכות סיחון מלך חשבון הירדן וגבל עד קצה ים כנרת
עבר הירדן מזרחה

[...and in the valley, Beth-haram, Beth-nimrah, Succoth, Zaphon, the remainder of the kingdom of Sihon, king of Hesbon, the Jordan and (its) territory/banks to the end of the Sea of Chinnereth across the Jordan, eastward.]

In this description of the territory of Gad it is obvious that the author perceives Succoth to be located in the "valley," clearly the Jordan River Valley.

Judg 8:4-9

ויבא גדעון הירדנה עבר הוא ושלש מאות האיש אשר אתו עיפים ורדפים ויאמר לאנשי סכות תנו נא
ככרות לחם לעם אשר ברגלי כי עיפים הם ואנכי רדף אחרי זבח וצל מנע מלכי מדין ויאמר שרי סכות
הכף זבח וצל מנע עתה בידך כי נתן לצבאך לחם ויאמר גדעון לכן בתת יהוה את זבח ואת צלמנע בידי
ודשתי את בשרכם את קוצי המדבר ואת הברקנים ויעל משם פנואל וידבר אליהם כזאת ויענו אותו
אנשי פנואל כאשר ענו אנשי סכות ויאמר גם לאנשי פנואל לאמר בשובי בשלום אתץ את המגדל הזה

[Then Gideon came toward the Jordan. He crossed and the three hundred men that were with him were tired and pursuing ("famished" in Septuagint). He said to the people of Succoth, "Please give loaves of bread to my followers because they are tired, for I am pursuing after Zebah and Zalmunah, the kings of Midian." And the leaders of Succoth said, "Are not the 'palms' of Zebah and Zalmunah now in your hands, that we should give your army bread?" Gideon said, "So, when YHWH gives Zebah and Zalmunah to me, then I will tread your flesh with the thorns of the wilderness and with the briars." So he went up from there to Penuel and spoke to them in the same manner. And the people of Penuel answered him as had answered the people of Succoth. He spoke similarly to the people of Penuel saying, "When I return intact I will break down this tower."]

This story of Gideon, as well as the next listed verses (Judg 8:14–16), relates events that occurred within the Jordan River Valley, near the community of Penuel. Succoth is consistently identified in the valley, as is the case with the previous verses.

1 Kgs 7:46

בככר הירדן יצקם המלך במעבה האדמה בין סכות ובין צרתן

[In the plain of the Jordan the king poured (cast) them in the compactness of the soil, between Succoth and Zarethan.]

Whether במעבה is written as here in 1 Kings or במעבי, as in various manuscripts, and in 2 Chr 4:17, בעבי (masculine singular vs plural), the geographical context of the described activity is the Jordan River Valley.

Pss 60:8; 108:8

אלהים דבר בקדשו
אעלזה אחלקה שכם
ועמק סכות אמדד

[God spoke in his holiness:
"Let me exult and let me divide Shechem,
and I will measure the Valley of Succoth."]

These two psalms are the only occurrences in the Hebrew Bible in which
חלק and מדד are used in apparent parallelism. Given the meaning of the roots,
"to divide" and "to measure," respectively, the parallelism would appear
valid. Given, as well, the context of the passages presented above, the geographical relationship of Succoth and Shechem is also supported within the
parallelism.

Summary and Analysis

Outside of the texts that are specifically involved in the exodus itinerary
narrative (Exod 12:37; 13:20; Num 33:6) it is possible to determine a location for Succoth. It is consistently placed somewhere within the Jordan River
Valley, possibly between Shechem and the Jabbok River. On no occasion do
biblical sources locate Succoth within Egypt itself.

Once again, comment must be directed toward the consistent identification of Succoth within especially the P and D sources. Even given a strong
"exodus from Egypt" tradition present from at least the middle of the 8th
century B.C.E., these sources continue to portray a contemporary geographical reality that contradicts the itinerary site-placements within Egypt and the
Sinai Peninsula. I again interpret this tendency to indicate the Egypt Presupposition as present within the biblical sources.

YAM SÛP—ים סוף

Perhaps the most critical geographical site to be considered is the textual location of Yam Sûp (including the Way of Yam Sûp and Sûp). Since it is mentioned various times in three different contextual forms, they will all be discussed here. The texts that indicate this location are as follows:

VERSE	Driver	Noth	Friedman
Exod 10:19	J	J	J
Exod 13:18	E	E	E
Exod 15:22	J	–	R
Exod 23:31	E	E	E
Num 14:25	JE	J	J
Num 21:4	P	J	R
Num 21:14–15	JE	Fragment	R
Num 33:11	P	Other	R
Deut 1:1	D	D	DTR[1]
Deut 2:1	D	D	DTR[1]
Judg 11:16	D	D	–
1 Kgs 9:26	D	pre-D	–
Jer 49:21	–	–	–

Exod 10:19

ויהפך יהוה רוח ים חזק מאד וישא את הארבה ויתקעהו ימה סוף לא נשאר ארבה אחד בכל גבול מצרים
[YHWH turned a very strong west wind and lifted the locusts. And he blew them toward Yam Sûp. Not one locust remained in all the borders of Egypt.]

I have included this verse in the sample because it is frequently used as evidence that Yam Sûp is a reference to the Gulf of Suez.[19] Revealing the "Canaanite" geographical perspective of the author, the text refers to the source of the wind, רוח ים, here meaning "a west wind." Nothing in the verse, however, indicates that the author is referring to the Gulf of Suez. It is just as likely to perceive Yam Sûp as referring to the Gulf of Elath. To the biblical authors, a west wind blowing locusts out of Egypt (which would include the Sinai Peninsula) would be blowing them toward Yam Sûp, the Gulf of Elath.

Exod 13:18

...ויסב אלהים את העם דרך המדבר ים סוף
[And God led the people around the way of the wilderness of Yam Sûp...]

The minor difficulty encountered in the form דרך המדבר ים סוף, i.e., the definite article present on a noun in construct form, can be alleviated by understanding the genitive as that of a geographical name (the "Way of the Wilderness of Yam Sûp").[20] Verse 18, taken in context, describes the decision to take the Israelites away from the Way of the Land of the Philistines. It is possible to interpret this road (דרך) as referring to the Way of Horus, the road leading along the northern coast of the Sinai Peninsula.[21] As before, there is nothing in the context of the passage to indicate that such is necessarily the case.

When indicating a road, דרך suggests the direction of travel by the name of the road.[22] Hence, the Way of the Land of the Philistines is a road leading toward Philistia. The Way of the Wilderness of Yam Sûp is a road leading toward Yam Sûp. With no firm indication as to the author's fixed perspective, we cannot state the starting point of the journey with any certainty.

Exod 15:22

ויסע משה את ישראל מים סוף ויצאו אל מדבר שור...

[So Moses led Israel from Yam Sûp and they went out into the Wilderness of Shur.]

Yam Sûp is identified as in close proximity to the Wilderness of Shur (described below). For the first time the text identifies a site known within the Hebrew Bible. The proper identification of Shur may assist in locating Yam Sûp.

Exod 23:31

ושתי את גבלך מים סוף ועד ים פלשתים וממדבר עד הנהר כי אתן בידכם את ישבי הארץ וגרשתמו מפניך

[I will set your border from Yam Sûp to the Sea of the Philistines, and from the Wilderness to the Euphrates. For I will give into your hands the inhabitants of the land and you drive them out before you.]

With this description of the general, perhaps idealized, borders of ancient Israel, the author fixes the location of Yam Sûp. This border is presented as the contrast of two extremes. One is in the general direction of south to north, or, more specifically, southwest to northeast. In order to define a complementary, defining border, a perpendicular direction must be applied. Hence, from the southeast toward the northwest. If Yam Sûp is defined as the Gulf of Suez, the author will have defined Israel's borders with two "south to north" demarcation lines. Only within the context of Yam Sûp being the Gulf of Elath does this boundary description make any sense.

Num 14:25

והעמלקי והכנעני יושב בעמק מחר פנו וסעו לכם המדבר דרך ים סוף

[The Amalekites and the Canaanites dwell in the valley. Tomorrow, turn and travel to the wilderness via the Way of Yam Sûp.]

B. A. Levine would attempt to expain the supposed inconsistencies in the textual placement of the Amalekites and Canaanites.[23] This is not necessary. There is no reason to restrict the location and/or movements of the local inhabitants to one of only mountains, plains or valleys. They may quite readily have inhabited all of these regions. The point of this verse is that, in order for the Israelites to proceed from Kadesh-barnea to the north, they will need to circle around. The route through the Amalekites and Canaanites to the north is blocked. Hence, they are instructed to turn toward Yam Sûp. Once again, there is no indication in the Hebrew Bible that the Israelites turned toward Egypt and the Gulf of Suez at any time in their journey. The only possible body of water is the Gulf of Elath.

Num 21:4

...ויסעו מהר ההר דרך ים סוף לסבב את ארץ אדום

[Then they journeyed from Mt. Hor via the Way of Yam Sûp, in order to go around the land of Edom.]

Yam Sûp, located here in proximity to Edom, can be no other body of water besides the Gulf of Elath.

Num 21:14–15

על כן יאמר בספר מלחמות יהוה
את והב בסופה ואת הנחלים
ארנון ואשד הנחלים
אשר נטה לשבת ער   ונשען לגבול מואב

[For thus it was stated in the Book of the Wars of YHWH:
With Waheb in Sûpāh, and at the wadis;
(At the) Arnon and the cataract of the wadis.
Where it bends toward the settlement of Ar, and leans toward the boundary of
Moab.]

D. L. Christensen and M. Weippert have suggested that this difficult
verse be altered to the extent that YHWH is the subject of the passage,
acting from the midst of a whirlwind (סופה). Their translation, however,
alters the text to an unnecessary extent.[24] Levine is correct that with a minor
alteration in the Masoretic phrasing a clear contextual translation may be
derived.[25]

The passage is a description of the border region of Moab with a portion
of the Amorites. As with others, I would identify the סופה mentioned here
with סוף of Deut 1:1. Even should they be separate sites, they are both
located in proximity to Moab. The Arnon River is consistently associated
with Moab as a border site (Num 21:13–15, 24–28; 22:36; Deut 2:18–24;
3:8, 12, 16; 4:48; Josh 12:1–2; 13:8–9; Judg 11:18; 2 Kgs 10:33; Isa 16:2;
Jer 48:20). Ar, itself, is consistently associated with Moab as well (Num
21:28; Deut 2:9, 16, 29; Isa 15:1).

It is worth considering Deut 1:1 at this point in the investigation,
although slightly out of order.

Deut 1:1

אלה הדברים אשר דבר משה אל כל ישראל בעבר הירדן במדבר בערבה מול סוף בין פרן ובין תפל ולבן
וחצרת ודי זהב

[These are the words that Moses spoke to all Israel in the region of the Jordan, in the
Wilderness, in the Arabah, near Sûp, between Paran and Tophel, Laban, Hazeroth
and Di-zahab.]

Although the preposition בעבר most often means "on the other side of"
or "beyond" (Gen 50:11; Deut 3:8; 4:41, 46, 47; Josh 5:1; 9:10; 22:4, 7; Judg
10:8; Jer 25:22), it is possible to follow B. Gemser's suggestion.[26] He would
translate בעבר as "in the region of" or "in X's borderland" on various occasions. Either translation would seem appropriate here, although I have

chosen Gemser's suggestion here as it gives a broader geographical sense, as implied by the context of the verse.

The only identifiable sites mentioned in this verse are Sûp, Paran, Hazeroth and, of course, the Jordan and the Arabah. Paran will be discussed below; Hazeroth is identified on only one occasion (Num 11:35) as next to the Wilderness of Paran. Hazeroth is also mentioned further in the investigation. Sûp is located, in this text, next to the Arabah. As previously described, the Arabah is the region of the Jordan River Valley including the Dead Sea. It does not extend southward from there toward the Gulf of Elath. The preposition מול occurs singularly in the Hebrew Bible 11 times (as in Exod 18:19; Deut 2:19; 3:29; 11:30; 1 Sam 14:5), and an additional 14 times as the closer-in-proximity אל מול. The meaning is generally "near" or "next to," and identifies סוף as located next to the Arabah, thus south of the Dead Sea.

It is interesting to note that the Aramaic Targumim noted previously in this study (Chapter Three, pp. 69, 71–72) translated this verse with ים סוף rather than סוף. In addition, although the rabbinic commentator Rashi (1040–1105 C.E.) identifies *sûp* as reeds, the later commentator Ibn Ezra (1089–1164 C.E.) is the first to suggest that *sûp* may have a totally different intent. He states the following in his comment on Exod 13:18:

סוף. הוא שם מקום וי"א שהוא מגזרת סוף דבר כי הוא סוף העולם והים אוקינוס כאשר כבר זכרתי
וזאת טאות גדולה כי הואים מזרחי כנגד מצרים וים ספרדי גדול ממנו

[Sûp: This is the name of a place. Others say that sûp comes from the same root as sôp (as) in *the end of the matter* (Eccl 12:13). It is so called because it lies at the end of the world. The reference is to the Atlantic, which I have already mentioned. However, this is a major mistake, because it (Yam Sûp) lies in the east, opposite Egypt, while the Mediterranean (?) is larger than it is.]

Ibn Ezra does not indicate in his writings just where he would locate the place Sûp. His is the first interpretation, however, that identifies the derivation of the name Yam Sûp as from a neighboring locale, not from plants or a mythological (or perceived) geographical end of the world. Although no comment is made concerning Num 21:14–15 and Deut 1:1, there would appear to have been some awareness of the geographical identification of Sûp at least as early as Ibn Ezra.

Returning to the verses mentioning Yam Sûp:

Num 33:11

וסעו מים סוף ויחנו במדבר סין

[They journeyed from Yam Sûp and camped in the Wilderness of Sin.]

Although this verse does not locate Yam Sûp next to a fixed locale, it does place it near the Wilderness of Sin. The Wilderness of Sin, as detailed below, is also near Edom, confirming the identification of Yam Sûp as the Gulf of Elath.

Deut 2:1

ונפן ונסע המדברה דרך ים סוף כאשר דבר יהוה אלי ונסב את הר שעיר ימים רבים

[Then we journeyed back toward the wilderness via the Way of Yam Sûp as YHWH said to me. We traveled around Mt. Seir for many days.]

Again, the general area in which Yam Sûp is located is associated with Edom and Mt. Seir (discussed later in this chapter).

Judg 11:16

כי בעלותם ממצרים וילך ישראל במדבר עד ים סוף ויבא קדשה

[For when they came up from Egypt, Israel went in the wilderness until Yam Sûp, and they came to Kadesh.]

It is true that this verse does not eliminate the possiblility that Yam Sûp is located in the western Sinai Peninsula. On the other hand, the Hebrew clearly reads with the connotation that Kadesh and Yam Sûp are closely associated with each other. As an analogy, and perhaps somewhat too closely associated with the geography of California, it is as if one says, "They came up from Los Angeles and went along the coast until San Francisco Bay, and they came to Oregon." The analogy makes more sense, contextually and geographically, to say, "They came up from Los Angeles and went along the coast until San Francisco Bay, and they came to Oakland." It is this sense with which the Hebrew Bible seems to agree. Thus, Yam Sûp must be closer to Kadesh than it is to the western Sinai.

1 Kgs 9:26

ואני עשה המלך שלמה בעציון גבר אשר את אלות על שפת ים סוף ים בארץ אדום

[King Solomon built a fleet of ships at Ezion-geber, which is near ("with") Elath on the shore of Yam Sûp, in the land of Edom.]

As important in the Hebrew Bible as it is within the Septuagint, this verse clearly identifies Yam Sûp (as well as Ezion-geber and Elath) as being located in the region of Edom. The only body of water in that vicinity is the Gulf of Elath.

Jer 49:21

מקול נפלם רעשה הארץ צעקה בים סוף נשמע קולה

[From the sound of their fall (collapse) the earth will tremble; the sound of their cry will be heard at Yam Sûp.]

The second half of this verse is difficult. It is possible to delete צעקה and read קולה as קולם, thus following many other manuscripts as well as the reading of Jer 50:46. Even with those changes, the context of this verse is Jeremiah's prophecy against Edom. Yam Sûp is here identified as part of Edom, consistent with the above examples.

Summary and Analysis

Yam Sûp—As indicated above, the texts that identify a location for Yam Sûp consistently locate it near Edom. There is no reason not to identify Yam Sûp as the present day Gulf of Elath. Consistent also with the geographical traditions from other Hebrew and Aramaic, Greek and Latin texts, the Hebrew Bible supports the identification of Yam Sûp as separate from the Gulf of Suez. It is only the later interpretations influenced by the Septuagint and Vulgate that create the presupposition that Yam Sûp must be either of the two Sinai Peninsula gulfs. In actuality, it is only the Gulf of Elath.

Way of Yam Sûp—From the discussion above, the Way of Yam Sûp is the road that leads to Yam Sûp.

Sûp—Although Sûp is perhaps mentioned twice in the Hebrew Bible, its location (in the book of Numbers) on the border of Moab lends itself to an identification with Sûp in Deut 1:1. Given the meaning of מול as described above, I suggest that Sûp is the region south of the Arabah, i.e., the land south of the Dead Sea. Hence, the name given to the Gulf of Elath (or the Aelanite Gulf) by biblical sources may well be derived from the region adjoining it. Thus, Yam Sûp is the Sea of the region Sûp.

The next four sites, Etham to Migdol, will be considered together.

ETHAM—אתם

VERSE	Driver	Noth	Friedman
Exod 13:20	P	J	R
Num 33:6	P	Other	R
Num 33:7	P	Other	R

Exod 13:20

ויסעו מסכת ויחנו באתם בקצה המדבר

[Then they journeyed from Succoth and camped at Etham, at the edge of the wilderness.]

Two possibilities exist for locating Etham in this verse. First: Succoth is an anachronistic addition representing the Egypt Presupposition of P and R (and perhaps J, if one accepts a late dating for J). Second: if Succoth is an original itinerary site, then the location of Etham would necessarily be in the Jordan River Valley. Unfortunately there is no corroboration for either Etham position.

Num 33:6–7

ויסעו מסכת ויחנו באתם אשר בקצה המדבר ויסעו מאתם וישב על פי החירות אשר על פני בעל צפן ויחנו לפני מגדל

[Then they journeyed from Succoth and camped at Etham, which is at the edge of the wilderness. Then they journeyed from Etham and turned back upon Pi-hahiroth, which is next to Baal-zephon; and they camped before Migdol.]

Other than recognizing that Pi-hahiroth is located next to the sea (see discussion below), it is not possible, based on these verses, to identify an exact location for these several sites.

PI-HAHIROTH—פי החירות

VERSE	Driver	Noth	Friedman
Exod 14:2	P	P	P
Exod 14:9	P	P	P
Num 33:7	P	Other	R

Exod 14:2

דבר אל בני ישראל וישבו ויחנו לפני פי החירת בין מגדל ובין הים לפני בעל צפן נכחו תחנו על הים

[Speak to the children of Israel, and turn back and camp before Pi-hahiroth, between Migdol and the sea, before Baal-zephon. You shall camp opposite it, against the sea.]

Again, the only referent for these sites is "the sea." I will consider the possible identification of this sea in the discussion that follows.

Exod 14:9

וירדפו מצרים אחריהם וישיגו אותם חנים על הים כל סורכב פרעה ופרשיו וחילו על פי החירת לפני בעל צפן

[Egypt pursued after them and they overtook them encamped at the sea, all of Pharaoh's horses, chariots, drivers and soldiers (overtook them) in front of Pi-hahiroth before Baal-zephon.]

As with the previous verses, the only indication of location here is in proximity to "the sea."

BAAL-ZEPHON—בעל צפן

VERSE	Driver	Noth	Friedman
Exod 14:2	P	P	P
Exod 14:9	P	P	P
Num 33:7	P	Other	R

As in the case with Pi-hahiroth, Baal-zephon may only be discussed in relationship to these very localized sites. In particular, only the identification of "the sea" (or perhaps even a firm identification of Migdol) will provide a geographical location for these sites. These possibilities are discussed below.

MIGDOL—מגדל

VERSE	Driver	Noth	Friedman
Exod 14:2	P	P	P
Num 33:7	P	Other	R
Jer 44:1	–	–	–
Jer 46:14	–	–	–
Ezek 29:10	–	–	–
Ezek 30:6	–	–	–

Jer 44:1

הדבר אשר היה אל ירמיהו אל כל היהודים הישבים בארץ מצרים הישבים במגדל ובתחפנחס ובנף
ובארץ פתרוס לאמר...

[The word that came to Jeremiah, to all the Judeans who dwell in the land of Egypt, those who dwell in Migdol, in Tahpanhes, in Noph (Memphis), and in the land of Pathros, saying...]

Although at least four separate sites named Migdol have been identified by archaeologists,[27] there would appear to be no reason that the Migdol of P and R, in their versions of the itinerary sites, would necessarily be a different location. The question remains, just where is it? Jeremiah lists Migdol in association with Tahpanhes, Memphis and Pathros. He repeats the association in 46:14, as stated:

Jer 46:14

הגידו במצרים והשמיעו במגדול והשמיעו בנף ובתחפנחס...

[Proclaim in Egypt and cause them to hear in Migdol; cause them to hear in Memphis and Tahpanhes...]

It is worth considering these passages from Jeremiah together with the two occasions when Migdol is mentioned in Ezekiel.

Ezek 29:10

לכן הנני אליך ואל יאריך ונתתי את ארץ מצרים לחרבות חרב שממה ממגדל סונה ועד גבול כוש

[...thus I am against you and against your Nile. I have made the land of Egypt to be dry ground; a desolation of waste from Migdol to Syene to the border of Ethiopia.]

Ezek 30:6

כה אמר יהוה

ונפלו סמכי מצרים   וירד גאון עזה

ממגדל סונה   בחרב יפלו בה   נאם אדני יהוה

[Thus said YHWH:

The supporters of Egypt will fall, the excellence of her strength will descend;

From Migdol to Syene they will fall within it (Egypt), says the lord YHWH.]

The pertinent grammatical concern in these verses is the question regarding the nature of מגדל. Is it to be understood as a place name or a noun in construct with סונה? It is possible in 29:10 to translate in construct, based upon the correspondence with the concluding words of the verse, גבול כוש. I have chosen to translate based upon the reading in 30:6. The genitive renders the meaning of this verse unwieldy. If, however, the ה of סונה is that of direction, as translated here, Ezekiel's comments concerning the entire land of Egypt are thus consistent within his remarks.

Summary and Analysis

As mentioned above, there are a number of sites that archaeologists identify as Migdol. Perhaps one of them is the Migdol of the exodus itineraries. Perhaps none could be identified as such. Perhaps the Migdol of which Jeremiah speaks is different even from that of Ezekiel. It is my assumption that the Migdol of the exodus itineraries is the same as that spoken of by the prophets. This is assumed because of the nature of the site as described by both prophets. It appears to be at an extremity of the Egyptian territory, either north or east.

The other sites mentioned in association with Migdol also appear in other parts of the Hebrew Bible. Tahpanhes is described as perhaps the initial point of entry into Egypt by Jeremiah (43:7), as well as associated with Egypt on several other occasions (Jer 2:16; 43:8, 9; Ezek 30:18). In describing the flight of Judeans to Egypt, Jeremiah mentions the first of the refugees' stops. Jeremiah's perspective, reflecting those of his day, is that the border with Egypt begins at the Wadi of Egypt, or perhaps Shihor (see discussion above regarding Jer 2:18, p. 84). Tahpanhes could thus be located anywhere between the Nile Delta and the Wadi of Egypt. Memphis (נף) is also identified within the Hebrew Bible as part of Egypt (Isa 19:13; Jer 2:16; 46:19; Ezek 30:13, 16), although Pathros (Gen 10:14; Isa 11:11; Ezek 29:14; 30:14) appears to be physically separate. It is apparently located in the south.[28] Syene is the final site associated with Migdol. In addition to the verses cited, it appears on two other occasions (Isa 49:12; Ezek 30:16). From Ezek 29:10 and 30:6, it would seem that Syene is to be located in the southern regions of Egypt.

Based upon the apparent location of Tahpanhes in the northern region of Egypt and Pathros and Syene in the south, it appears that Jer 44:1 represents a north to south placement of the sites listed. If Tahpanhes is the first, or one of the first, entry points along the Egyptian border, just where is Migdol? Either further north, further to the east or perhaps adjacent to Tahpanhes. Even assuming Jeremiah's geographical perspective as well as the knowledge that the Egyptians built fortified sites along the northern-Sinai Route of Horus,[29] it is not possible to locate Migdol with any greater precision. I would speculate, however, that based upon the name *Migdol* it implies a fortified location. With the textual perspective placing the Egyptian border in the eastern Sinai, perhaps Migdol is located in the east and not in the Nile Delta.

A more pertinent question arises out of the realization that the source of Migdol within the itineraries is overwhelmingly Priestly (P[N] at the earliest). Even with a late 8th century date for P[N] his redaction of the earlier itinerary raises the question, why has he placed several Egyptian (perhaps) locations in the site list? It is evident from the 8th century prophets (Amos, Hosea, Micah, Isaiah 1–39) that the exodus tradition is already firmly established within the tradition of Israel (Northern Kingdom only). Thus, to any author of the text, the Israelites *must* have fled from Egypt proper. As mentioned previously, the Egypt Presupposition is already evident within the Hebrew Bible, within P in particular. P's dilemma would be based upon his geographical awareness. How is it possible that the Israelites crossed Yam Sûp at the very beginning of the flight from Pharaoh? With the gap between Rameses and Yam Sûp needing to be filled, the later authors simply inserted the sites that they knew existed in their own day, i.e., Etham, Pi-hahiroth, Baal-zephon and Migdol.

Of the four, Etham, Pi-hahiroth and Baal-zephon are impossible to locate, other than the references to "the Sea" in the case of Pi-hahiroth and Baal-zephon. Only with an accurate identification of הים would there be any indication as to the authors' location of these sites (see below).

The same consideration applies to Migdol. If it is located next to a sea identified as the Gulf of Suez then it would clearly be in Egypt. If, however, the sea is Yam Sûp then Migdol would possibly be different from the Migdol of Jeremiah and Ezekiel. If the Migdol of Jeremiah and Ezekiel is located in the Eastern Sinai (although not considered "Egypt" proper by Egyptians) the identification would be consistent.

THE SEA—הים

Is it possible to determine the contextual frame of reference for הים? Does it refer to the Gulf of Suez, or perhaps to a body of water between the Gulf and the Mediterranean Sea? Perhaps within the specific context of the exodus narrative הים refers to Yam Sûp.

The term itself occurs over 350 times in the Hebrew Bible. It is utilized in several contexts, with several bodies of water as its referent. By far the most frequent usage is as the generic "ocean(s)" (Gen 1:26; 22:17; 41:49; Exod 20:11; Num 11:22; Deut 30:13; Josh 11:4; Judg 7:12; 1 Sam 13:5; Isa 50:2; Jer 15:8; Prov 23:34 + many others). Often it is utilized in the sense of "westward" (Gen 28:14; Exod 26:22; Num 2:18; Deut 3:27; Josh 12:7; Isa 24:14; Ezek 48:1–8 +). On several occasions ים designates the "molten sea" of the Jerusalem Temple (1 Kgs 7:23–25, 39, 44; 2 Kgs 16:17; Jer 27:19; 2 Chr 4:2–15).

Nevertheless, הים is often indicative of specific bodies of water. Most frequently it refers to the Mediterranean Sea (Exod 23:31; Deut 11:24; 34:2; Josh 1:4; 9:1; 15:4, 11, 12; 16:6, 8; 1 Kgs 5:23; Isa 23:4, 11; Jer 46:18 ++), less frequently to the Dead Sea as well (Gen 14:3; Num 34:3, 12; Deut 3:17; 4:49; Josh 3:16; 12:3; 15:2, 5; 2 Kgs 14:25; Ezek 47:8; 2 Chr 20:2). It can indicate the distant waters of the Persian Gulf (Jer 51:36) and perhaps even the Indian Ocean and Today's Red Sea (Isa 11:11; 24:15; Jer 25:22; Ezek 26:18; Esth 10:1). ים also designates Chinnereth (Num 34:11; Isa 8:23) as well as Yam Sûp from the context of its usage (Exod 10:19; 15:8, 10; Josh

24:6; Ps 106:7; Neh 9:11; 2 Chr 8:17). As an indicator of the "Sea of the Exodus" (Pss 77:20; 78:53; 114:3, 5) there is no context that would permit a determination as to the exact location or referent.

Reference is also made to the possible use of ים to indicate the Nile River (as perhaps in Isa 18:2; 19:5; Nah 3:8).[30] R. E. Clements has suggested that Isa 18:2 is better understood as referring to the Mediterranean.[31] Nevertheless, from the context of the passage, it is more simply and clearly rendered as referring to the Gulf of Elath. As the Ethiopians would send ambassadors to Jerusalem via the oceans rather than the Nile River, the most direct route to Israel would have been to Elath, on the shore of Yam Sûp.

It is possible to understand ים as Nile River in the other two instances. The context of Isa 19:5, however, could indicate the Mediterranean Sea, since the Nile (יאור) is designated throughout in verses 6–8. The text in Nahum could also be understood as either the Nile or the Mediterranean, as the Nile would be viewed as an extension of the ים, and not necessarily identical to it. Within the Hebrew Bible, ים does not refer to a river other than perhaps on these two occasions. If a clearer meaning may be derived by translating ים as Mediterranean Sea, then that meaning should be given.

What is noticed, however, is that הים is never utilized within the Hebrew Bible to designate the Gulf of Suez. As noted in Chapter Three (pp. 66–68), the only possible textual reference to this gulf is to be found in Isa 11:15 (לשון ים מצרים). Thus, based upon context, I would identify the unidentified "Sea of the Exodus" as indicating Yam Sûp.

WILDERNESS OF ETHAM—מדבר אתם

This site is described in only one place, in reference to Marah.

VERSE	Driver	Noth	Friedman
Num 33:8	P	Other	R

Num 33:8

ויסעו מפני החירת ויעברו בתוך הים המדברה וילכו דרך שלשת ימים במדבר אתם ויחנו במרה
[They journeyed from Pi-hahiroth and crossed in the midst of the sea toward the wilderness. Then they walked a three day journey in the Wilderness of Etham, and camped at Marah.]

If the Wilderness of Etham can be localized near Marah and thus the Wilderness of Shur (see below), then it may be possible to consider its textual identification somewhat pinpointed. Otherwise, this wilderness should perhaps be considered another of the sites added by later authors, although it would appear to be located by them in the eastern Sinai.

SHUR AND THE WILDERNESS OF SHUR—שור

VERSE	Driver	Noth	Friedman
Gen 20:1	E	E	E
Gen 25:18	J	Other	P
Exod 15:22	J	J	R
1 Sam 15:7	D	D	–
1 Sam 27:8	D	D	–

Gen 20:1

ויסע משם אברהם ארצה הנגב וישב בין קדש ובין שור ויגר בגרר

[Then Abraham journeyed toward the land of the Negeb, and he settled between Kadesh and Shur. And he dwelled in Gerar.]

Gen 25:18

וישכנו מחוילה עד שור אשר על פני מצרים באכה אשורה

[They settled from Havilah to Shur, which is next to Egypt, as you go toward Assyria.]

Although על פני has been discussed previously (pp. 82–83) it is worth briefly revisiting that information here. על פני most often carries the meaning "on the surface of" (see, in addition to that discussion, Gen 11:4; Num 12:3; 1 Kgs 17:14; Isa 18:2; Job 18:17). Within the context of lateral physical proximity, על פני readily may be translated as "next to" (Gen 11:28; 19:28; Num 21:11, 20; Deut 32:49; Josh 15:8; 1 Sam 15:7; 1 Kgs 6:13; 2 Kgs 23:13), or "east of," as is also the sense of Gen 25:18.

Regarding באכה, the long form of the pronominal suffix, attached to the infinitive, is attested on several occasions in the Hebrew Bible (Gen 10:19, 30; 13:10; 1 Kgs 18:46 with the root ב–ו–א).

Exod 15:22

ויסע משה את ישראל מים סוף ויצאו אל מדבר שור...

[So Moses led the Israelites from Yam Sûp and they went out to the Wilderness of
Shur...]

The verbal root נ–ס–ע may be parsed as either hiphil (as done here) or as
qal, in which case the text would read, "Moses journeyed with the
Israelites...." Either reading makes sense within the context.

1 Sam 15:7

ויך שאול את עמלק מחוילה בואך שור אשר על פני מצרים

[Saul smote Amalek from Havilah as you go toward Shur, which is next to Egypt.]

1 Sam 27:8

ויעל דוד ואנשיו ויפשטו אל הגשורי והגרזי והעמלקי כי הנה ישבות הארץ אשר מעולם בואך שורה ועד
ארץ מצרים

[David went up, and his men, and they raided the Geshurites, the Girzites and the
Amalekites (because these are the settled of the land from of old) as you come
toward Shur until the land of Egypt.]

Although the Septuagint reads "from Teman..." in place of "...from of
old...," the context does not change. Shur is still located outside of Egypt,
toward the east.

Summary and Analysis

As is evident from these texts, the biblical authors are consistent in identifying Shur and the Wilderness of Shur. Assuming Shur to be located within
its own wilderness, they can be placed northwest of Yam Sûp and near the
Negeb. In all cases, they are to be located east of Egypt.

The next series of stops, at Marah, Elim, the Wilderness of Sin, Dophkah, Alush, Rephidim, Massah and Meribah are presented together. They are
listed in the itineraries as located between Yam Sûp and Mt. Sinai. Although
they are mentioned infrequently in the text, the following analysis will
demonstrate their proximity to the eastern side of the Sinai Peninsula.

MARAH—מרה

VERSE	Driver	Noth	Friedman
Exod 15:23	J	J	J
Num 33:8	P	Other	R

Exod 15:23

ויבאו מרתה ולא יכלו לשתת מים ממרה כי מרים הם על כן קרא שמה מרה

[Then they came toward Marah, but they were not able to drink the water of Marah, because it was bitter. Therefore the name of the place was called Marah.]

As the Israelites are described as having left Yam Sûp and journeying toward the Wilderness of Shur, they would appear to be (in the mind of J) in the region north of the Gulf of Elath.

Num 33:8 has been described above within the context of the Wilderness of Etham. Besides the apparent interchangeability of Etham for Shur (as far as P, Other or R is concerned), the general description of Marah places it in the vicinity of Yam Sûp.

ELIM—אילם

VERSE	Driver	Noth	Friedman
Exod 15:27	J	P	R
Num 33:10	P	Other	R

Exod 15:27

...ויבאו אילמה ושם שתים עשרה עינת מים

[Then they came toward Elim, and (at Elim) there were twelve springs of water...]

Num 33:10

ויסעו מאילם ויחנו על ים סוף

[Then they journeyed from Elim and camped at Yam Sûp.]

The geographical meanderings of the Israelites, as detailed in Num 33:8–10, have caused much discussion and consternation among scholars.

To many, the fact that "the sea" is mentioned in v. 8 while Yam Sûp is mentioned here, clearly indicates two separate bodies of water. This conclusion
is not warranted. There are at least two simple explanations. First, the exact
location of Pi-hahiroth (v. 8) is never clarified, nor are the geographical conditions through which the Israelites are wandering. It is simple enough to
picture them "crossing the sea" (v. 8), moving away from the sea (vv. 8–9)
and then returning to the sea at another place (v. 10). Second, perhaps
another California analogy would be appropriate. When journeying to
Berkeley from Sacramento last Monday, I drove along the highway next to
the bay. Having completed my business in Berkeley, I proceeded to visit
friends in San Francisco. I crossed over San Francisco Bay, into the City and
enjoyed a lovely afternoon there. The bay is the same. There is no reason to
assume two bodies of water.

WILDERNESS OF SIN—מדבר סין

VERSE	Driver	Noth	Friedman
Exod 16:1	P	P	R
Num 33:11	P	Other	R

Exod 16:1

ויסעו מאילם ויבאו כל עדת בני ישראל אל מדבר סין אשר בין אילם ובין סיני...
[Then they journeyed from Elim and the entire congregation of the children of Israel
came to the Wilderness of Sin, which is between Elim and Sinai...]

The Priestly source (or perhaps R) has previously located Elim at Yam
Sûp, as noted above. Depending on the location of Sinai (see below) we will
be able to fix more precisely the location of the Wilderness of Sin.

Num 33:11

ויסעו מים סוף ויחנו במדבר סין
[Then they journeyed from Yam Sûp and camped in the Wilderness of Sin.]

DOPHKAH—דפקה

VERSE	Driver	Noth	Friedman
Num 33:12	P	Other	R

Num 33:12

ויסעו ממדבר סין ויחנו בדפקה

[They journeyed from the Wilderness of Sin and camped at Dophkah]

ALUSH—אלוש

VERSE	Driver	Noth	Friedman
Num 33:13	P	Other	R

Num 33:13

ויסעו מדפקה ויחנו באלוש

[They journeyed from Dophkah and camped at Alush.]

REPHIDIM—רפידים

VERSE	Driver	Noth	Friedman
Exod 17:1	P	P	R
Exod 17:8	E	J	E
Exod 19:2	P	P	R
Num 33:15	P	Other	R

Exod 17:1

ויסעו כל עדת בני ישראל ממדבר סין למסעיהם על פי יהוה ויחנו ברפידים...

[The entire congregation of the children of Israel journeyed from the Wilderness of Sin in stages, by the word of YHWH. And they camped at Rephidim...]

Exod 17:8

ויבא עמלק וילחם עם ישראל ברפידם

[Then Amalek came and made war with the Israelites at Rephidim.]

This verse locates Rephidim in a geographical association with the Amalekites. Whenever the Amalekites are identified within the Hebrew Bible as located near any particular fixed locale, they are to be located in the region of the Negeb and Edom.[32] Of particular interest is Judg 12:15:

Judg 12:15

...ויקבר בפרעתון בארץ אפרים בהר העמלקי

[...then they buried him at Pirathon, in the land of Ephraim, in the hill country of the Amalekites.]

R. G. Boling's comment that this verse "has geographical sense, if the location of Pirathon near the southern border of Manasseh is correct," reflects another common presupposition that Ephraim is strictly to be located north of Jerusalem.[33] Other evidence, supported by Judg 5:14, indicates that the Ephraimites were indeed associated with the Amalekites and the area south of Judah.[34]

Judg 5:14

מני אפרים שרשם בעמק...

[...from Ephraim, their root is in Amalek...]

The references within the biblical text that indicate the presence of Israelites living in territory normally associated with Judah must be taken into consideration by scholars. The common references to Israel as "Northern" and Judah as "Southern" reflect the period of the Divided Monarchy. These references are inappropriately carried back into the understanding of Israelite history. Even scholars who would date the existence of Judah after the development of Israel (Finkelstein[35] is a notable example) will identify sites in the region from Jerusalem to Elath as Judean. Although the elaboration of these issues is the focus of future research, this presupposition has its effect on the view toward certain biblical material. For example, the stories of Isaac, associated with Beer-sheba and the southern region of Canaan, are identified as Judean. Even given the association of Northerners with Beer-sheba as a holy site (Amos 5:5), the Isaac tradition is viewed as Judean. I contend that there is no reason not to consider Isaac as an Israelite patriarch.

It is very likely that the Judean authors rewrote and elaborated upon the stories of the patriarchs and the exodus. Nevertheless, the origins of these stories, perhaps most of them, are likely to be found within the "Northern" Israelites.

Exod 19:2

ויסעו מרפידים ויבאו מדבר סיני ויחנו במדבר ויחן שם ישראל נגד ההר

[They journeyed from Rephidim, came to the Wilderness of Sinai and camped in the wilderness. Israel camped there in the presence of the mountain.]

I have chosen to translate נגד in the sense with which it is most commonly used. Although it frequently is understood with the meaning "next to" or "up against" (as in Gen 31:37; Josh 8:11; Ezek 40:23), its most common usage is with the meaning given here (Josh 8:35; 1 Sam 12:3; 16:6; 2 Sam 12:12; Hos 7:2; Pss 22:26; 31:20; 52:11; Eccl 6:8; 2 Chr 6:12–13). In any case, it does not change the meaning of the verse. Rephidim is the last stop before the Wilderness of Sinai, which itself contains Mt. Sinai.

Num 33:15

ויסעו מרפידם ויחנו במדבר סיני

[They journeyed from Rephidim and camped in the Wilderness of Sinai.]

MASSAH—מסה

VERSE	Driver	Noth	Friedman
Exod 17:7	J	J	E
Deut 33:8	JE	Special	Other
Ps 95:8	—	—	—

Exod 17:7

ויקרא שם המקום מסה ומריבה...

[He called the name of the place Massah and Meribah...]

The geographical context of the events surrounding the naming of Massah and Meribah is Rephidim. The specific location is thus adjoining the Wilderness of Sinai.

Deut 33:8

וללוי אמר
תמיך ואוריך לאיש חסידך
אשר נסיתו במסה   תריבהו על מי מריבה

[Concerning Levi he said:
(Septuagint—Give to Levi) your Thummim and your Urim to your pious one,
the one you tested at Massah, with whom you contested at the waters of Meribah.]

This verse, with its difficulties and alternate readings, still maintains the parallelism between Massah and Meribah. As with Exod 17:7 and Ps 95:8 (to follow) the biblical tradition maintains the close, perhaps identical, association of these two sites.

Ps 95:8

אל תקשו לבבכם כמריבה   כיום מסה במדבר

[Do not harden your hearts as at Meribah; as on the day of Massah in the wilderness.]

MERIBAH—מריבה

VERSE	Driver	Noth	Friedman
Num 20:13	P	P	P
Num 27:14	P	P	P
Deut 32:51	P	Dtr	Other
Deut 33:8	JE	Special	Other
Ezek 47:19	–	–	–
Ezek 48:28	–	–	–
Ps 95:8	–	–	–

Num 20:13

המה מי מריבה אשר רבו בני ישראל את יהוה...

[These are the waters of Meribah where the children of Israel contested with YHWH...]

Although not clear from this verse, the geographical context here is the vicinity of Kadesh and the Wilderness of Zin. The location of Kadesh is described below.

Num 27:14

כאשר מריתם פי במדבר צן במריבת העדה להקדישני במים לעיניהם הם מי מריבת קדש מדבר צן

[...because you contested my word in the Wilderness of Zin during the rebellion of the congregation; you failed to sanctify me in their eyes by means of the water. These are the waters of Meribath-kadesh in the Wilderness of Zin.]

As a reiteration of the events of Num 20:12–13, the text must be altered slightly to read as modeled on Deut 32:51 (see next). As with other verses, the geographical context remains unchanged. In this case, Meribah appears to be associated again with the Wilderness of Zin and perhaps even Kadesh as well.

Deut 32:51

על אשר מעלתם בי בתוך בני ישראל במי מריבת קדש מדבר צן על אשר לא קדשתם אותי בתוך בני ישראל

[...because you acted unfaithfully to me amongst the children of Israel at the waters of Meribath-kadesh in the Wilderness of Zin, because you did not sanctify me amongst the children of Israel.]

Deut 33:8 has been discussed above, as has Ps 95:8.

Ezek 47:19

ופאת נגב תימנה מתמר עד מי מריבות קדש נחלה אל הים הגדול ואת פאת תימנה נגבה

[The side of the Negeb, toward the south: from Tamar until the waters of Meribath-kadesh, its wadi to the Great Sea. This is the side to the south, toward the Negeb.]

I choose to read, along with a few manuscripts and the Syriac, Targumim and Vulgate, that Meribath-kadesh was intended, not Meriboth-kadesh. In either case, however, the location would be the same. It is not necessary to add "the Wadi of Egypt," as does the NRSV, although it would be very convenient to then identify the wadi at Meribath-kadesh (identified above as Kadesh) as the same Wadi of Egypt discussed previously. As is indicated in v. 20, ואת should be emended to read וזאת. In any case, Ezekiel is describing the location of Meribath-kadesh in the Negeb region.

Ezek 48:28

ועל גבול גד אל פאת נגב תימנה והיה גבול מתמר מי מריבת קדש נחלה על הים הגדול

[And upon (adjoining) the border of Gad, at the side of the Negeb, toward the south: the border will be from Tamar until the waters of Meribath-kadesh, its wadi to the Great Sea.]

As indicated in 47:19, and supported by various manuscripts plus the Syriac and Vulgate versions, ועד should be added before מי מריבת קדש. Ezekiel's locating of Meribath-kadesh is consistent, and placed in the Negeb.

Summary and Analysis

From the investigation above, the various sources consistently locate the sites discussed above in the region from Yam Sûp to the Wilderness of Sinai. The location of Kadesh-barnea will be described below, but suffice to say at this juncture, that it is located within the Negeb. Thus, the Israelite journey at this stage takes place entirely within the lands adjoining Edom and the eastern Sinai Peninsula.

I would, however, separate the identification of Massah and Meribah from including Meribath-kadesh. It is possible that at some point confusion entered the identification of these sites, likely based on the similarities in their names. The sources appear to locate Meribath-kadesh at Kadesh-barnea. Massah/Meribah, on the other hand, appears to be closer to the Wilderness of Sinai, separate from the Wilderness of Zin, which is in association with Kadesh-barnea.

WILDERNESS OF SINAI AND MT. SINAI—סיני

VERSE	Driver	Noth	Friedman
Exod 19:1–2	P	P	R/P
Exod 19:11, 18	J	J	J
Exod 19:20, 23	J	J	J
Lev 7:38	P	P Add.	P
Num 10:12	P	P	P
Deut 33:2	JE	Special	Other
Judg 5:4–5	Pre-D	Pre-D	–

Exod 19:1-2

בחדש השלישי לצאת בני ישראל מארץ מצרים ביום הזה באו מדבר סיני ויסעו מרפידים ויבאו מדבר
סיני ויחנו במדבר ויחן שם ישראל נגד ההר

[At the third month after the exodus of the children of Israel from the land of Egypt, on the very day, they came to the Wilderness of Sinai. They journeyed from Rephidim, came to the Wilderness of Sinai and camped in the wilderness. Israel camped there in the presence of the mountain.]

These verses, taken in conjunction with Exod 19:11, 18, 20 and 23, locate Mt. Sinai as the mountain against which the Israelites are camped. As

would seem obvious, Mt. Sinai is located within the Wilderness of Sinai, as
also indicated in Leviticus:

Lev 7:38

אשר צוה יהוה את משה בהר סיני ביום צותו את בני ישראל להקריב את קרבניהם ליהוה במדבר סיני

[...which YHWH commanded Moses at Mt. Sinai, in his commanding the children
of Israel to bring their sacrifices to YHWH in the Wilderness of Sinai.]

Num 10:12

ויסעו בני ישראל למסעיהם ממדבר סיני וישכן הענן במדבר פארן

[So the children of Israel journeyed in their stages from the Wilderness of Sinai.
Then the cloud settled in the Wilderness of Paran.]

YHWH is leading the Israelites, via the cloud, toward the Wilderness of
Paran (discussed below as well as in the context of Deut 33:2, see next).

Deut 33:2

ויאמר
יהוה מסיני בא   וזרח משעיר למו
הופיע מהר פארן   ואתה מרבבת קדש
מימינו אשדת למו

[He said:
YHWH came from Sinai, and dawned from Seir upon us.
He shined forth from Mt. Paran, and came from Meribath-kadesh.
– (corrupt, see below)]

This verse is extremely difficult. Nevertheless, the geographical context
will remain clear. The parallelistic structure of this opening verse is carried
throughout the entire chapter. There are four verbs associated with action
attributed to YHWH. In three out of the four actions a clear geographical
reference is made. Thus it is expected that the fourth verb would also have a
physical site associated with it. It is possible that there was a place named
רבבת קדש but it is unattested in the Hebrew Bible. Many emendations to this
line have been suggested, including את רבבת קדש (Septuagint), ואתו רבבת קדש
(Syriac, Targumim and the Vulgate) and ואתה ממרבת קדש (as suggested in
BHS). This latter suggestion has much appeal. It involves little emendation
of the text and it refers to a known geographical site, one that is in direct
association and proximity to the other locales in the verse.

The final line, מימינו אשדת למו appears corrupt. It has been suggested, based upon the Samaritan and Vulgate manuscripts, that a reference to YHWH's law is intended, i.e., אש דת. This is difficult as דת is used only in the Persian period, and is too late a date for this text.[36] I would consider two other possibilities. First, the structure of the verse is unbalanced. There is no corresponding phrase to accompany this final line. It may simply be too corrupt to translate.

Nevertheless, the challenge presents itself. Assuming the phrase was composed with a pre- or ante-cedent clause we may analyze it further. The second possibility is in translating אשדת as "foundation" or perhaps "mountain side" from išdu, as in Deut 3:17; 4:49; Josh 10:40; 12:3, 8; 13:20. This understanding then translates, "at his right is the foundation/mountain slope of/upon/to/for X." In keeping with the geographical context of this verse, ימין may easily be understood as "south." Dropping the suffix as a late emendation is a possibility, but it perhaps refers to another site, in keeping with the context of the entire verse. Thus I would offer as a translation at this juncture, "from/at its south is the mountain slope of/upon/to/for X."

In addition, consideration must be given to the word למו. It is used strictly in poetry and can be translated as "to him/them."[37] It is translated in the Septuagint, Syriac, Targumim and Vulgate as לנו, "upon us," in the first line of the verse, but "to him" in its final usage. Perhaps both meanings are intended in this verse. On the other hand, "upon us" is not a proper translation, as למו is third person. Perhaps then, the first occurrence should be "to him/them." If that is the case, the parallel structure of the verse would have to be reinterpreted. YHWH would be seen as shining forth upon himself (which would require a form change in זרח to hithpael) or upon them. This latter is possible, but would then require a comparable change in אתה, which would make no sense. As למו is only translated in the first person in this location, it would seem more likely that a consistent translation would be more appropriate.

In the spirit of emendation that is prevalent regarding this verse, I would suggest that another emendation is required, reading לעמו in both instances.[38] If this poem has its origins within an oral tradition, it would be a simple matter of improper hearing when transcribing the text in writing. Otherwise, a simple scribal error could be to blame. In this case, I would translate v. 2 as follows:

He said:
YHWH came from Sinai, and dawned from Seir upon his people.
He shined forth from Mt. Paran, and came from Meribath-kadesh.
[missing], at its south is the mountain slope of his people.

As mentioned above, the geographical context of Mt. Sinai (and Paran, for that matter) remains unchanged. Both are located in the region of Seir, which, as detailed below, is Edom.

Judg 5:4-5

יהוה בצאתך משעיר   בצעדך משדה אדום
ארץ רעשה גם שמים נטפו   גם עבים נטפו מים
הרים נזלו מפני יהוה   זה סיני   מפני יהוה אלהי ישראל

[YHWH, when you went out from Seir, when you marched from the land of Edom, the earth rumbled, the heavens also dropped; the clouds also dropped water. The mountains flooded in the presence of YHWH, the one of Sinai, in the presence of YHWH, the God of Israel.]

Given the minor difficulty in translating זה סיני, Sinai is once again associated as the abode of YHWH, situated in the direction of Seir.[39]

Summary and Analysis

The biblical authors, though specifically locating Mt. Sinai on only a few occasions, are consistent in situating the mountain within the Wilderness of Sinai. Both are placed in close proximity to the region of Edom and the Negeb. Mt. Sinai is closely associated with Mt. Seir and the region of Paran. These all appear to be located in the eastern Sinai, north of Yam Sûp. Moreover, the preceding sites (detailed between Yam Sûp and Sinai), whether specifically located on other occasions or not, may still be placed in the same region. The various sources locate them in relationship to the land between the Gulf of Elath and the central Negeb, approaching Kadesh-barnea, thus they reflect their perception of the region's geography.

MT. HOREB—חרב

VERSE	Driver	Noth	Friedman
Exod 17:6	E	J	E
Deut 1:2	D	D	DTR[1]
Deut 1:19	D	D	DTR[1]
1 Kgs 19:8	D	D	–

Exod 17:6

הנני עמד לפניך שם על הצור בחרב והכית בצור ויצאו ממנו מים ושתה העם ויעש כן משה לעיני זקני ישראל

["Here I am standing before you there on the rock at Horeb. Now, strike the rock and water will come out of it and the people will drink." Moses did this in the sight of the elders of Israel.]

The context of this incident is the period right after leaving the Wilderness of Sin and arriving at Rephidim. This site, from this point in time called Massah and Meribah, is located at Mt. Horeb, thus situating the mountain in the region of the Negeb and Edom.

Deut 1:2

אחד אשר יום מחרב דרך הר שעיר עד קדש ברנע

[It is eleven days from Horeb, via the Way of Mt. Seir, to Kadesh-barnea.]

Irrespective of the accuracy concerning travel time between Horeb and Kadesh-barnea, it may be assumed that the Way of Mt. Seir is that road between Kadesh-barnea and Mt. Seir. Locating Horeb in proximity to that road also locates Horeb between Mt. Seir and Kadesh-barnea. Thus, Horeb is to be placed at some location between Edom and the Negeb.

Deut 1:19

ונסע מחרב ונלך את כל המדבר הגדול והנורא ההוא אשר ראיתם דרך הר האמרי כאשר צוה יהוה אלהינו אתנו ונבא עד קדש ברנע

[Then we journeyed from Horeb and traveled the entire great and terrible wilderness that you saw via the Way of the Hill Country of the Amorites, just as YHWH our God commanded us. Then we came to Kadesh-barnea.]

The Amorites are identified on numerous occasions within th
Bible. The term appears to be a cultural designation of a people in
number of areas north and northeast of Kadesh-barnea, from Canaan to the
Bashan (Gen 14:7; Num 13:29; 21:13; 21:21–26; Deut 3:8; 4:46–47; Josh
5:1; 7:7; 9:10; 12:2 + others). The Hill Country of the Amorites is described
on occasion (Deut 1:6–7, 19–20, 44; Josh 10:6; Judg 1:35–36), indicating
that the דרך described in Deut 1:19 indicates a north to northeast direction of
movement. Based on the itinerary descriptions that follow, from Kadesh-
barnea to the east bank of the Jordan River, this 'Way' is understood as
extending toward Moab, to the northeast.

1 Kgs 19:8

ויקם ויאכל וישתה וילך בכח האכילה ההיא ארבעים יום וארבעים לילה עד הר האלהים חרב
[Then he arose, ate and drank. He went in the strength of that meal forty days and
forty nights until the mountain of God, Horeb.]

This story about Elijah fleeing from Ahab and Jezebel takes place in and
around the wilderness south of Beer-sheba. The source locates Mt. Horeb,
given the common poetic use of "forty days and forty nights" within biblical
literature, in the region of the Negeb.

Summary and Analysis

A judgment on the relationship between Mt. Horeb and Mt. Sinai need
not be made here. If they are identical then these verses strongly support that
"they" are to be localized in the region of the Negeb, toward Edom. If not
identical, then the sources are still consistent in locating Mt. Horeb in the
same region as Mt. Sinai. Again, they would both be placed between Edom
and Kadesh-barnea, in the Negeb.

MT. SEIR AND SEIR—שעיר

VERSE	Driver	Noth	Friedman
Gen 14:6	Special	Special	J
Gen 32:4	J	J	E
Gen 36:8–9, 21	P	P	P
Num 24:18	J,E	J	E

VERSE	Driver	Noth	Friedman
Deut 2:1, 5	D	D	DTR[1]
Deut 2:8, 29	D	D	DTR[1]
Deut 33:2	JE	Special	Other
Josh 15:10	P	D	–
Josh 24:4	E	D	–
Judg 5:4	Pre-D	D	–
Ezek 35:15	–	–	–
2 Chr 20:10	–	–	–
2 Chr 25:11, 14	–	–	–

Gen 14:6

ואת החרי בהררם שעיר עד איל פארן אשר על המדבר

[...and the Horites in their mountains, Seir to the Terebinth of Paran, which is at the wilderness...]

The Terebinth of Paran (or El-paran) has been suggested as located at the tip of the Gulf of Elath, perhaps identical to Elath.[40] There is no textual support for this conclusion. In fact, the Hebrew Bible identifies the Horites on a few occasions, most notably Gen 36:20; Deut 2:12, 20. In these instances they are consistently associated with Edom/Seir. Thus, the Terebinth of Paran may not exactly be located at Elath, but at least associated clearly with Edom.

Gen 32:4

וישלח יעקב מלאכים לפניו אל עשיו אחיו ארצה שעיר שדה אדום

[So Jacob sent messengers before him to Esau, his brother, toward the land of Seir, the country of Edom.]

Gen 36:8, 9, 21

וישב עשו בהר שעיר עשו הוא אדום

ואלה תלדות עשו אבי אדום בהר שעיר

ודשון ואצר ודישן אלה אלופי החרי בני שעיר בארץ אדום

[So Esau settled in the hill country of Seir. Esau is Edom.

These are the generations of Esau, ancestor of Edom, in the hill country of Seir.

...Dishon, Ezer and Dishan. These are the chiefs of the Horites, the children of Seir in the land of Edom.]

Num 24:18

והיה אדום ירשה   והיה ירשה שעיר איביו

וישראל עשה חיל

[For Edom will be possessed; Seir—possessed by his enemies,
but Israel will triumph.]

This is another difficult verse, missing a preposition in the second clause
to denote the relationship to Edom's enemies. Levine's suggestion that it is
not necessary makes sense, rejecting the tendency to move איביו to the subsequent comment concerning Israel's success.[41] As is common, the identification of Edom and Seir is unaffected.

Deut 2:1, 5, 8, 29

ונפן ונסע המדברה דרך ים סוף כאשר דבר יהוה אלי ונסב את הר שעיר ימים רבים

אל תתגרו בם כי לא אתן לכם מארצם עד מדרך כף רגל כי ירשה לעשו נתתי את הר שעיר

ונעבר מאת אחינו בני עשו הישבים בשעיר מדרך הערבה מאילת ומעצין גבר

כאשר עשו לי בני עשו הישבים בשעיר והמואבים הישבים בער עד אשר אעבר את הירדן אל הארץ

אשר יהוה אלהינו נתן לנו

[...we turned back and journeyed toward the wilderness via the Way of Yam Sûp, as
YHWH said to me, and we went around Mt. Seir many days.
...do not stir up trouble with them because I will not give you from their land even a
stepping place for the sole of the foot because I have given Mt. Seir as a possession
to Esau.
Then we passed by our kin, the children of Esau, who dwell in Seir, away from the
Way of the Arabah, away from Elath and Ezion-geber.
...just as the children of Esau, the ones who dwell in Seir, and the Moabites, the
ones who dwell in Ar, did for me—until I cross the Jordan to the land that YHWH
our God is giving to us.]

Deut 33:2, as well as Judg 5:4, has been previously discussed.

Josh 15:10

ונסב הגבול מבעלה ימה אל הר שעיר ועבר אל כתף הר יערים מצפונה היא כסלון וירד בית שמש ועבר

תמנה

[...then the border circles from Baalah westward to Mt. Seir, passes to the slope of
Mt. Jearim (that is, Chesalon) from the north. Then it drops down to Beth-shemesh
and crosses by Timnah...]

In this description of the southern border of Judah, the text notes its proximity to Mt. Seir.

Josh 24:4

ואתן ליצחק את יעקב ואת עשו ואתן לעשו את הר שעיר...

[...and to Isaac I gave Jacob and Esau. And I gave to Esau Mt. Seir...]

Ezek 35:15

כשמחתך לנחלת בית ישראל על אשר שממה כן אעשה לך שממה תהיה הר שעיר וכל אדום כלה וידעו
כי אני יהוה

[As was your joy for the inheritance of the house of Israel, for the reason that it was desolate, thus I will do to you. You will become desolate, Mt. Seir and all of Edom, its entirety. Thus they will know that I am YHWH.]

2 Chr 20:10

ועתה הנה בני עמון ומואב והר שעיר אשר לא נתתה לישראל לבוא בהם בבאם מארץ מצרים כי סרו
מעליהם ולא השמידום

[Now, behold the children of Ammon, Moab and Mt. Seir, through whom you would not permit Israel to go when they came from the land of Egypt because they turned away from them and did not destroy them...]

The context of this verse, from 20:2, is that a force is moving against Judah from Edom. The allied countries are here listed from the north to the south, Mt. Seir again being associated with the region of Edom.

2 Chr 25:11, 14

ואמציהו התחזק וינהג את עמו וילך גיא המלח ויך את בני שעיר עשרת אלפים
ויהי אחרי בוא אמציהו מהכות את אדומים ויבא את אלהי בני שעיר ויעמידם לו לאלהים ולפניהם
ישתחוה להם יקטר

[Then Amaziah strengthened himself and led his people. They went to the Valley of Salt and slew ten thousand of the children of Seir.

Now, after Amaziah came from the slaughter of the Edomites, he brought the gods of the children of Seir, set them up as his gods, bowed down to them and made sacrifices to them.]

Summary and Analysis

The Valley of Salt is also located within Edom/Seir on other occasions in the Hebrew Bible (2 Sam 8:13–14; Ps 60:2; and possibly 2 Kgs 14:7). It is

also evident from the material cited that the sources consistently identify
Seir as Edom. Mt. Seir is located in proximity to the Negeb and Judah's
southern border. Again, the sources maintain their consistency in site identification.

The next 19 sites, from Kibroth-hataavah to Abronah, will be considered
as a group, as they are mentioned so infrequently in the Hebrew Bible.

KIBROTH-HATAAVAH—קברות התאוה

VERSE	Driver	Noth	Friedman
Num 11:35	J	J	E
Num 33:16–17	P	Other	R

Num 11:35

מקברות התאוה נסעו העם חצרות...

[From Kibroth-hataavah the people journeyed to Hazeroth...]

Num 33:16–17

ויסעו ממדבר סיני ויחנו בקברת התאוה ויסעו מקברות התאוה ויחנו בחצרת

[They journeyed from the Wilderness of Sinai and camped at Kibroth-hataavah.
They journeyed from Kibroth-hataavah and camped at Hazeroth.]

HAZEROTH—חצרות

VERSE	Driver	Noth	Friedman
Num 12:16	JE	J	E

Num 12:16

ואחר נסעו העם מחצרות ויחנו במדבר פארן

[Afterward, the people journeyed from Hazeroth and camped in the Wilderness of
Paran.]

RITHMAH—רתמה

VERSE	Driver	Noth	Friedman
Num 33:18–19	P	Other	R

Num 33:18–19

ויסעו מחצרת ויחנו ברתמה ויסעו מרתמה ויחנו ברמן פרץ

[They journeyed from Hazeroth and camped at Ritmah. They journeyed from Ritmah and camped at Rimmon-perez.]

RIMMON-PEREZ—רמן פרץ

VERSE	Driver	Noth	Friedman
Num 33:20	P	Other	R

Num 33:20

ויסעו מרמן פרץ ויחנו בלבנה

[They journeyed from Rimmon-perez and camped at Libnah.]

LIBNAH—לבנה

VERSE	Driver	Noth	Friedman
Num 33:21	P	Other	R
Josh 10:29–31	D²	D	–
Josh 15:42	P	D	–

Num 33:21

ויסעו מלבנה ויחנו ברסה

[They journeyed from Libnah and camped at Rissah.]

Josh 10:29–31

ויעבר יהושע וכל ישראל עמו ממקדה לבנה וילחם עם לבנה ויתן יהוה גם אותה ביד ישראל ואת מלכה
ויכה לפי חרב ואת כל הנפש אשר בה לא השאיר בה שריד ויעש למלכה כאשר עשה למלך יריחו ויעבר
יהושע וכל ישראל עמו מלבנה לכישה ויחן עליה וילחם בה

[Then Joshua and all Israel with him crossed from Makkedah toward Libnah, and he
fought with Libnah. And YHWH gave it, also, as well as its king into the hand of
Israel. And he struck it, and all life that was in it, with the edge of the sword. He left
no escapee remaining in it, and he did to its king as he had done to the king of
Jericho. Then Joshua and all Israel with him crossed from Libnah toward Lachish,
and he camped against it and fought with it.]

Josh 15:42

לבנה ועתר ועשן

[Libnah, Ether and Ashan...]

If these sites identified as Libnah are the same as that of the itinerary list, it would appear to be located near the Shephelah, in the southern region of Judah. The sites associated with Libnah, especially in Josh 10:29–31, are also consistently located in the same region. Makkedah (in Josh 15:41) is described as in the lowlands of Judah. Lachish is also described as situated in the Shephelah and southern portion of Judah (Josh 15:39; Isa 36:1–2; Jer 34:7; Neh 11:30). The Shephelah itself is described as extending along a north-south axis, between the coast and the hill country further inland. It continues south alongside Philistia and borders the Negeb (Deut 1:7; Josh 9:1; 10:40; 11:16–17; 12:8; Obad 19).

RISSAH—רסה

VERSE	Driver	Noth	Friedman
Num 33:22	P	Other	R

Num 33:22

ויסעו מרסה ויחנו בקהלתה

[They journeyed from Rissah and camped at Kehelathah.]

KEHELATHAH—קהלתה

VERSE	Driver	Noth	Friedman
Num 33:23	P	Other	R

Num 33:23

ויסעו מקהלתה ויחנו בהר שפר

[They journeyed from Kehelathah and camped at Mt. Shepher.]

MT. SHEPHER—הר שפר

VERSE	Driver	Noth	Friedman
Num 33:24	P	Other	R

Num 33:24

ויסעו מהר שפר ויחנו בחרדה

[They journeyed from Mt. Shepher and camped at Haradah.]

HARADAH—חרדה

VERSE	Driver	Noth	Friedman
Num 33:25	P	Other	R

Num 33:25

ויסעו מחרדה ויחנו במקהלת

[They journeyed from Haradah and camped at Makheloth.]

MAKHELOTH—מקהלת

VERSE	Driver	Noth	Friedman
Num 33:26	P	Other	R

Num 33:26

ויסעו ממקהלת ויחנו בתחת

[They journeyed from Makheloth and camped at Tahath.]

TAHATH—תחת

VERSE	Driver	Noth	Friedman
Num 33:27	P	Other	R

Num 33:27

ויסעו מתחת ויחנו בתרח

[They journeyed from Tahath and camped at Terah.]

TERAH—תרח

VERSE	Driver	Noth	Friedman
Num 33:28	P	Other	R

Num 33:28

ויסעו מתרח ויחנו במתקה

[They journeyed from Terah and camped at Mithkah.]

MITHKAH—מתקה

VERSE	Driver	Noth	Friedman
Num 33:29	P	Other	R

Num 33:29

ויסעו ממתקה ויחנו בחשמנה

[They journeyed from Mithkah and camped at Hashmonah.]

HASHMONAH—חשמנה

VERSE	Driver	Noth	Friedman
Num 33:30	P	Other	R

Num 33:30

ויסעו מחשמנה ויחנו במסרות

[They journeyed from Hashmonah and camped at Moseroth.]

MOSEROTH—מסרות

VERSE	Driver	Noth	Friedman
Num 33:31	P	Other	R

Num 33:31

ויסעו ממסרות ויחנו בבני יעקן

[They journeyed from Moseroth and camped at Bene-jaakan.]

BENE-JAAKAN—בני יעקן

VERSE	Driver	Noth	Friedman
Num 33:32	P	Other	R
Deut 10:6	D	D	DTR[1]

Num 33:32

ויסעו מבני יעקן ויחנו בחר הגדגד

[They journeyed from Bene-jaakan and camped at Hor-haggidgad.]

Deut 10:6

ובני ישראל נסעו מבארת בני יעקן מוסרה שם מת אהרן ויקבר שם ויכהן אלעזר בנו תחתיו

[The children of Israel journeyed from the wells of Bene-jaakan to Moserah. There Aaron died and was buried. And Eleazar his son succeeded him as priest.]

HOR-HAGGIDGAD—חר הגדגד

VERSE	Driver	Noth	Friedman
Num 33:33	P	Other	R

VERSE	Driver	Noth	Friedman
Deut 10:7	D	D	DTR[1]

Num 33:33

ויסעו מחר הגדגד ויחנו ביטבתה

[They journeyed from Hor-haggidgad and camped at Jotbathah.]

Deut 10:7

משם נסעו הגדגדה ומן הגדגדה יטבתה ארץ נחלי מים

[From there they journeyed toward Gudgodah, and from Gudgodah to Jotbathah, a land of wadis of water (flowing wadis).]

JOTBATHAH—יטבתה

VERSE	Driver	Noth	Friedman
Num 33:34	P	Other	R
Deut 10:7	D	D	DTR[1]

Num 33:34

ויסעו מיטבתה ויחנו בעברנה

[They journeyed from Jotbathah and camped at Abronah.]

Deut 10:7 is translated above. These previous four sites, Moseroth/Moserah, Bene-jaakan, Hor-haggidgad/Gudgodah and Jotbathah occur in both the Numbers and Deuteronomy descriptions. Although they occur in different arrangements and two with different versions of their spelling, it is assumed that the sources are writing about the same four sites.

ABRONAH—עברנה

VERSE	Driver	Noth	Friedman
Num 33:35	P	Other	R

Num 33:35

ויסעו מעברנה ויחנו בעציון גבר

[They journeyed from Abronah and camped at Ezion-geber.]

Summary and Analysis

It is nearly impossible to locate the above detailed sites. There are some points that are apparent. First, with the exception of one text identifying Kibroth-hataavah, they are all late additions to the exodus narrative itinerary, dating to the late 8th century B.C.E., at the earliest. As previously discussed, the exodus story was part of the Northern Kingdom's national origin tradition by that time (pp. 98, 110, 118, 247 n.15). As a result, these additions may be considered anachronistic expansions of an earlier itinerary narrative. Second, when they are identified outside of Numbers 33, as in the case of Libnah (located in the southern Shephelah) and Bene-jaakan, the locations appear to remain consistent with other sites in the itinerary. In other words, the sources place these sites in and around the vicinity of the Negeb and Edom.

Considering the anachronistic nature of these itinerary sites, it seems appropriate to discount them as accurate, "historical" exodus route sites. Nevertheless, because of their consistent proximity to the Negeb, Edom and eventually Yam Sûp, the authors apparently construed their locations within that region and context.

EZION-GEBER—עציון גבר

VERSE	Driver	Noth	Friedman
Num 33:36	P	Other	R
Deut 2:8	D	D	DTR[1]
1 Kgs 9:26	D	Pre-D	–
1 Kgs 22:49	D	Pre-D	–
2 Chr 8:17	–	–	–

Num 33:36

ויסעו מעציון גבר ויחנו במדבר צן הוא קדש

[They journeyed from Ezion-geber and camped in the Wilderness of Zin, that is, Kadesh.]

Deut 2:8

ונעבר מאת אחינו בני עשו הישבים בשעיר מדרך הערבה מאילת ומעצין גבר

[We passed over before our kin the children of Esau, those who dwell in Seir, away from the Way of the Arabah, from Elath and from Ezion-geber.]

1 Kgs 9:26

ואני עשה המלך שלמה בעציון גבר אשר את אלות על שפת ים סוף בארץ אדום

[King Solomon built a fleet of ships at Ezion-geber, which is near ("with") Elath on
the shore of Yam Sûp, in the land of Edom.]

1 Kgs 22:49

יהושפט עשר אניות תרשיש ללכת אופירה לזהב ולא הלך כי נשברה אניות בעציון גבר
[Jehoshaphat made ships of Tarshish to go to Ophir for gold. They did not go
because the ships were wrecked at Ezion-geber.]

The geographical context of this verse is Edom, locating Ezion-geber at
the northern tip of the Gulf of Elath (1 Kgs 22:48).

2 Chr 8:17

אז הלך שלמה לעציון גבר ואל אילות על שפת הים בארץ אדום
[Thus Solomon went to Ezion-geber and to Elath, on the shore of the sea, in the land
of Edom.]

Summary and Analysis

From these texts that localize Ezion-geber, the biblical sources consistently place it near Yam Sûp, between Edom and the sea. 2 Chr 8:17 specifically identifies the sea, הים, as Yam Sûp, affirming the contextual reading
of הים in other pertinent instances, as discussed previously (pp. 111–12).

ELATH—אילת

VERSE	Driver	Noth	Friedman
Deut 2:8	D	D	DTR[1]
1 Kgs 9:26	D	Pre-D	–
2 Kgs 16:6	D	D	–
2 Chr 8:17	–	–	–

As three of these verses have been discussed previously, I will proceed
with the remaining text.

2 Kgs 16:6

בעת ההיא השיב רצין מלך ארם את אילת לארם וינשל את היהודים מאילות וארמים באו אילת וישבו
שם עד היום הזה

[At that time King Rezin of Aram recovered Elath for Aram and cleared away the Judeans from Elath. The Arameans then came to Elath and they dwell there to this day.]

While this verse appears to bear little upon the concerns here, it has been suggested that it be emended (see BHS critical notes). As the Edomites were the residents of Elath, and not the Arameans, then emendation is considered justified. From this perspective it appears to be a textual corruption based upon the preceding v. 5, plus the easy similarity between ר and ד. As noted by M. Cogan and H. Tadmor, the corrupted reading has even tempted a number of scholars to propose an Aramean involvement in the region on behalf of Edom.[42] This latter interpretation is also supported by J. K. Kuan in suggesting that the verse be emended to change only the *ketib* (וארמים) to the *qere* (ואדמים).[43] This is intriguing in that it permits a reasonable translation of the text with minimal emendation. Moreover, as seen from the texts that identify the location of Elath and Ezion-geber, the biblical location of Edom appears to extend southward to the region of the Gulf of Elath.[44] Locating Edomites in Elath would maintain the geographical consistency observed to this point in the investigation.

Summary and Analysis

Although described by later sources, the authors are consistent in locating Elath in the region of Edom, at Yam Sûp.

WILDERNESS OF ZIN—מדבר צן

VERSE	Driver	Noth	Friedman
Num 13:21	P	P	P
Num 33:36	P	Other	R
Num 34:3	P	Other	P
Josh 15:1	P	Additions	—

Num 13:21

ויעלו ויתרו את הארץ ממדבר צן עד רחב לבא חמת

[They went up and they spied out the land, from the Wilderness of Zin to the expanse of Lebo-hamath.]

Lebo-hamath is consistently located in the north, in the vicinity of Mt. Hermon and Damascus (Josh 13:5; Judg 3:3; Jer 49:23; Ezek 47:16–17; 48:1; Amos 6:14). It is also, as here, described in association with the northern extent of Israel (1 Kgs 8:65; Zech 9:2; 1 Chr 13:5). This context identifies the Wilderness of Zin as located in the southern reaches of Israelite territory.

Num 33:36

ויסעו מעציון גבר ויחנו במדבר צן הוא קדש

[They journeyed from Ezion-geber and camped in the Wilderness of Zin, which is Kadesh.]

Num 34:3

והיה לכם פאת נגב ממדבר צן על ידי אדום והיה לכם גבול נגב מקצה ים המלח קדמה

[…and your southern side will be from the Wilderness of Zin, along the side of Edom. Your southern border will be from the end of the Dead Sea toward the east…]

Josh 15:1

ויהי הגורל למטה בני יהודה למשפחתם אל גבול אדום מדבר צן נגבה מקצה תימן

[The lot for the tribe of the children of Judah, according to their families, will be from the border of Edom, the Wilderness of Zin southward from the edge of Teman.]

Summary and Analysis

Teman is consistently identified with Edom in the Hebrew Bible (Gen 36:11, 15, 34, 42; Jer 49:7, 20; Ezek 25:13; Amos 1:12; Obad 9; Hab 3:3). As is the case for the previous sites, the sources consistently locate the Wilderness of Zin in the region between Kadesh (perhaps identified as containing Kadesh) and Edom.

PARAN AND THE WILDERNESS OF PARAN—מדבר פארן

VERSE	Driver	Noth	Friedman
Gen 14:6	Special	Special	J
Gen 21:21	E	E	E
Num 10:12	P	P	P

VERSE	Driver	Noth	Friedman
Num 13:3	P	P	P
Num 13:26	P	P	P
Deut 33:2	JE	Special	Other
1 Kgs 11:18	D	Pre-D	–
Hab 3:3	–	–	–

Gen 14:6

ואת החרי בהררם שעיר עד איל פארן אשר על המדבר

[...and the Horites in their mountains, Seir to the Terebinth of Paran, which is at the wilderness...]

Gen 21:21

וישב במדבר פארן ותקח לו אמו אשה מארץ מצרים

[He dwelled in the Wilderness of Paran, and his mother took a wife for him from the land of Egypt.]

The context of this verse is the story of Hagar, living in the wilderness south of Beer-sheba.

Num 10:12

ויסעו בני ישראל למסעיהם ממדבר סיני וישכן הענן במדבר פארן

[The children of Israel journeyed in their stages from the Wilderness of Sinai. The cloud then settled in the Wilderness of Paran.]

Num 13:3

וישלח אתם משה ממדבר פארן על פי יהוה...

[Then Moses sent them from the Wilderness of Paran, as instructed by YHWH...]

The geographical context of this verse is in the wilderness south of Canaan, as the spies are instructed to proceed north to the Negeb (v. 17).

Num 13:26

וילכו ויבאו אל משה ואל אהרן ואל כל עדת בני ישראל אל מדבר פארן קדשה...

[They went and came to Moses and to Aaron and to all the congregation of the children of Israel, to the Wilderness of Paran toward Kadesh...]

Deut 33:2 has been previously discussed. It locates Paran within the geographical context of Edom.

1 Kgs 11:18

ויקמו ממדין ויבאו פארן ויקחו אנשים עמם מפארן ויבאו מצרים...

[They arose from Midian and came to Paran. They took people with them from Paran and came to Egypt...]

Within the context of Hadad's rebellion against Solomon, this description locates Paran between Midian and Egypt. Midian is not often geographically fixed within the Hebrew Bible. Nevertheless, when the sources do write about its location (Gen 36:35; Num 22:1–7; 31:8; Josh 13:21; Judg 6:3) it appears to be east of the Negeb, perhaps in some association with Moab and the Amalekites. Thus, for Paran to be between Midian and Egypt, it would have to be located somewhere near the Negeb and Edom.

Hab 3:3

אלוה מתימן יבוא   וקדוש מהר פארן

[Eloha came from Teman, the Holy from Mt. Paran...]

Summary and Analysis

Paran and its wilderness are also consistently located within the area touching on Edom and the Negeb. It is possible that there existed an overlapping in territory when considering the identification of various wilderness areas. Thus, the Wilderness of Paran was likely perceived as bordering the Wilderness of Zin at Kadesh. Although it is extremely difficult to pinpoint the location of Midian, it does appear to be consistently identified in association with Moab. Thus, the Wilderness of Paran could be located (based on 1 Kgs 11:18) extending from eastward of Egypt toward Moab, hence across the same region described in the other texts.

KADESH AND KADESH-BARNEA—קדש ברנע/קדש

VERSE	Driver	Noth	Friedman
Gen 14:7	Special	Special	J
Gen 20:1	E	E	E

VERSE	Driver	Noth	Friedman
Num 13:26	P	P	P
Num 20:1	P	P	R
Num 20:16	JE	E	J
Num 20:22	P	J	R
Num 33:36	P	Other	R
Deut 1:2	D	D	DTR[1]
Deut 1:19	D	D	DTR[1]
Deut 1:46	D	D	DTR[1]
Josh 10:41	D[2]	D	–
Josh 15:3	P	Additions	–
Judg 11:16–17	D	D	–

Gen 14:7

וישבו ויבאו אל עין משפט הוא קדש ויכו את כל שדה העמלקי...

[Then they turned back to En-mishpat, which is Kadesh, and they struck all the land
of the Amalekites...]

The geographical context of these events is described above. From v. 6
the text describes the location as in and around Edom, thus locating both
Kadesh and the Amalekites.

Gen 20:1

ויסע משם אברהם ארצה הנגב וישב בין קדש ובין שור ויגר בגרר

[Abraham journeyed from there toward the land of the Negeb. And he settled
between Kadesh and Shur. Thus he lived in Gerar.]

Num 13:26

וילכו ויבאו אל משה ואל אהרן ואל כל עדת בני ישראל אל מדבר פארן קדשה...

[Then they came to Moses, Aaron and the entire congregation of the children of
Israel, to the Wilderness of Paran toward Kadesh...]

Num 20:1

ויבאו בני ישראל כל העדה מדבר צן בחדש הראשון וישב העם בקדש...

[The children of Israel, the entire congregation, came to the Wilderness of Zin in the
first month. The people settled in Kadesh...]

Num 20:16

ונצעק אל יהוה וישמע קלנו וישלח מלאך ויצאנו ממצרים והנה אנחנו בקדש עיר קצה גבולך

[...and we cried to YHWH and he heard our voice. So, he sent an angel and brought us out of Egypt. Now, we are in Kadesh, a city on the edge of your border.]

This verse, and the next, are in the context of comments made to the king of Edom (v. 14) as well as proximity to the border of his country (v. 23).

Num 20:22

ויסעו מקדש ויבאו בני ישראל כל העדה הר ההר

[They journeyed from Kadesh and the children of Israel, the entire congregation, came to Mt. Hor.]

Num 33:36

ויסעו מעציון גבר ויחנו במדבר צן הוא קדש

[They journeyed from Ezion-geber and camped in the Wilderness of Zin, which is Kadesh.]

Deut 1:2

אחד עשר יום מחרב דרך הר שעיר עד קדש ברנע

[It is eleven days from Horeb to Kadesh-barnea via the Way of Mt. Seir.]

Deut 1:19

ונסע מחרב ונלך את כל המדבר הגדול והנורא ההוא אשר ראיתם דרך הר האמרי כאשר צוה יהוה
אלהינו אתנו ונבא עד קדש ברנע

[Then we journeyed from Horeb and traveled the entire great and terrible wilderness that you saw via the Way of the Hill Country of the Amorites, just as YHWH our God commanded us. Then we came to Kadesh-barnea.]

Deut 1:46–2:1

ותשבו בקדש ימים רבים כימים אשר ישבתם ונפן ונסע המדברה דרך ים סוף כאשר דבר יהוה אלי ונסב
את הר שעיר ימים רבים

[Then you dwelled in Kadesh for the many days that you dwelled there. We then turned back and journeyed toward the wilderness via the Way of Yam Sûp, as YHWH had commanded me. We went around Mt. Seir for many days.]

Josh 10:41

ויכם יהושע מקדש ברנע ועד עזה ואת כל ארץ גשן...

[Joshua defeated them from Kadesh-barnea until Gaza, and all the land of Goshen...]

As suggested in v. 40, the region conquered by Joshua is the region of the southern section of Canaan, around the southern hills to the Negeb and Shephelah.

Josh 15:3

ויצא אל מנגב למעלה עקרבים ועבר צנה ועלה מנגב לקדש ברנע...

[...and it goes out from south of the ascent of Akrabbim, crosses toward Zin and goes up from the south of Kadesh-barnea...]

This description of the southern border of Judah (Josh 15:1–4) is included within a geographical context extending from Edom and the southern tip of the Dead Sea south and westward toward the Mediterranean at the Wadi of Egypt.

Judg 11:16–17

כי בעלותם ממצרים וילך ישראל במדבר עד ים סוף ויבא קדשה וישלח ישראל מלאכים אל מלך אדום
לאמר אעברה נא בארצך ולא שמע מלך אדום וגם אל מלך מואב שלח ולא אבה וישב ישראל בקדש

[...for when they came up from Egypt, Israel then traveled through the wilderness to Yam Sûp, and they came to Kadesh. Israel sent messengers to the king of Edom saying, "Let me please cross through your land." But the king of Edom did not listen. Israel also sent to the king of Moab, but he would not consent. So, Israel dwelled in Kadesh.]

Summary and Analysis

Consistent within the biblical sources, Kadesh (=Kadesh-barnea) is located in the Negeb, near the border with Edom. I am here identifying Kadesh as Kadesh-barnea. Even if the identification is not valid, both sites are consistently located by the sources within the same geographical region.

MT. HOR—הר ההר

VERSE	Driver	Noth	Friedman
Num 20:22	P	P	R
Num 20:23	P	P	P

VERSE	Driver	Noth	Friedman
Num 21:4	P	J	R
Num 33:37	P	Other	R
Num 34:7	P	Other	R

Num 20:22

ויסעו מקדש ויבאו בני ישראל כל העדה הר ההר

[They journeyed from Kadesh. The children of Israel, the entire congegation, arrived at Mt. Hor.]

Num 20:23

ויאמר יהוה אל משה ואל אהרן בהר ההר על גבול ארץ אדום...

[YHWH spoke to Moses and Aaron at Mt. Hor, at the border of the land of Edom...]

Num 21:4

ויסעו מהר ההר דרך ים סוף לסבב את ארץ אדום...

[They journeyed from Mt. Hor via the Way of Yam Sûp, encircling the land of Edom...]

Num 33:37

ויסעו מקדש ויחנו בהר ההר בקצה ארץ אדום

[They journeyed from Kadesh and camped at Mt. Hor, at the edge of the land of Edom...]

Num 34:7

וזה יהיה לכם גבול צפון מן הים הגדל תתאו לכם הר ההר

[And this shall be your northern border: from the Mediterranean Sea you will mark off for yourselves to Mt. Hor.]

The context of this verse will be discussed below. Nevertheless, the verb used to designate the border "marking" appears to be from the root ת–א–ה, as discussed by Levine, with the sense of "to draw a line." Gesenius would read this root as well, understanding an intended תתאוו, an imperfect piel.[45]

Summary and Analysis

Mt. Hor occurs relatively infrequently in the Hebrew Bible, considering its importance as the site where Aaron died. Nevertheless, the sources are again consistent in locating Mt. Hor in the region of Kadesh and Edom. A fascinating reading is found in Num 34:7 that commonly leads scholars to locate another Mt. Hor in the north; I would suggest that the text remain untouched. As discussed previously, the Hebrew Bible tradition strongly indicates the presence of Israelite (Northern) communities within the region extending through Judah southward into the Negeb, and at a time prior to the United Kingdom. With the creation of Judah, these communities would have then had a border with Judah, a northern border in the perspective of these southern Israelites. In keeping with my proposal that the exodus represents an allegorical rendering of the division of the Davidic/Solomonic kingdom,[46] I would also suggest that Num 34:7 represents an older, Israelite tradition. It reflects the border of the Negeb Israelite communities with Judah to the north.

The next series of itinerary sites, from Zalmonah to Bamoth/Bamoth-baal, describe the journey from Kadesh to the Moabite side of the Jordan River. Many of these sites are described only once, and will thus be considered as a single group.

ZALMONAH—צלמנה

VERSE	Driver	Noth	Friedman
Num 33:41	P	Other	R

Num 33:41

ויסעו מהר ההר ויחנו בצלמנה

[They journeyed from Mt. Hor and camped at Zalmonah.]

PUNON—פונן

VERSE	Driver	Noth	Friedman
Num 33:42	P	Other	R

Num 33:42

ויסעו מצלמנה ויחנו בפונן

[They journeyed from Zalmonah and camped at Punon.]

OBOTH—אבת

VERSE	Driver	Noth	Friedman
Num 21:10–11	P	Fragments	R
Num 33:43	P	Other	R

Num 21:10–11

ויסעו בני ישראל ויחנו באבת ויסעו מאבת ויחנו בעיי העברים במדבר אשר עלפני מואב ממזרח השמש

[The children of Israel journeyed and camped at Oboth. They journeyed from Oboth and camped at Iye-abarim, in the wilderness that is next to Moab at the east.]

Num 33:43

ויסעו מפונן ויחנו באבת

[They journeyed from Punon and camped at Oboth.]

IYE-ABARIM—עיי העברים

VERSE	Driver	Noth	Friedman
Num 21:11	P	Fragments	R
Num 33:44–45	P	Other	R
Josh 15:29	P	D	–

Num 21:11

ויסעו מאבת ויחנו בעיי העברים במדבר אשר על פני מואב ממזרח השמש

[They journeyed from Oboth and camped at Iye-abarim, in the wilderness that is next to Moab at the east.]

Num 33:44–45

ויסעו מאבת ויחנו בעיי העברים בגבול מואב ויסעו מעיים ויחנו בדיבן גד

[They journeyed from Oboth and camped at Iye-abarim, at the border of Moab. They journeyed from Iyim and camped at Dibon-gad.]

DIBON-GAD/DIBON—דיבן גד/דיבן

VERSE	Driver	Noth	Friedman
Num 21:30	JE	E	J
Num 32:34	JE	Other	P
Num 33:45	P	Other	R

VERSE	Driver	Noth	Friedman
Josh 13:9	D^2	D	–
Josh 13:17	P	D	–
Isa 15:2	–	–	–
Jer 48:18, 22	–	–	–
Neh 11:25	–	–	–

Num 21:30

ונירם אבד   חשבון עד דיבון ונשים עד נפח   אשר עד מידבא

[Their cultivated fields perished, from Heshbon to Dibon, and the women from Nophah, which is next to Medeba.]

I have chosen to translate ונשים in order to reflect the context of vv. 27–30. This context, as well as that of the geographical references, is also reflected in the translation of Nophah as a place name. It is possible to translate this verse in several ways. The NRSV translates as:

> So their prosperity perished
> > from Heshbon to Dibon,
> > and we laid waste until fire
> > > spread to Medeba.

Levine renders the verse as follows:

> Their prosperity has vanished,
> > from Heshbon to Dibon;
> They are devastated down to Nophah,
> > located near Medeba.[47]

In either case, the geographical context of the verse locates Dibon within the region of Moab.

Num 32:34

ויבנו בני גד את דיבן ואת עטרת ואת ערער

[The children of Gad built Dibon, Atharoth, Aroer...]

Num 33:45

ויסעו מעיים ויחנו בדיבן גד

[They journeyed from Iyim and camped at Dibon-gad.]

Josh 13:9

מערוער אשר על שפת נחל ארנון והעיר אשר בתוך הנחל וכל המישר מידבא עד דיבון

[From Aroer, which is on the bank of the Wadi Arnon, and the city that is in the midst of the wadi, and all the Tableland of Medeba until Dibon.]

Josh 13:17

חשבון וכל עריה אשר במישר דיבון ובמות בעל ובית בעל מעון

[...Heshbon and all its cities that are in the tableland: Dibon, Bamoth-baal and Beth-baal-meon...]

Isa 15:2

עלה הבית ודיבן   הבמות לבכי
על נבו ועל מידבא   מואב ייליל
בכל ראשיו קרחה   כל זקן גרועה

[The daughter of Dibon has gone up to the high places to weep.
Concerning Nebo and concerning Medeba, Moab wails.
On all its heads is baldness, all beards are shaven.]

This is another difficult verse. I have chosen to translate with the Syriac and Targumim, which have עלתה בת דיבון. This also reflects the text in Jer 48:18 (see next) and would seem to be the intention here as well. As noticed frequently, the intricacies of these translation difficulties do not alter the geographical context of the verse. Dibon, as well as Medeba and Nebo, is located in Moab.

Jer 48:18, 22

רדי מכבוד ישבי בצמא   ישבת בת דיבון
כי שדד מואב עלה בך   שחת מבצריך

[Descend from glory! Dwell in thirst! the reigning daughter of Dibon.
Because the destroyer of Moab has come up against you, he has slaughtered your strongplaces.]

Although it is suggested that בצמא is corrupt and should be read as בצאה, "filth, corruption,"[48] the imagery is one of destruction and suffering. The geographical context, once again, remains the region of Moab, as in v. 22:

ועל דיבון ועל נבו ועל בית דבלתים

[...and upon Dibon, Nebo and Beth-diblathaim...]

Neh 11:25

ואל החצרים בשדתם מבני יהודה ישבו בקרית הארבע ובנתיה ובדיבן ובנתיה וביקבצאל וחצריה

[Concerning the villages and their fields, from the children of Judah they dwelled in Kiriath-arba and its towns, and in Dibon and its towns, and in Jekabzeel and its towns...]

ALMON-DIBLATHAIM—עלמן דבלתים

VERSE	Driver	Noth	Friedman
Num 33:46	P	Other	R

Num 33:46

ויסעו מדיבן גד ויחנו בעלמן דבלתימה

[They journeyed from Dibon-gad and camped at Almon-diblathaim.]

WADI-ZERED—נחל זרד

VERSE	Driver	Noth	Friedman
Num 21:12	JE	Other	?
Deut 2:13	D	D	DTR

Num 21:12

משם נסעו ויחנו בנחל זרד

[They journeyed from there and camped at the Wadi Zered.]

The geographical context of the Wadi Zered is known from the previous verse (Num 21:11), i.e., the wilderness bordering Moab.

Deut 2:13

עתה קמו ועברו לכם את נחל זרד ונעבר את נחל זרד

[Now, arise and get yourselves across the Wadi Zered. So, we crossed the Wadi Zered.]

As related in Deut 2:8–9, the Israelites are here moving into Moab from Edom.

BEER—באר

VERSE	Driver	Noth	Friedman
Num 21:16	JE	Other	?

Num 21:16

ומשם בארה הוא הבאר אשר אמר יהוה למשה אסף את העם ואתנה להם מים

[From there toward Beer. This is the Beer where YHWH said to Moses, "Bring the people together and I will give them water."]

From Num 21:11–15, it is clear that the geographical context is within Moab.

MATTANAH—מתנה

VERSE	Driver	Noth	Friedman
Num 21:18–19	JE	Other	?

Num 21:18–19

...וממדבר מתנה וממתנה נחליאל ומנחליאל במות

[...and from the wilderness toward Mattanah, and from Mattanah to Nahaliel, and from Nahaliel to Bamoth...]

NAHALIEL—נחליאל

VERSE	Driver	Noth	Friedman
Num 21:19	JE	Other	?

See under Mattanah, above.

BAMOTH/BAMOTH-BAAL—במות/במות בעל

VERSE	Driver	Noth	Friedman
Num 21:19–20	JE	Other	?

VERSE	Driver	Noth	Friedman
Num 22:41	JE	E	E
Josh 13:17	P	D	–

Num 21:19–20

וממתנה נחליאל ומנחליאל במות ומבמות הגיא אשר בשדה מואב ראש הפסגה ונשקפה על פני הישימן

[...and from Mattanah to Nahaliel, and from Nahaliel to Bamoth, and from Bamoth to the valley that is in the country of Moab at the top of Pisgah that overlooks the face of the Jeshimon.]

Num 22:41

ויהי בבקר ויקח בלק את בלעם ויעלהו במות בעל...

[Then at morning Balak took Balaam up to Bamoth-baal...]

Once again, the geographical context of this verse is within the territory of Moab.

Josh 13:17

חשבון וכל עריה אשר במישר דיבון ובמות בעל ובית בעל מעון

[...Heshbon and all its cities that are in the tableland; Dibon, Bamoth-baal and Beth-baal-meon...]

Josh 13:17 is a description of the communities within the boundaries of the tribe of Reuben, these particular sites located within the territory of Moab.

Summary and Analysis

As mentioned, many of these sites are listed only once, or within only one context. Their identity as actual, physical locations may be difficult to support, and the possiblility of anachronistic editing into a pre-existent itinerary is quite likely. Nevertheless, at this stage of the journey, the Israelites are moving from Kadesh, around Edom and through Moab. When these sites are specifically located, the sources maintain their consistency in placing them within the traveled region.

To this point, the only inconsistent identification of a particular site is the case of Dibon. Neh 11:25 identifies a Dibon within the territory of Judah.

It is possible that Nehemiah has mistakenly placed the Moabite Dibon. An alternative explanation is that, during Nehemiah's time, Judah's territory was perceived as extending into Moabite territory. Thus, the older site would be included in post-exilic Judean territory. It is more likely, however, that the Dibon of Neh 11:25 represents another site named Dibon, this one located within Judah.

It is possible as well, that Bamoth and Bamoth-baal are the same site. Even if not, the sources locate them both in association with Moab.

Two possible approaches regarding the above sites are warranted. Discounting those sites that are mentioned only once (Zalmonah, Punon, Almon-diblathaim, Beer, Mattanah and Nahaliel), the other sites are consistently located by the sources within this segment of the journey. Taking the singular sites into consideration, the sources perceive them as being located within the same geographical parameters.

PISGAH—פסגה

VERSE	Driver	Noth	Friedman
Num 23:14	JE	E	E
Deut 3:17	D^2	D	DTR^1
Deut 3:27	D	D	DTR^1
Deut 4:49	D^2	D	DTR^1
Deut 34:1	JE	P	E
Josh 12:3	D^2	Pre-D	–

Num 23:14

ויקחהו שדה צפים אל ראש הפסגה ויבן שבעה מזבחת ויעל פר ואיל במזבח

[He took him to the field of Zophim, to the top of Pisgah. Then he built seven altars and offered a bull and ram on each altar.]

Since this verse is contained within the story of Balak and Balaam, the geographical context is clearly Moab.

Deut 3:17

והערבה והירדן וגבל מכנרת ועד ים הערבה ים המלח תחת אשדת הפסגה מזרחה

[...the Arabah and the Jordan and its edges, from Chinnereth until the Sea of the Arabah, the Dead Sea, below the slopes of Pisgah to the east.]

Deut 3:27

עלה ראש הפסגה ושא עיניך ימה וצפנה ותימנה ומזרחה וראה בעיניך כי לא תעבר את הירדן הזה

[Ascend to the top of Pisgah and lift up your eyes to the west, north, south and east, and look with your eyes, for you will not cross this Jordan.]

Deut 4:49

וכל הערבה עבר הירדן מזרחה ועד ים הערבה תחת אשדת הפסגה

[...and all the Arabah across the Jordan to the east until the Sea of the Arabah, below the slopes of Pisgah.]

Deut 34:1

...ויעל משה מערבת מואב אל הר נבו ראש הפסגה אשר על פני ירחו ויראהו יהוה את כל הארץ

[So Moses went up from the Plains of Moab to Mt. Nebo, to the top of Pisgah, which is opposite Jericho. And YHWH showed him all the land...]

Josh 12:3

והערבה עד ים כנרות מזרחה ועד ים הערבה ים המלח מזרחה דרך בית הישמות ומתימן תחת אשדות הפסגה

[...and the Arabah to the Sea of Chinnereth eastward, and until the Sea of the Arabah, the Dead Sea, eastward via the Way of Beth-jeshimoth, and from Teman beneath the slopes of Pisgah...]

Summary and Analysis

Pisgah is consistently placed by the sources on the eastern side of the Jordan River, near the Dead Sea, in Moab.

Associated with the Israelite sojourn in Moab, the sites between Jahaz and the Tablelands of Medeba will also be considered as a single group.

JAHAZ—יהצה

VERSE	Driver	Noth	Friedman
Num 21:23	JE	E	J
Josh 13:18	P	D	—
Judg 11:20	Pre-D	Pre-D	—
Isa 15:4	—	—	—
Jer 48:34	—	—	—
1 Chr 6:63	—	—	—

Num 21:23

ולא נתן סיחן את ישראל עבר בגבלו ויאסף סיחן את כל עמו ויצא לקראת ישראל המדברה ויבא יהצה
וילחם בישראל

[But Sihon would not permit Israel to pass across his border. So Sihon gathered his people and he went out toward the wilderness to meet Israel. He came toward Jahaz and fought with Israel.]

Josh 13:18

ויהצה וקדמת ומפעת

[…and Jahaz, Kedemoth and Mephaath…]

As in the case of Pisgah, these locales are within the Reubenite territory located within Moabite land.

Judg 11:20

...ויאסף סיחון את כל עמו ויחנו ביהצה וילחם עם ישראל

[…so Sihon gathered all of his people and camped at Jahaz. Then he fought with Israel.]

The geographical context of this verse is the same as Num 21:23, the events taking place while the Israelites are passing by Edom and heading into Moab.

Isa 15:4

ותזעק חשבון ואלעלה   עד יהץ השמע קולם
על כן חלצי מואב יריעו   נפשו ירעה לו

[Heshbon cries out; also Elealeh. Their voices are heard as far as Jahaz.
Therefore the loins of Moab trembles; his life trembles.]

Jer 48:34

מזעקת חשבון עד אלעלה עד יהץ נתנו קולם...

[From the cry of Heshbon, they utter their voices to Elealeh and to Jahaz.]

1 Chr 6:63

ומעבר לירדן ירחו למזרח הירדן ממטה ראובן את בצר במדבר ואת מגרשיה ואת יהצה ואת מגרשיה

[…and across the Jordan, Jericho. To east of the Jordan from the tribe of Reuben, Bezer in the wilderness and its pasturelands and Jahaz and its pasturelands…]

HESHBON—חשבון

VERSE	Driver	Noth	Friedman
Num 21:26	JE	E	J
Num 32:3	JE	Other	P
Deut 1:4	D	D	DTR¹
Deut 2:24	D	D	DTR¹
Deut 3:6	D	D	DTR¹
Deut 4:46	D²	D	DTR¹
Deut 29:6	D	D	DTR¹
Josh 9:10	D²	Pre-D	–
Josh 13:15–17	P	D	–
Josh 13:21	P	D	–
Judg 11:18–19	Pre-D	Later D	–
Isa 15:4	–	–	–
Isa 16:8–9	–	–	–
Jer 48:2	–	–	–
Jer 48:34	–	–	–
Jer 48:45	–	–	–

Num 21:26

כי חשבון עיר סיחן מלך האמרי הוא והוא נלחם במלך מואב הראשון ויקח את כל ארצו מידו עד ארנן

[Because Heshbon, it is the city of Sihon the king of the Amorites. He fought against the first king of Moab and took all his land into his own hand until the Arnon.]

It is clear from the context of this verse and the following (27–30) that Heshbon is to be located within Moab.

Num 32:3

עטרות ודיבן ויעזר ונמרה וחשבון ואלעלה ושבם ונבו ובען

[...Ataroth, Dibon, Jazer, Nimrah, Heshbon, Elealeh, Sebam, Nebo and Beon...]

Once again, from the geographical context of the surrounding material, these are all communities within Moab.

Deut 1:4

אחרי הכתו את סיחן מלך האמרי אשר יושב בחשבון...

[...after he defeated Sihon, the king of the Amorites, who dwelled in Heshbon...]

Deut 2:24

קומו סעו ועברו את נחל ארנן ראה נתתי בידך את סיחן מלך חשבון האמרי ואת ארצו...

[Continue journeying and cross the Wadi Arnon. See, I have given Sihon the king of Heshbon, the Amorite, and his land into your hand...]

Deut 3:6

ונחרם אותם כאשר עשינו לסיחן מלך חשבון...

[...and we destroyed them as we had done to Sihon, the king of Heshbon...]

The geographical context of this verse is seen in 3:8, again including the territory of Moab.

Deut 4:46

בעבר הירדן בגיא מול בית פעור בארץ סיחן מלך האמרי אשר יושב בחשבון...

[...beyond the Jordan in the valley near Beth-peor, in the land of Sihon, the king of the Amorites who lives in Heshbon...]

Considering again the context of v. 47, Heshbon is to be located on the eastern side of the Jordan, in Moab.

Deut 29:6

ותבאו אל המקום הזה ויצא סיחן מלך חשבון...

[And you came to this place, then Sihon the king of Heshbon...]

"This place," as described in 28:69, is the country of Moab.

Josh 9:10

ואת כל אשר עשה לשני מלכי האמרי אשר בעבר הירדן לסיחון מלך חשבון ולעוג מלך הבשן אשר בעשתרות

[...and all that he did to the two kings of the Amorites who are on the other side of the Jordan; to Sihon, the king of Heshbon, and to Og, the king of Bashan who was in Ashtaroth.]

The passages found in Josh 13:15–17, 21; Isa 15:4 and Jer 48:34 have been discussed previously. They all locate Heshbon within the territory of Moab.

Judg 11:18–19

וילך במדבר ויסב את ארץ אדום ואת ארץ מואב ויבא ממזרח שמש לארץ מואב ויחנון בעבר ארנון ולא

באו בגבול מואב כי ארנון גבול מואב וישלח ישראל מלאכים אל סיחון מלך האמרי מלך חשבון...

[They went in the wilderness and circled around the land of Edom and the land of Moab. Then they came from the east to the land of Moab, and they camped beyond the Arnon, but did not cross the border of Moab. Israel sent messengers to Sihon, the king of the Amorites, the king of Heshbon...]

Isa 16:8–9

כי שדמות חשבון אמלל   גפן שבמה

בעלי גוים   הלמו שרוקיה

עד יעזר נגעו   תעו מדבר

שלחותיה נטשו   עברו ים

על כן אבכה בבכי יעזר   גפן שבמה

אריוך דמעתי   חשבון ואלעלה

כי על קיצך ועל קצירך   הידד נפל

[Because the fields of Heshbon are feeble; the vines of Sibmah,

whose branches struck down the lords of nations,

that extended until Jazer, wandered in the wilderness,

its shoots extended out and crossed the sea.

Therefore, I shall cry with the weeping of Jazer, the vines of Sibmah,

I will flood you with my tears, Heshbon and Elealeh;

for concerning your summer fruit and concerning your harvest,

            cheering has ceased.]

Jer 48:2

אין עוד תהלת מואב   בחשבון חשבו עליה רעה...

[There is no more fame for Moab; in Heshbon they conspire evil against her...]

Jer 48:45

...כי אש יצא מחשבון   ולהבה מבין סיחון

ותאכל פאת מואב...

[...for a fire has come out from Heshbon; and a flame from the midst of Sihon.

It has consumed the border of Moab...]

JAZER—יעזר

VERSE	Driver	Noth	Friedman
Num 21:32	JE	E	J
Num 32:3	JE	Other	P
Num 32:35	JE	Other	P
Josh 13:25	P	D	–
2 Sam 24:5	P	D	–
Isa 16:8–9	–	–	–
Jer 48:32	–	–	–
1 Chr 6:66	–	–	–
1 Chr 26:31	–	–	–

Num 21:32

וישלח משה לרגל את יעזר...

[Moses sent out (those) to spy at Jazer...]

The Israelites are encamped in Moab. Thus Moses is investigating the surrounding territory, throughout this section.

The passages from Num 32:3; Isa 16:8–9 and Jer 48:32 have been discussed previously. They identify Jazer as located within Moab.

Num 32:35

ואת עטרת שופן ואת יעזר ויגבהה...

[...and Ataroth-shophan, Jazer, Jogbehah...]

As in v. 34, the text describes the building projects undertaken by the Gadites in territories belonging to Moab.

Josh 13:25

ויהי להם הגבול יעזר וכל ערי הגלעד...

[Their territory was at the border, Jazer and all the cities of Gilead...]

Gilead, indicated here in association with Jazer, is consistently located within the Hebrew Bible east of the Jordan River, between the Arnon (on the south) and northward to the Bashan and perhaps even Damascus (Gen 37:25; Num 26:29; 27:1; 32:25–26; Deut 2:36; 3:10, 16; 34:1; Josh 12:1–2; 13:8–12; 17:1, 5, 6; 22:32; Judg 5:17; 10:4, 8; 1 Sam 13:7; 17:24–26; 2 Kgs 10:33; Jer 22:6; 50:19; Ezek 47:18; Amos 1:3, 13; Mic 7:14).

2 Sam 24:5

ויעברו את הירדן ויחנו בערוער ימין העיר אשר בתוך הנחל הגד ואל יעזר

[Then they crossed the Jordan and camped at Aroer, to the south of the city that is in the midst of the Wadi of the Gadites, toward Jazer.]

I concur with the translation of P. K. McCarter, rendering from the Septuagint[L].[49] As we have seen previously, the difficulties in the Hebrew Bible do not reflect on the context of the verse. Jazer is located within the territory of Moab.

1 Chr 6:66

ואת חשבון ואת מגרשיה ואת יעזיר ואת מגרשיה

[Heshbon with its pasture lands, and Jazer with its pasture lands.]

In discussing locations east of the Jordan River (see above 1 Chr 6:63 with Jahaz) the text describes locations within Moab.

1 Chr 26:31

...וימצא בהם גבורי חיל ביעזיר גלעד

[...and there were found amongst them mighty ones of strength in Jazer, Gilead.]

EDREI—אדרעי

VERSE	Driver	Noth	Friedman
Num 21:33	JE	E	J
Deut 1:4	D	D	DTR[1]
Deut 3:1	D	D	DTR[1]
Deut 3:10	D	D	DTR[1]
Josh 12:4	D[2]	D	–
Josh 13:12	D[2]	D	–
Josh 13:31	P	D	–

Num 21:33

ויפנו ויעלו דרך הבשן ויצא עוג מלך הבשן לקראתם הוא וכל עמו למלחמה אדרעי

[They turned and went up via the Way of the Bashan. And Og, the king of the Bashan went out to meet them, he and all his people to battle at Edrei.]

The geographical location is found within the context of chapter 21. Moses is leading the Israelites northward through Moab in the direction of the Bashan.

Deut 1:4

...ואת עוג מלך הבשן אשר יושב בעשתרת באדרעי

[...and Og, the king of the Bashan who dwelled in Ashtaroth, (and) in Edrei]

Deut 3:1

ונפן ונעל דרך הבשן ויצא עוג מלך הבשן לקראתנו הוא וכל עמו למלחמה אדרעי

[We turned and went up via the Way of the Bashan. Then Og, the king of the Bashan came out to meet us, he and all his people to battle at Edrei.]

Deut 3:10

...וכל הבשן עד סלכה ואדרעי ערי ממלכת עוג בבשן

[...and all of the Bashan until Salecah and Edrei, cities of the kingdom of Og in the Bashan.]

Josh 12:4

וגבול עוג מלך הבשן מיתר הרפאים היושב בעשתרות ובאדרעי

[The border for Og, the king of the Bashan, among the remaining Rephaim, who lived at Ashtaroth and Edrei.]

Josh 13:12

כל הממלכות עוג בבשן אשר מלך בעשתרות ובאדרעי

[...all the kingdom of Og in Bashan who reigned in Ashtaroth and Edrei...]

Josh 13:31

...וחצי הגלעד ועשתרות ואדרעי ערי ממלכות עוג בבשן

[...and half of Gilead, and Ashtaroth and Edrei, cities in the kingdom of Og in Bashan...]

ASHTAROTH—עשתרות

VERSE	Driver	Noth	Friedman
Deut 1:4	D	D	DTR[1]

VERSE	Driver	Noth	Friedman
Josh 9:10	D^2	D	–
Josh 12:4	D^2	D	–
Josh 13:12	D^2	D	–
Josh 13:31	P	D	–
1 Chr 6:56	–	–	–

Four of these six passages, Deut 1:4; Josh 12:4; 13:12, 31, have been discussed previously. The sources consistently locate Ashtaroth within the region of the Bashan.

Josh 9:10

...ולעוג מלך הבשן אשר בעשתרות

[...and to Og, the king of Bashan, who is in Ashtaroth.]

1 Chr 6:56

לבני גרשום ממשפחת חצי מטה מנשה את גולן בבשן ואת מגרשיה ואת עשתרות ואת מגרשיה

[To the children of Gershom, from the family of the half-tribe of Manasseh: Golan in the Bashan and its pasture lands and Ashtaroth and its pasture lands.]

The final two verses have been discussed above and are consistent in their placement of Sibam/Sibmah.

TABLELANDS OF MEDEBA—מישר מידבא

VERSE	Driver	Noth	Friedman
Num 21:30	JE	E	J
Josh 13:9	D^2	D	–
Josh 13:16	P	D	–
Isa 15:2	–	–	–

Josh 13:16

ויהי להם הגבול מערוער אשר על שפת נחל ארנון והעיר אשר בתוך הנחל וכל המישר על מידבא

[Their border was from Aroer, which is on the bank of the Wadi Arnon, and the city that is in the midst of the wadi, and all the tableland next to Medeba...]

The remaining verses, which are discussed above, mention the Tablelands of Medeba, as well as Medeba, locating both within the region of

Moab east of the Jordan River and in the vicinity of the northern end of the
Dead Sea.

Summary and Analysis

The Israelites are depicted as spread between the region of the Dead Sea
to near the Bashan, through the territory of the Amorites and the nation of
Moab. Once again, the sources are consistent in locating the above sites.

Because the Hebrew Bible identifies the Mountains of Abarim in such
close association with Mt. Nebo, they will be considered together.

MOUNTAINS OF ABARIM—הרי העברים

VERSE	Driver	Noth	Friedman
Num 27:12	P	P	P
Num 33:48	P	Other	R
Deut 32:49	P	P	Other

Num 27:12

ויאמר יהוה אל משה עלה אל הר העברים הזה וראה את הארץ אשר נתתי לבני ישראל
[YHWH said to Moses, "Ascend this mountain of the Abarim range and view the
land that I am giving to the children of Israel."]

Num 33:48

ויסעו מהרי העברים ויחנו בערבת מואב על ירדן ירחו
[They journeyed from the Mountains of Abarim and camped in the Plains of Moab
next to the Jordan at Jericho.]

Deut 32:49

עלה אל הר העברים הזה הר נבו אשר בארץ מואב אשר על פני ירחו
[Ascend this mountain of the Abarim range, Mt. Nebo, which is in the land of
Moab, which is facing Jericho...]

MT. NEBO—הר נבו

VERSE	Driver	Noth	Friedman
Num 33:47	P	Other	R

VERSE	Driver	Noth	Friedman
Deut 32:49	P	P	Other
Deut 34:1	JE, P	P	E
Isa 15:2	–	–	–
Jer 48:1	–	–	–
Jer 48:22	–	–	–

Num 33:47

ויסעו מעלמן דבלתימה ויחנו בהרי העברים לפני נבו

[They journeyed from Almon-diblathaim and camped at the Mountains of Abarim before Nebo.]

Of the remaining verses, only Jer 48:1 has not been previously discussed.

Jer 48:1

למואב כה אמר יהוה צבאות אלהי ישראל
הוי אל נבו כי שדדה...

[Concerning Moab: thus says YHWH of hosts, the god of Israel;
Woe to Nebo because it is devastated...]

Summary and Analysis

The Mountains of Abarim and Mt. Nebo are perceived as associated with each other. Nebo may thus be one of the peaks in the Abarim range of mountains. They are consistently identified by the sources as located in the region east of Jericho, across the Jordan River in Moab.

PLAINS OF MOAB—ערבות מואב

VERSE	Driver	Noth	Friedman
Num 22:1	P	P	R
Num 26:3	P	Additions	P
Num 26:63	P	Additions	P
Num 31:12	P	Other	P
Num 33:48	P	Other	R
Num 33:50	P	Other	P

VERSE	Driver	Noth	Friedman
Num 35:1	P	Other	P
Num 36:13	P	Other	P
Deut 34:1	JE, P	P	E
Josh 13:32	P	D	–

Num 22:1

ויסעו בני ישראל ויחנו בערבות מואב מעבר לירדן ירחו

[The children of Israel journeyed and camped in the Plains of Moab, across from the Jordan at Jericho.]

Num 26:3

וידבר משה ואלעזר הכהן אתם בערבת מואב על ירדן ירחו... Num 26:3

[Then Moses and Eleazar the priest spoke with them in the Plains of Moab, next to the Jordan at Jericho…]

Num 26:63

...אשר פקדו את בני ישראל בערבת מואב על ירדן ירחו

[…who appointed the children of Israel in the Plains of Moab, next to the Jordan at Jericho.]

Num 31:12

...אל ערבת מואב אשר על ירדן ירחו

[…on the Plains of Moab, which are next to the Jordan at Jericho.]

Num 33:48

ויסעו מהרי העברים ויחנו בערבת מואב על ירדן ירחו

[They journeyed from the Mountains of Abarim and camped in the Plains of Moab, next to the Jordan at Jericho.]

Num 33:50

וידבר יהוה אל משה בערבת מואב על ירדן ירחו...

[YHWH spoke to Moses in the Plains of Moab, next to the Jordan at Jericho…]

Num 35:1

וידבר יהוה אל משה בערבת מואב על ירדן ירחו...

[YHWH spoke to Moses in the Plains of Moab, next to the Jordan at Jericho…]

Num 36:13

אלה המצות והמשפטים אשר צוה יהוה ביד משה אל בני ישראל בערבת מואב על ירדן ירחו

[These are the commandments and the laws that YHWH commanded by the hand of Moses to the children of Israel in the Plains of Moab, next to the Jordan at Jericho.]

Deut 34:1 has been discussed previously, and locates the Plains of Moab at Mt. Nebo, at the Jordan River Valley, east of the Jordan River.

Josh 13:32

אלה אשר נחל משה בערבות מואב מעבר לירדן יריחו מזרחה

[These are what Moses gave as an inheritance in the Plains of Moab, on the other side of the Jordan, toward the east from Jericho.]

Summary and Analysis

The Plains of Moab form the context for locating the final two itinerary sites, Beth-jeshimoth and Abel-shittim. Obviously, the name ערבות מואב locates the plains within Moab. It is worth noting, however, that the biblical sources are, once again, consistent in locating this region. The Plains are situated on the eastern side of the Jordan River, opposite Jericho.

BETH-JESHIMOTH—בית הישמת

VERSE	Driver	Noth	Friedman
Num 33:49	P	Other	R
Josh 12:3	D²	Pre-D	–

Num 33:49

ויחנו על הירדן מבית הישמת עד אבל השטים בערבת מואב

[They camped beside the Jordan between Beth-jeshimoth and Abel-shittim, in the Plains of Moab.]

Josh 12:3

והערבה עד ים כנרות מזרחה ועד ים הערבה ים המלח מזרחה דרך בית הישמות ומתימן תחת אשדות הפסגה

[...and the Arabah to the Sea of Chinnereth eastward, and until the Sea of the Arabah, the Dead Sea, eastward via the Way of Beth-jeshimoth, and from Teman beneath the slopes of Pisgah...]

ABEL-SHITTIM—אבל השטים

VERSE	Driver	Noth	Friedman
Num 33:49	P	Other	R

VERSE	Driver	Noth	Friedman
Num 25:1	JE	J	J
Josh 2:1	JE	D	–
Josh 3:1	JE	Pre-D	–
Mic 6:5	–	–	–

Num 33:49 has been presented above with Beth-jeshimoth, locating Abel-shittim within the area of the Jordan River Valley and Moab.

Num 25:1

...וישב ישראל בשטים

[Israel dwelled in Shittim...]

The geographical context of this verse and the surrounding material is within Moab.

Josh 2:1

...וישלח יהושע בן נון מן השטים

[Then Joshua, the son of Nun sent from Shittim...]

Joshua sends the spies into Jericho from across the Jordan River, while still in Moab.

Josh 3:1

וישכם יהושע בבקר ויסעו מהשטים ויבאו עד הירדן הוא וכל בני ישראל וילנו שם טרם יעברו

[Joshua rose in the morning and they journeyed from Shittim. And they came to the Jordan, he and all the children of Israel. They rested there before crossing.]

Mic 6:5

...עמי זכר נא מה יעץ בלק מלך מואב ומה ענה אתו בלעם בן בעור מן השטים עד הגלגל

[My people: please remember what Balak, the king of Moab, planned. (and remember) what Balaam, the son of Beor, answered him from Shittim to Gilgal...]

Summary and Analysis

With these two locations we conclude the list of exodus itinerary sites. Shittim may or may not be identified with Abel-shittim. If not, then Abel-shittim has only one reference, again perceived by the authors as located in Moab. Shittim itself, is consistently placed in Moab as well. This follows the pattern noticed throughout the itinerary, as elaborated in the chapter.

It is necessary to consolidate the data presented in this chapter. This consolidation is to be found in Chapter Five, in which I have gathered the geographical source definitions in tables, sorted by individual scholars. Finally, the data in the charts are transferred to a map format in the Appendix to represent the site locations of the exodus itineraries.

CHAPTER FIVE

SUMMARY AND CONCLUSIONS: FROM WHENCE THE EXODUS?

> ...and home there's no returning.
> *The Oracles.* A. E. Housman (1859-1936)

It is possible to compile and pictorially represent the data presented in Chapter Four. Tables 4–6 display the itinerary sites in relationship to the Fixed Locales, as described by Driver, Noth and Friedman. Within each table is the listing of each source. For each reference noted within Chapter Four that situated a site in proximity to a Fixed Locale, one entry has been made in the appropriate location in each table. Multiple listings are designated by a number following the source. For example, if a particular site is identified by D on three separate occasions it will be noted as "D-3."

Map 6 is presented following the tables to indicate the dispersion of the exodus itinerary sites. The consistency of the biblical authors is evident, as is the necessity to shift our geographical understanding of the exodus event. This is discussed later in this chapter.

A cursory reading of the biblical text obviously reveals the presence of more geographical sites than those investigated here. The hypothesis of this investigation seeks to test and to clarify the consistency with which biblical sources situate the exodus itinerary sites relative to known locales (see below). It is possible to test this consistency even further. I accounted for the sites that are described in association with the exodus itinerary sites. For example, Hebron is not an itinerary site. Yet, it is described in association with Kadesh-barnea as the first location visited by the spies Moses sent to Canaan (Num 13:22). Wadi Eshcol is also an associated location, identified as also visited by the spies (Num 13:23–24).

	Egypt	Edom	Negeb	Judah	Shephelah	Jordan R.V.	Chinnereth	Moab	Bashan
Goshen			D²-2	P					
Rameses									
Succoth						J, P-3, Pre-D-2, Pss-2, 2 Chr-2			
Derech Yam Sûp/ Yam Sûp		J, E-2, P, D-2, Jer							
Sûp								JE, D	
Etham									
Pi-hahiroth		P-2 the sea							
Baal-zephon		P, the sea							
Migdol	Jer, Ezek unclear	P-2 the sea							
Wilderness of Etham									
Shur/Wilderness of Shur			J-2, E, D-2						
Marah			J						
Elim			J, P unclear						
Wilderness of Sin			P-2						

Table 4—SOURCE DISTRIBUTION: DRIVER (continued on pp. 173–76)

	Egypt	Edom	Negeb	Judah	Shephelah	Jordan R.V.	Chinnereth	Moab	Bashan
Dophkah									
Alush									
Rephidim			E, P-2						
Massah			J, JE, Pss						
Meribah			JE, P-3, Ezek-2, Pss						
Sinai/Wilderness of Sinai		J, JE, P-2, pre-D							
Mt. Horeb			E-2, D-3						
Mt. Seir/Seir		J-2, E-2, JE, pre-D, D, special, Ezek, 1 Chr, 2 Chr-2							
Kibroth-hataavah			P						
Hazeroth			JE						
Rithmah									
Rimmon-perez									
Libnah					P, D^2				
Rissah									
Kehelathah									

Table 4—SOURCE DISTRIBUTION: DRIVER (continued)

	Egypt	Edom	Negeb	Judah	Shephelah	Jordan R.V.	Chinnereth	Moab	Bashan
Mt. Shepher									
Haradah									
Makheloth									
Tahath									
Terah									
Mithkah									
Hashmonah									
Moseroth									
Bene-jaakan									
Hor-haggidgad									
Jotbathah									
Abronah		P possibly							
Ezion-geber		P, D-3, 2 Chr							
Elath		D-3, 2 Chr							
Wilderness of Zin			P-4						
Paran/Wilderness of Paran		E, JE, P-3, D, special, Hab							
Kadesh/ Kadesh-barnea			E, JE, special, P-4						

Table 4–SOURCE DISTRIBUTION: DRIVER (continued)

	Egypt	Edom	Negeb	Judah	Shephelah	Jordan R.V.	Chinnereth	Moab	Bashan
Mt. Hor		P-5							
Zalmonah		P							
Punon									
Oboth								P-2	
Iye-abarim								P-2	
Dibon gad/Dibon								JE-2, P-2, D², Isa, Jer, Neh	
Almon-diblathaim								P	
Wadi Zered								JE, D	
Beer								JE	
Mattanah								JE	
Nahaliel								JE	
Bamoth/Bamoth-baal								JE-2, P	
Pisgah								JE-2, D, D²	
Jahaz								JE, P, pre-D, Isa, Jer-2, 1 Chr	

Table 4–SOURCE DISTRIBUTION: DRIVER (continued)

	Egypt	Edom	Negeb	Judah	Shephelah	Jordan R.V.	Chinnereth	Moab	Bashan
Heshbon								JE-2, P-2, pre-D, D^2-4, Isa-2, Jer-4	
Jazer								JE-3, P-2, Isa, Jer, 1 Chr-2	
Edrei									JE, P-2, D-3, D^2
Ashtaroth									P, D, D^2-3, 2 Chr
Tablelands of Medeba								JE, P, D^2, Isa-2, Jer	
Mts. of Abarim								P-3	
Mt. Nebo								JE, P-3, Isa, Jer-2	
Plains of Moab								JE, P-10	
Beth-jeshimoth								P, D^2	
Abel-shittim								JE-3, P, Mic	

Table 4–SOURCE DISTRIBUTION: DRIVER (continued)

	Egypt	Edom	Negeb	Judah	Shephelah	Jordan R.V.	Chinnereth	Moab	Bashan
Goshen			D-2	D					
Rameses									
Succoth						J-3, pre-D-2, D-3, other, Pss-2, 2 Chr-2			
Derech Yam Sûp/ Yam Sûp		J, E-2, pre-D, D-3, other, Jer							
Sûp								tradition fragment, D	
Etham									
Pi-hahiroth		P-2 the sea							
Baal-zephon		P, the sea							
Migdol	Jer, Ezek unclear	P, other the sea							
Wilderness of Etham									

Table 5—SOURCE DISTRIBUTION: NOTH (continued on pp. 178–82)

	Egypt	Edom	Negeb	Judah	Shephelah	Jordan R.V.	Chinnereth	Moab	Bashan
Shur/Wilderness of Shur			J, E, other, D-2						
Marah			J						
Elim			P, other - unclear						
Wilderness of Sin			P, other						
Dophkah									
Alush									
Rephidim			J, P, other						
Massah			J, special, Pss						
Meribah			P-2, Dtr, Ezek-2, Pss						
Sinai/Wilderness of Sinai		J, P-2, Add. to P, pre-D, special							
Mt. Horeb			J-2, D-3						

Table 5—SOURCE DISTRIBUTION: NOTH (continued)

	Egypt	Edom	Negeb	Judah	Shephelah	Jordan R.V.	Chinnereth	Moab	Bashan
Mt. Seir/Seir		J-2, P, D-4, special-2, Ezek, 1 Chr, 2 Chr-2							
Kibroth-hataavah			other						
Hazeroth			J						
Rithmah									
Rimmon-perez									
Libnah					D-2				
Rissah									
Kehelathah									
Mt. Shepher									
Haradah									
Makheloth									
Tahath									
Terah									
Mithkah									
Hashmonah									
Moseroth									
Bene-jaakan									
Hor-haggidgad									
Jotbathah									
Abronah		other - possible							

Table 5—SOURCE DISTRIBUTION: NOTH (continued)

	Egypt	Edom	Negeb	Judah	Shephelah	Jordan R.V.	Chinnereth	Moab	Bashan
Ezion-geber		D, pre-D-2, other, 2 Chr							
Elath		pre-D, D-2, 2 Chr							
Wilderness of Zin			P-2, Add. to P, other						
Paran/Wilderness of Paran		E, P-3, pre-D, special-2, Hab							
Kadesh/ Kadesh-barnea			J, E-2, P-2, special, other						
Mt. Hor		J, P-2, other-2							
Zalmonah		other							
Punon									
Oboth								tradition fragment D	
Iye-abarim								other, D	

Table 5—SOURCE DISTRIBUTION: NOTH (continued)

	Egypt	Edom	Negeb	Judah	Shephelah	Jordan R.V.	Chinnereth	Moab	Bashan
Dibon gad/Dibon								E, D-2, other-2, Isa, Jer, Neh	
Almon-diblathaim								other	
Wadi Zered								D, other	
Beer								other	
Mattanah								other	
Nahaliel								other	
Bamoth/								E, D,	
Bamoth-baal								other	
Pisgah								E-2,P, pre-D, D-2	
Jahaz								E, pre-D, D, Isa, Jer-2, 1 Chr	
Heshbon								E, pre-D, D-10, later-D, other, Isa-2, Jer-4	

Table 5—SOURCE DISTRIBUTION: NOTH (continued)

	Egypt	Edom	Negeb	Judah	Shephelah	Jordan R.V.	Chinnereth	Moab	Bashan
Jazer								E, D-2, other-2, Isa, Jer, 1 Chr-2	
Edrei									E, D-7
Ashtaroth									D-5, 1 Chr
Tablelands of Medeba								E, D-2, Isa-2, Jer	
Mts. of Abarim								P-2, other	
Mt. Nebo								P-2, other, Isa, Jer-2	
Plains of Moab								P-2, Add. to P-2, D, other-5	
Beth-jeshimoth							other, pre-D		
Abel-shittim								J, pre-D, D, other, Mic	

Table 5—SOURCE DISTRIBUTION: NOTH (continued)

	Egypt	Edom	Negeb	Judah	Shephelah	Jordan R.V.	Chinnereth	Moab	Bashan
Goshen			D-2	D					
Rameses									
Succoth						E, R-3, Pss-2, 2Chr-2			
Derech Yam Sûp/ Yam Sûp		E-2, DTR¹, R, Jer							
Sûp								R	
Etham									
Pi-hahiroth		P, R - the sea							
Baal-zephon		P, R - the sea							
Migdol	Jer, Ezek unclear	P, R - the sea							
Wilderness of Etham									
Shur/Wilderness of Shur			E, P, R						
Marah			J						
Elim			R-2 - unclear						

Table 6—SOURCE DISTRIBUTION: FRIEDMAN (continued on pp. 184–87)

	Egypt	Edom	Negeb	Judah	Shephelah	Jordan R.V.	Chinnereth	Moab	Bashan
Wilderness of Sin			R-2						
Dophkah									
Alush									
Rephidim			E, R-3						
Massah			E, other, Pss						
Meribah			E-2, other-2, Ezek-2, Pss						
Sinai/Wilderness of Sinai		J, P-2, R/P, other							
Mt. Horeb			E-2, DTR¹-2						
Mt. Seir/Seir		J, E-2, P, DTR¹, other, Ezek, 1Chr, 2 Chr-2							
Kibroth-hataavah			R						
Hazeroth			E						

Table 6—SOURCE DISTRIBUTION: FRIEDMAN (continued)

	Egypt	Edom	Negeb	Judah	Shephelah	Jordan R.V.	Chinnereth	Moab	Bashan
Rithmah									
Rimmon-perez									
Libnah					R				
Rissah									
Kehelathah									
Mt. Shepher									
Haradah									
Makheloth									
Tahath									
Terah									
Mithkah									
Hashmonah									
Moseroth									
Bene-jaakan									
Hor-haggidgad									
Jotbathah									
Abronah		R possibly							
Ezion-geber		DTR¹, R 2 Chr							
Elath		DTR¹ 2 Chr							
Wilderness of Zin			P, R-3						

Table 6—SOURCE DISTRIBUTION: FRIEDMAN (continued)

	Egypt	Edom	Negeb	Judah	Shephelah	Jordan R.V.	Chinnereth	Moab	Bashan
Paran/Wilderness of Paran		J, E, P-3, other, Hab							
Kadesh/Kadesh-barnea			J-2, E, P, R-3						
Mt. Hor		P-2, R-3							
Zalmonah		R							
Punon									
Oboth									
Iye-abarim								R	
Dibon gad/Dibon								J, P, R, Isa, Jer, Neh	
Almon-diblathaim								R	
Wadi Zered								DTR[1], ?	
Beer								?	
Mattanah								?	
Nahaliel								?	
Bamoth/Bamoth-baal								E, ?	
Pisgah								E-2, DTR[1]	

Table 6—SOURCE DISTRIBUTION: FRIEDMAN (continued)

	Egypt	Edom	Negeb	Judah	Shephelah	Jordan R.V.	Chinnereth	Moab	Bashan
Jahaz								J, Isa, Jer-2, 1 Chr	
Heshbon								J, P, DTR^1-6, Isa-2, Jer-4	
Jazer								J, P-2, Isa, Jer, 1 Chr-2	
Edrei									E, D-7
Ashtaroth									D-5, 1 Chr
Tablelands of Medeba								J, Isa-2, Jer	
Mts. of Abarim								P, R, other,	
Mt. Nebo								E, other, R, Isa, Jer-2	
Plains of Moab								E, P-7, R	
Beth-jeshimoth							R		
Abel-shittim								J, R, Mic	

Table 6—SOURCE DISTRIBUTION: FRIEDMAN (continued)

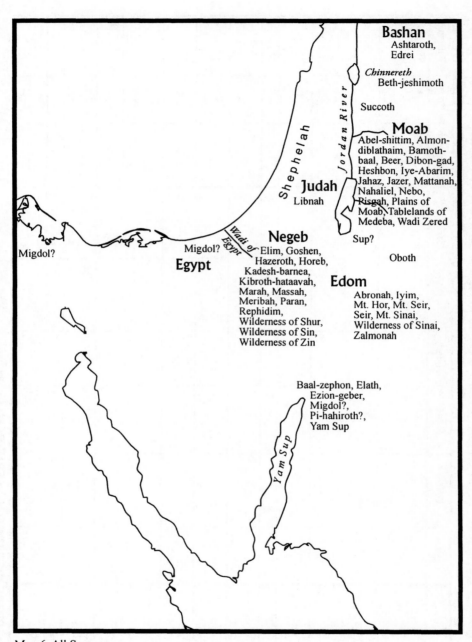

Map 6. All Sources

Of the more than 75 associated sites investigated, all of those for which a clear location could be identified were consistently situated by their various textual references. I selected a number of them (43) to identify in relation to the particular fixed locale with which they are associated. The following detail clarifies this relationship; the sites are listed in alphabetical order.

EDOM

Amalek (located in region of Edom and Negeb)
Gen 14:7; 36:12; Num 13:29; Judg 12:15; 1 Sam 15:7; 27:8; 1 Chr 1:36

Dedan
Isa 21:13; Jer 49:8

Mt. of God
Exod 3:1; 4:27; 18:5; 24:13–16; 1 Kgs 19:8

Teman
Gen 36:11, 15, 34, 42; Jer 49:7, 20; Ezek 25:13; Amos 1:22; Obad 9; Hab 3:3; 1 Chr 1:36, 45, 53

Valley of Salt
2 Sam 8:13–14; 2 Kgs 14:7; Ps 60:2; 2 Chr 25:11–14

JUDAH

Beer-sheba
Gen 21:14, 31–33; 26:23; 28:10, 19; 46:1, 5; Josh 15:28; 19:2; 20:1; 1 Sam 3:20; 2 Sam 3:10; 17:11; 24:2, 7, 15; 1 Kgs 5:5; 19:3; 23:8; Amos 5:5; Neh 11:27, 30; 1 Chr 4:24–33; 21:2; 2 Chr 30:5

Beth-lehem
Gen 48:7; Judg 17:7–9; 19:1–2, 18; 1 Sam 17:12; 2 Sam 2:32; Jer 41:17; Mic 5:1; Ruth 1:1–2; 2 Chr 11:6

Ephrath
Gen 35:19; 48:7; Mic 5:1; Ruth 1:2; 4:11

Gederah (-oth)

Josh 15:36, 41; 2 Chr 28:18

Gibeah

Josh 15:57; 18:28; Judg 19:14; 20:4, 10, 31; 1 Sam 7:1; 13:2, 15; 14:16; 2 Sam 23:29; Isa 10:29; Hos 5:8; 10:9; 1 Chr 11:31

Gibeon

Josh 10:41; 18:25; 21:17; 2 Sam 20:8; 1 Chr 8:29, 32; 9:35, 38

Hebron

Gen 13:18; 23:2, 19; 35:27; Num 13:22; Josh 10:5; 12:10; 15:54; 20:7; 21:11; Judg 16:3; 1 Chr 6:40

Kiriath-arba

Gen 23:2; 35:27; Josh 14:15; 15:13, 54; 20:7; 21:11; Judg 1:10

Kiriath-jearim

Josh 15;10, 60; 18:14; Judg 18:12; 1 Chr 13:6

Lachish

Josh 15:39; Isa 36:1–2; Jer 34:7; Neh 11:30

Mt. of YHWH

Isa 2:3; 30:29; Mic 4:2; Zech 8:3 (the Mt. of Yahweh is only Jerusalem)

Negeb of Judah

1 Sam 27:10; 2 Sam 24:7

Socoh

Josh 15:35, 48; 2 Chr 11:7; 28:18

Wadi Eshcol

Num 13:23; 32:9; Deut 1:24

PHILISTIA

Ashdod

Josh 11:22; 13:3; 15:46–47; 1 Sam 5:1–7; 6:17; Jer 25:20; Amos 1:8; Zeph 2:4–5; Zech 9:6; 2 Chr 26:6

Ekron

Josh 13:3; 15:11, 46; 1 Sam 5:10; 6:16–17; Jer 25:20; Amos 1:8; Zeph 2:4; Zech 9:5–7

Gaza

Gen 10:19; Josh 10:40–41; 11:21–22; 13:3; 15:47; Judg 16; 1 Sam 6:17; 1 Kgs 5:4; 2 Kgs 18:8; Jer 25:20; 47:1, 5; Amos 1:6–7; Zeph 2:4–5; Zech 9:5

EPHRAIM

Bethel

Gen 12:8; 13:3; 28:19; 35:6, 16; Josh 16:1; 18:21; Judg 4:5; 20:18, 26, 31; Neh 11:31

Beth-horon

Josh 16:3; 21:22; 1 Chr 6:53; 7:24

Shechem

Gen 12:6; 33:18; 35:1; Josh 17:1; 20:7; 21:21; Judg 9:7, 48; 21:19; 1 Kgs 12:25; Pss 60:8; 108:8; 1 Chr 6:52; 7:28

JORDAN RIVER VALLEY

Arabah

Num 22:1; 26:3, 63; 31:12; 33:48–50; 35:1; 36:13; Deut 1:1, 7; 2:8; 3:17; 4:49; 11:30; 34:1, 8; Josh 3:16; 4:13; 5:10; 8:14; 11:2, 16; 12:1, 3; 13:32; 18:18; 1 Sam 23:24; 2 Sam 2:29; 2 Kgs 25:4–5; Jer 39:4–5; 52:7–8; Ezek 47:8

Beth-haram

Num 32:36; Josh 13:27

Beth-nimrah

Num 32:3, 36; Josh 13:27

Gilgal

Num 11:30; Deut 11:29–30; Josh 4:19; 2 Sam 19:16, 41; 2 Kgs 2:1; Amos 4:4; 5:5

Penuel

Gen 32:31–32; Judg 8:8–9; 1 Kgs 12:25

Zaphon

Josh 13:27; Judg 12:1

Zarethan

Josh 3:16; 1 Kgs 4:12; 7:46

MOAB

Ar

Num 21:15, 28; Deut 2:9, 16, 29; Isa 15:1

Arnon

Num 21:13–15, 24–28; 22:36; Deut 2:18–24; 3:8, 12, 16; 4:48; Josh 12:1–2; 13:8–9; Judg 11:18; 2 Kgs 10:33; Isa 16:2; Jer 48:20

Aro'er

Num 32:34; Deut 2:36; 3:12; 4:48; Josh 12:2; 13:9, 16, 25; Judg 11:26, 32–33; 1 Sam 30:26–31; 2 Sam 24:5; 2 Kgs 10:33; Isa 17:2; Jer 48:19

Elealeh

Num 32:37; Isa 15:4; 16:9; Jer 48:34

Midian

Gen 36:35; Num 22:1–7; 31:8; Josh 13:21; Judg 6:3

Sebam

Num 32:38; Josh 13:19; Isa 16:8–9; Jer 48:32

THE NORTH (CHINNERETH, BASHAN, DAMASCUS)

Hazar-enan

Num 34:9–10; Ezek 47:17; 48:1

Lebo-hamath

Num 34:8; Josh 13:5; Judg 3:3; 1 Kgs 8:65; 2 Kgs 14:25, 28; 23:33;

25:21; Isa 10:9; 36:19; 37:13; Jer 39:5; 49:23; 52:9, 27; Ezek 47:16–17; 48:1; Amos 6:14; Zech 9:2; 1 Chr 13:5; 18:3; 2 Chr 7:8

Rehob

Num 13:21; Josh 19:28; 21:31

Salecah

Deut 3:10; Josh 12:5; 13:11

Sharon

Isa 33:9; 35:2; 1 Chr 5:11–17

The evidence gathered from these secondary, and non-itinerary, sites lends strong support to the conclusions to be drawn from the itinerary evidence. To reiterate the investigation's hypothesis:

if the geographical sites that pertain to the exodus are known to the various biblical sources, then they may be described on occasion in relative proximity to known regional locales.

Three conclusions are immediately evident from the data presented.

● The sources are consistent in their presentation of site identification (any site) throughout the Hebrew Bible.
● The previously stated assumptions regarding the accuracy of geographical perspectives and knowledge are apparently consistent as well.
● The identification of sites is consistent across the sources. In other words, no matter the era, no matter the political or theological agenda of the particular sources, they describe the geography of the region consistently.

Based upon this consistency, we may also state other conclusions and ramifications from the findings of this study.

● The geographical origin of the exodus.
Even a quick glance at any of the maps reveals the most telling observation. The exodus event involves locations associated with the Negeb, the Gulf of Elath, Edom and Moab. No site can be located in the western side of

the Sinai Peninsula (or even the Peninsula itself) nor in the Nile Delta. Thus, the Egypt Presupposition is proven to be a false assumption. The exodus narrative (even with "Egypt" in the story) is describing a movement of people within and out of the region between the Negeb and the Gulf of Elath.

- The Egypt Presupposition is also present in the Hebrew Bible.

As described in Chapter Four (pp. 93–94), it is possible to detail evidence for an Egypt Presupposition within even the Hebrew Bible. An interesting statistic emerges from the itinerary site data. Of the 72 sites investigated in the exodus itinerary, 21 are described in such meager detail within the Hebrew text, that it is impossible to locate them. Most are mentioned only once, in Numbers 33, and only in association with the site from which the Israelites left and/or the site to which they are journeying. The interesting feature of these 21 is that 20 of them are visited by the Israelites within and around the Sinai, Negeb and Edom. All appear to fill in a "Geographical Gap" suggested earlier in Chapter Four.

All of these 20 sites are later additions (most identified by Driver as P) to a received exodus tradition. Most of them fill the relatively small region between Mt. Sinai and Ezion-geber. If Driver is correct, this is perplexing, for P clearly identifies both of these known locations in close proximity to Edom. It would appear impossible to determine the path, or the motivation, P had in mind when adding these sites. In any event, by consciously adding sites between Mt. Sinai and Ezion-geber, this source was reinforcing the site identification/location within the eastern Sinai Peninsula region.

The other sites that are impossible (or very difficult) to place, Pi-hahiroth, Baal-zephon, Migdol, Etham, etc. appear to be additions intended to fill the Geographical Gap between Rameses (by the time of P and D, clearly accepted as in Egypt) and Yam Sûp. It may well be possible that the Josianic period is that in which many of these additional sites were added.[1] It is entirely possible that the later sources were adding contemporary Egyptian sites to the itinerary list in order to make sense of the gap they knew existed between Rameses and Yam Sûp. In any case, no matter when these sites became part of the story, one notices an expected phenomenon if the "later-added-sites" are removed from the lists/maps. Not only are the initial exodus locations extremely sparse when compared to the "Edom to Moab" component, but the "Eastern Sinai" location of the exodus event is all the more evident.

- The source of the exodus event itself.

As the geographical perspective locates the exodus event outside of Egypt, so must our understanding of the event itself be altered. Egypt, no matter that it is a "character" in the play, played no role in the events themselves. It is no wonder that the attempts to link the archaeological sites into the biblical text are so difficult and controversial. The Egyptian sources are silent regarding the events described in the Bible. Moreover, the sites are not to be found within Egypt, and not within the Late Bronze Age. The exodus tradition narrative clearly exists within the traditions of (Northern) Israel in the mid-8th century B.C.E. I suggest that the traditions of Israel will thus hold the key for understanding and discovering the event described as the exodus.

As noted above (pp. 22–23), Finkelstein and Silberman support the notion that the Josianic influence is seen in the addition of much geographical material to the exodus story. Nevertheless, the origin of the story is to be found within the Northern tradition. Hints and suggestions to these origins have been proposed previously by Gevirtz and myself.[2] The event in Israelite history that may be seen as an independence and liberation watershed is the freedom acquired from the oppression under Davidic/Solomonic rule. If an "exodus" slavery and liberation is to be sought, it would appear reasonable to find it within the division of the kingdom following Solomon's death.

The geographical memory residing within the biblical texts indicates a movement of Israelites from the south, then toward the northeast around Edom. They are traveling in avoidance of Judah because the enemy is there. Eventually they rejoin their compatriots in Ephraim/Samaria. With such a deeply felt event forming the core of this narrative, it is little wonder that it was able to stabilize, evolve and develop as Israel's story of its national origin.

EXCURSUS

Having proposed an altogether different model for the exodus itinerary, I am further tempted to suggest a route for this exodus. This is a rather complex, albeit speculative, undertaking. The attempt to propose what I envision as an originally disjointed movement of refugees is hindered by the oft-repeated redaction of the original exodus narrative, if indeed a travel itinerary were initially associated with the events. Nevertheless, a reinterpretation of the exodus is warranted. In order to set the stage for this discussion I will revisit some of the arguments set forward in this text.

If we assume that the exodus occurred, the biblical text appears to present two geographical scenarios. The Israelites proceeded from either the western (Nile Delta) or the eastern side of the Sinai Peninsula. In addition, the tradition of the exodus is either an Israelite (Northern Kingdom) event or one that also included Judah.

An exodus from the Nile Delta is not supported within the geographical memory of the biblical authors. At the same time, it is conceivable to suggest that the Egyptians enslaved the Israelites within the eastern Sinai Peninsula. The exodus events could have occurred there. This explanation is possible, but I consider it unlikely. It would require that the biblical authors, totally aware of their geographic context, identified royal Egyptian cities in the eastern Sinai. This identification lacks both biblical as well as archaeological support.

With an exodus from the eastern Sinai firmly entrenched in the geographical memory of the Hebrew Bible, another explanation for the story's Egyptian setting is required. Rather then incorrectly re-invent the physical geography and governmental structure of ancient Egypt, it is entirely possible to read the exodus narrative as representing another time and another antagonist. It may be read as allegory. As such, and taking into consideration the constraints imposed by a consistent geographical memory, the question is asked, "from whom were the Israelites fleeing?"

As mentioned previously in this text, the evidence from the prophetic corpus indicates that the exodus tradition was original to the Israelites (Northern Kingdom). They were responsible for the creation of the exodus narrative, as a condemnation of the slavery imposed and enforced by Solomon and Rehoboam. The following speculation is derived with that perspective in mind.

- The exodus narrative is an allegorical tale, created out of whole cloth, to describe the Israelite struggle for independence against the Davidic monarchy.

● As an allegorical tale, Pithom and Rameses represent Solomon's Temple and royal palace in Jerusalem.

● There is no association with Egypt.

● The eventual description and detailing of an intricate journey-in-stages is a representation of a much evolved story. It represents the authors' acceptance of the Egypt Presupposition. The journey described in the received text also represents the compilation of the various sites into an organized travel itinerary.

● The original itinerary, if it existed, represents the flight of various Israelite groups within Israel/Judah, away from the Judeans and toward northern Canaan. This eventual coalescing of Israelite groups would become known as the "Northern Kingdom."

From the itinerary investigation presented in Chapter Four it is apparent that there were at least four Negeb/Edomite centers around which the Israelites gathered. There were two in and around the Negeb (i.e., Kadesh-barnea and Mt. Hor). There were two in and around Edom (i.e., Mt. Horeb and Mt. Sinai). There also appear to have been several "paths of flight" for the Israelites. These are derived primarily from Exod 12:37–19:25 with a possible consideration of Numbers 13 and 21.

The historical context of the exodus narrative (recognizing that there is also no archaeological corroboration of the early Davidic dynasty) is Solomon's enslavement of the Israelite people, the subsequent rebellion under Jeroboam and the eventual independance war fought against Solomon's son Rehoboam. It is commonly assumed that the late 10th century B.C.E. destructions evident in Israel, Judah and the Negeb are the result of the invasion of Sheshonq I.[3] These destruction levels could easily be associated with the decades of war between Israel and Judah: or perhaps a combination of the two.

The end result of the independence war was the division of Israel/Judah into a northern Israel and southern Judah. The exodus represents the account of that division. I would suggest that the narrative originally told the story of groups of Israelites leaving their settlements in the Negeb and Jerusalem/Judah and seeking refuge in one or more of the four main locales mentioned above. Thus, they fled Jerusalem/Judah toward the north, perhaps toward Samaria, but clearly toward Succoth. In the Negeb/Edom region, the Israelites gathered in Kadesh-barnea, Mt. Horeb, Mt. Hor and/or Mt. Sinai. The "sea-crossing" story may be the result of some military action near Ezion-geber and Yam Sûp that saw the defeat of Rehoboam's chariots. As this story was retold as the Song of the Sea (Song of Miriam) and thus associated with Miriam (who is also closely associated with Kadesh-barnea), perhaps the group(s) responsible for its creation moved to Kadesh-barnea seeking shelter and protection within the fortress there.[4]

A proposed compilation of routes is indicated in Map 6a. Journey "A" represents the movement from Rameses to Succoth (Exod 12:37; 13:20). Perhaps Etham is also to be understood as in this region, but the text is unclear, only associating Etham with Succoth. Journey "B" represents the movements in and around Baal-zephon, Migdol, Pi-hahiroth and "The Sea." It is extremely difficult to locate what are probably anachronistic entries into the narrative. Nevertheless, as I have identified the sea of the exodus crossing as Yam Sûp, this is the only location possible for these particular sites (assuming their validity). Journey "C" represents the general movements described in Exod 15:22–19:25, from Yam Sûp to Mt. Sinai. The gathering and prolonged stay in Kadesh-barnea is represented by the directional arrows around "D." I would speculate further that the spies that were sent from Kadesh-barnea (Numbers 13) could also represent a movement of refugees north to Samaria ("E").

In summary, I propose that the exodus journey was more of a gradual migration north by the southern-dwelling Israelites along with those living in Judah (1 Kgs 12:17). The destruction levels discovered at numerous regional sites represent, at the very least, the abandonment and/or destruction of these settlements during the war for Israelite independence from Judah. It is only later (from the 8th through the 6th centuries B.C.E.) that the "exodus journey" evolves into the wilderness journey-by-stages that is portrayed in the Canonical version of the exodus narrative.

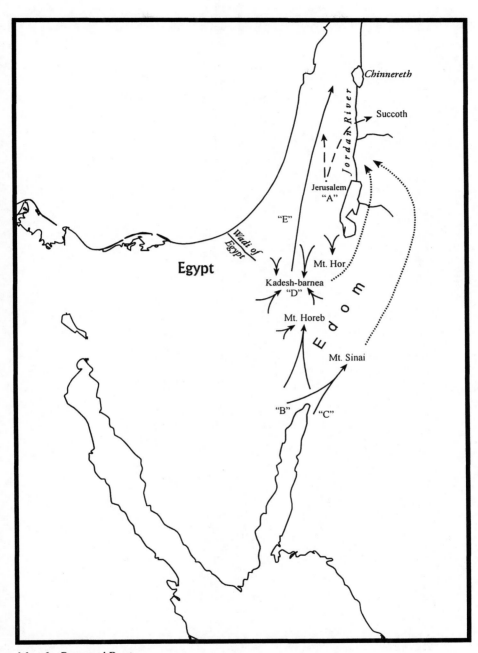

Map 6a. Proposed Routes

APPENDIX

THE JOURNEY—A NEW PERSPECTIVE: THE MAPS OF THE EXODUS ITINERARY SOURCES

The following pages present the maps drawn from the Source Distribution Tables in Chapter Five. They are ordered as follows:

Maps 7–26 present the itinerary sites as divided into the various pentateuchal sources according to the models of Driver, Noth and Friedman. Many of the sites are mentioned in the Hebrew Bible on more than one occasion, and by one or more of the sources. On several occasions a site may be mentioned only once by a particular source. Maps 27–35 present those three situations, each group of three maps identified by the particular scholar. Map 36 displays the site locations as presented by non-pentateuchal sources. As will be noted, an additional map of those sites with duplicated positions (located in proximity to more than one Fixed Locale) is not necessary, as there were no such sites.

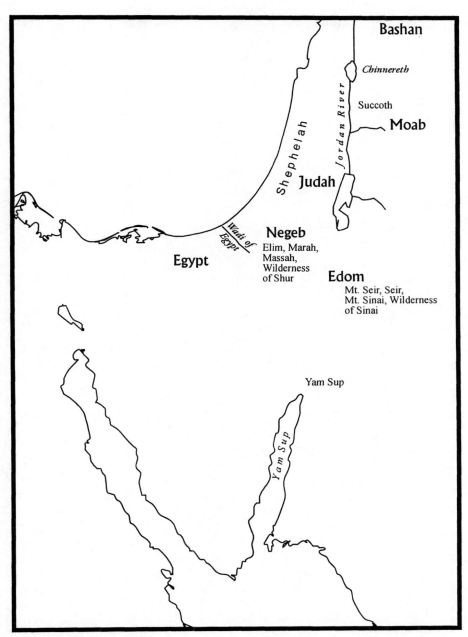

Map 7. Driver: (J)

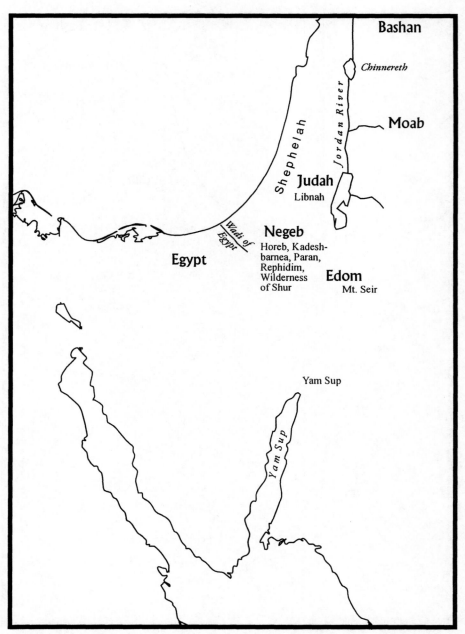

Map 8. Driver: (E)

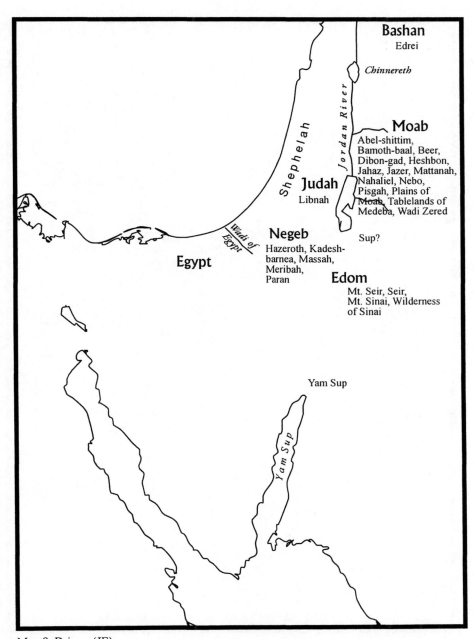

Map 9. Driver: (JE)

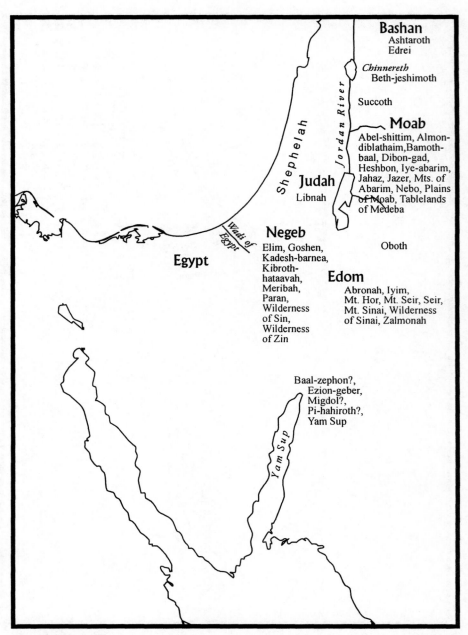

Map 10. Driver: (P)

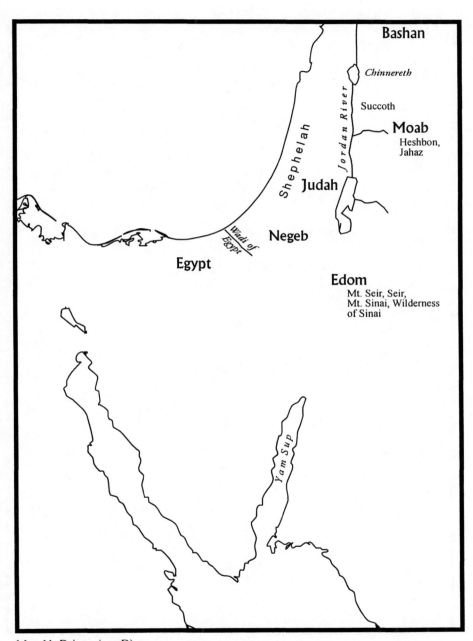

Map 11. Driver: (pre-D)

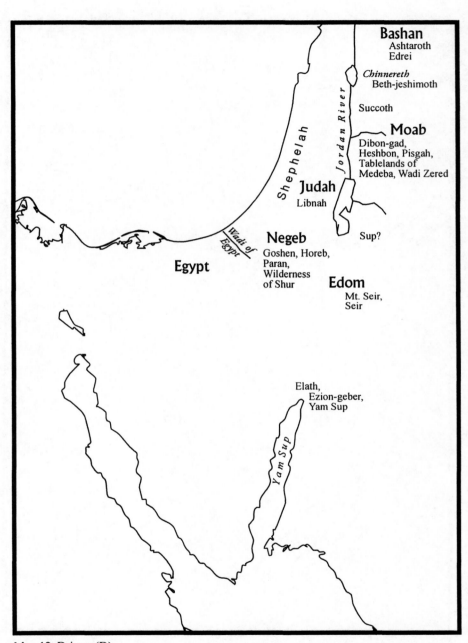

Map 12. Driver: (D)

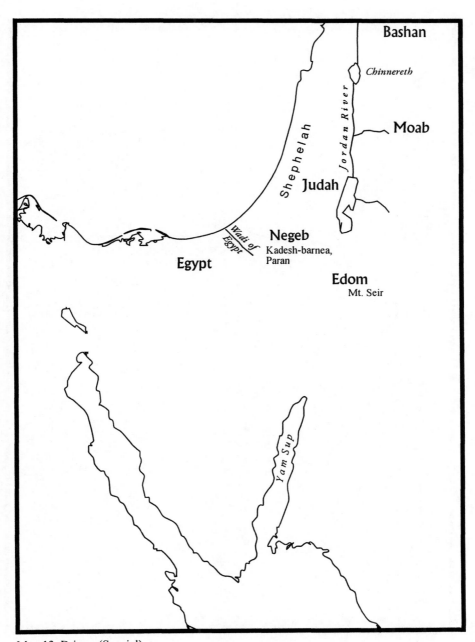

Map 13. Driver: (Special)

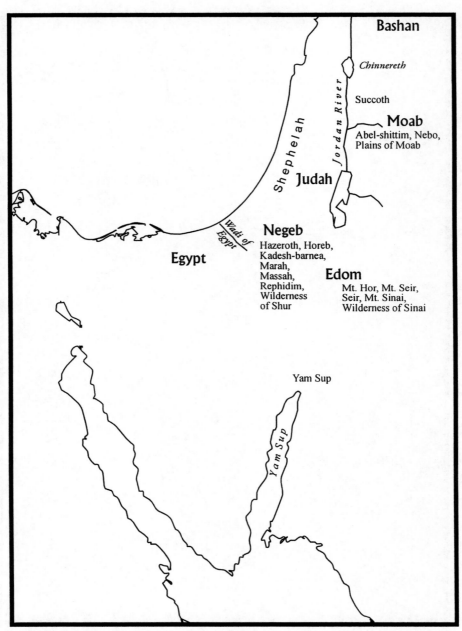

Map 14. Noth: (J)

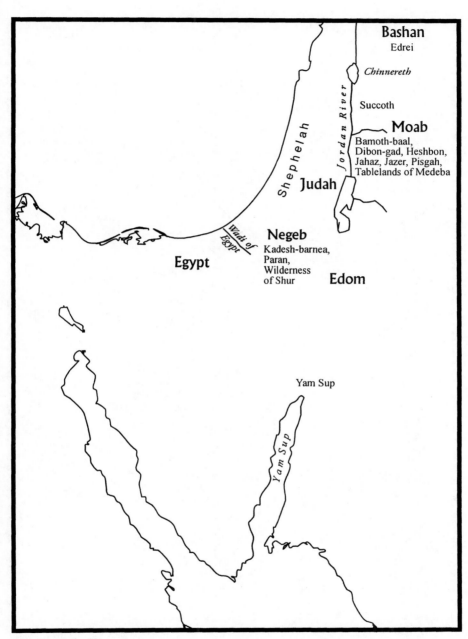

Map 15. Noth: (E)

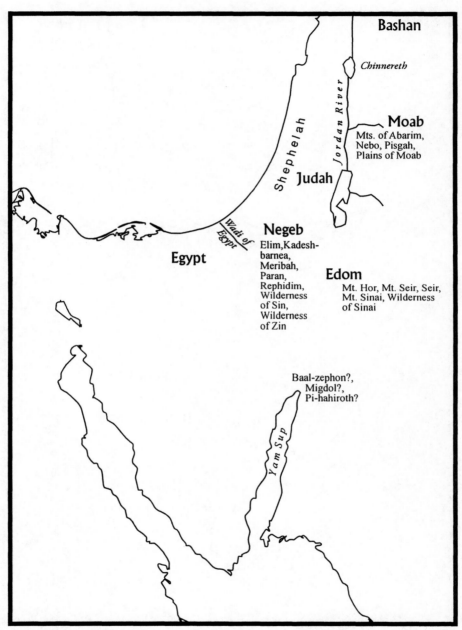

Map 16. Noth: (P)

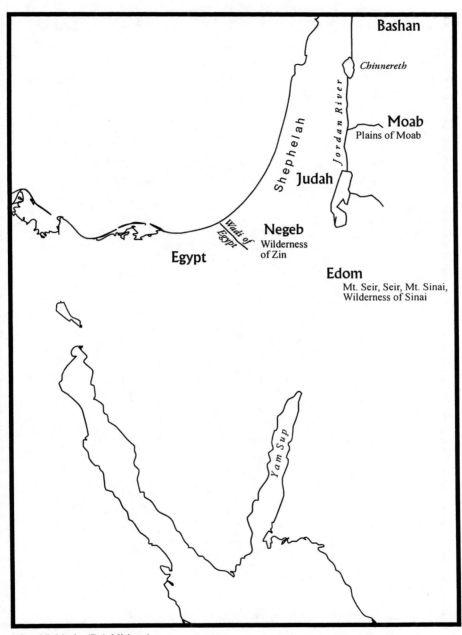

Map 17. Noth: (P Additions)

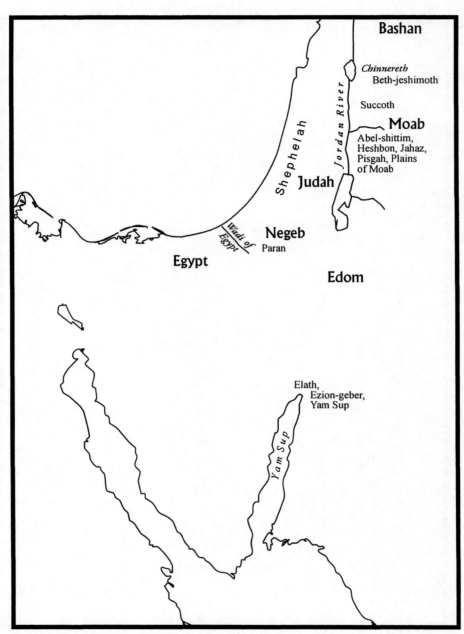

Map 18. Noth: (pre-D)

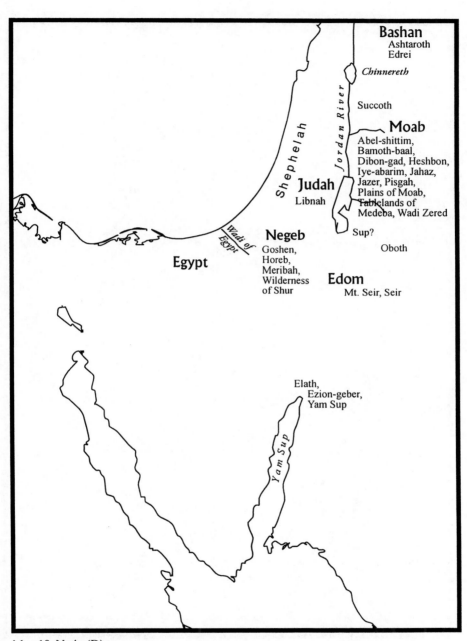

Map 19. Noth: (D)

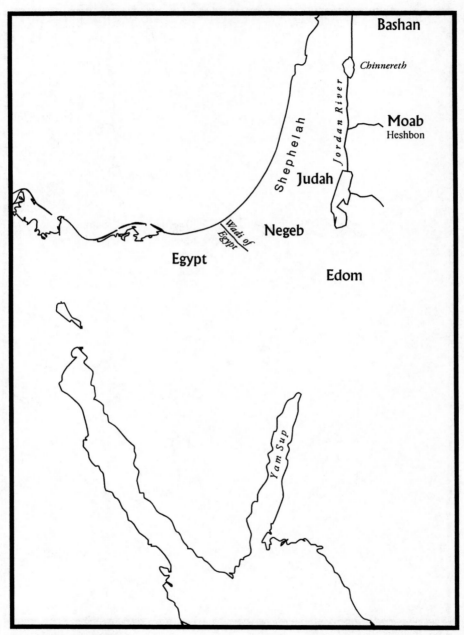

Map 20. Noth: (later D)

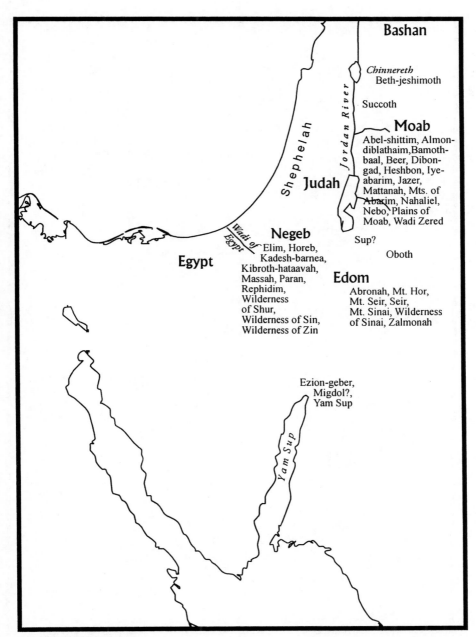

Map 21. Noth: (Special)

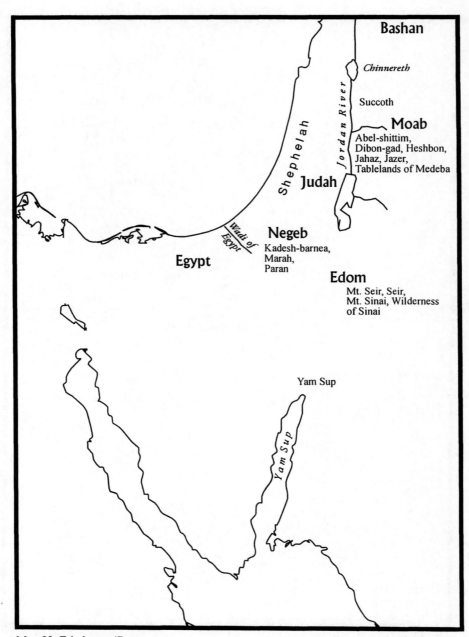

Map 22. Friedman: (J)

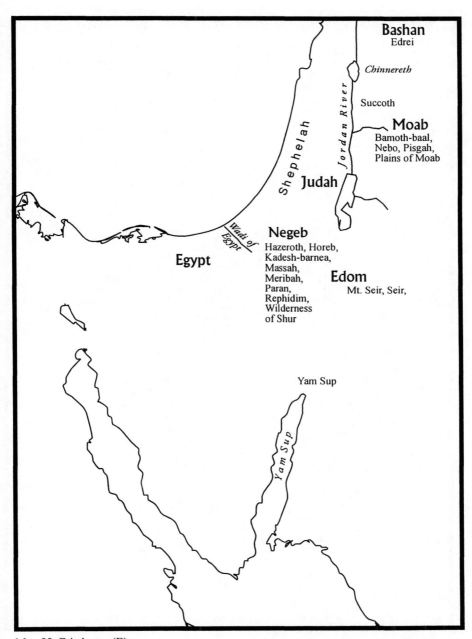

Map 23. Friedman: (E)

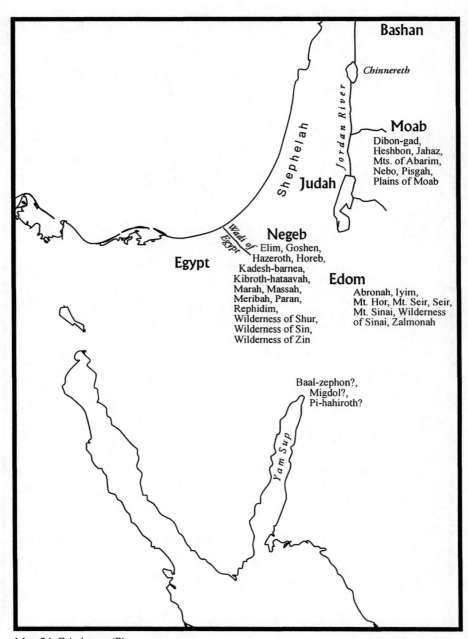

Map 24. Friedman: (P)

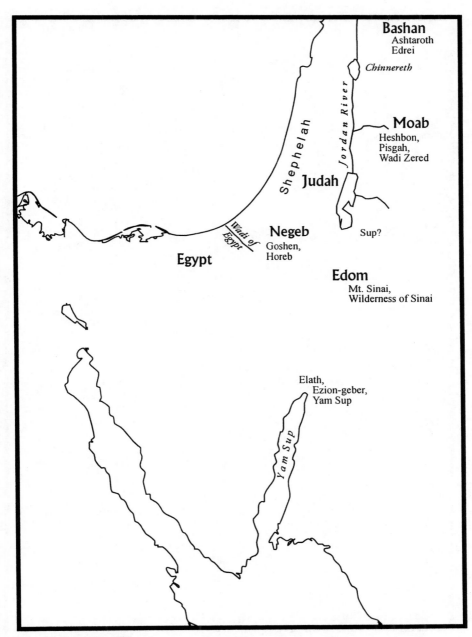

Map 25. Friedman: (D)

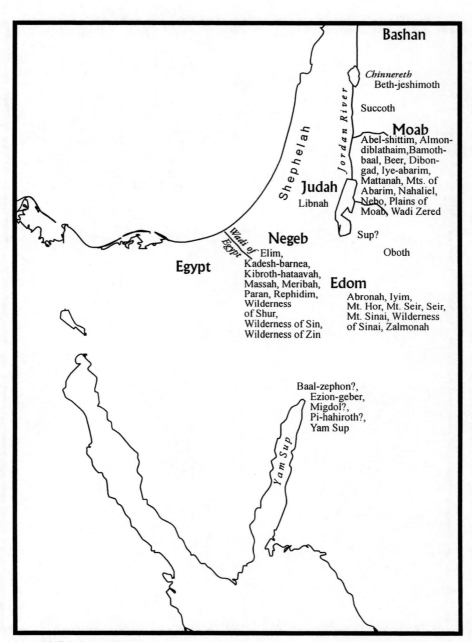

Map 26. Friedman: (R+)

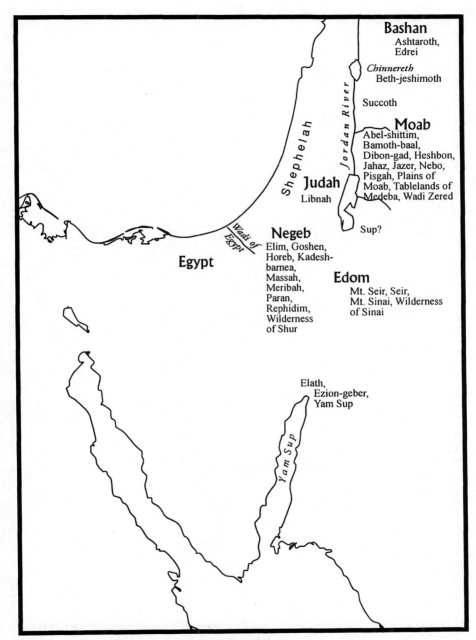

Bashan
Ashtaroth,
Edrei

Chinnereth
Beth-jeshimoth

Succoth

Moab
Abel-shittim,
Bamoth-baal,
Dibon-gad, Heshbon,
Jahaz, Jazer, Nebo,
Pisgah, Plains of
Moab, Tablelands of
Medeba, Wadi Zered

Sup?

Judah
Libnah

Shephelah

Jordan River

Wadi of Egypt

Negeb
Elim, Goshen,
Horeb, Kadesh-
barnea,
Massah,
Meribah,
Paran,
Rephidim,
Wilderness
of Shur

Egypt

Edom
Mt. Seir, Seir,
Mt. Sinai, Wilderness
of Sinai

Elath,
Ezion-geber,
Yam Sup

Yam Sup

Map 27. Driver: (Sites with two or more references)

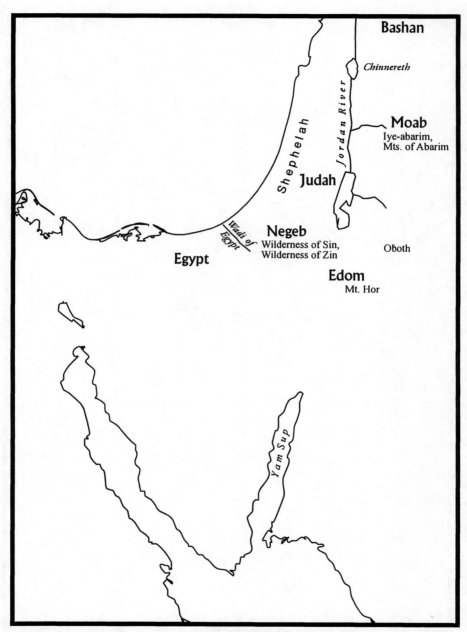

Map 28. Driver: (One source—two or more references/site)

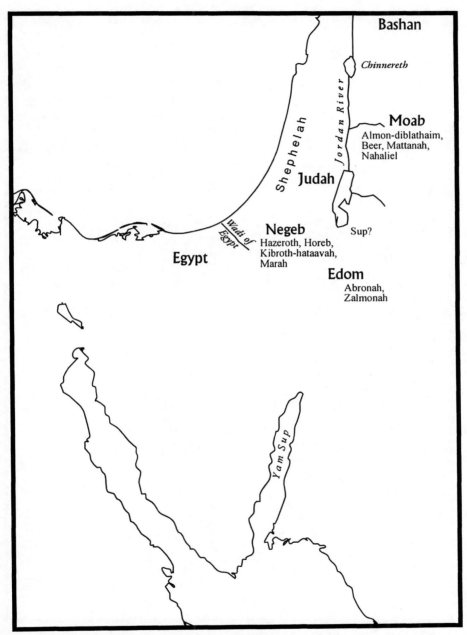

Map 29. Driver: (One source—one reference/site)

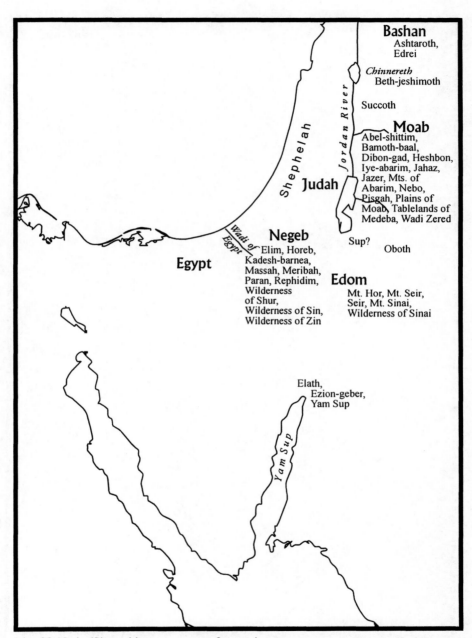

Map 30. Noth: (Sites with two or more references)

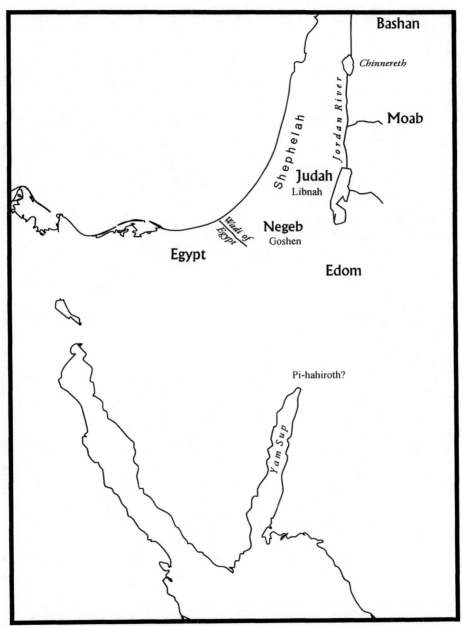

Map 31. Noth: (One source—two or more references per site)

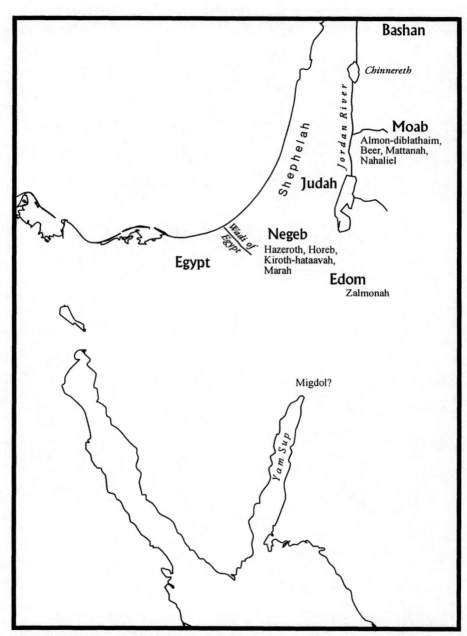

Map 32. Noth: (One source—one reference per site)

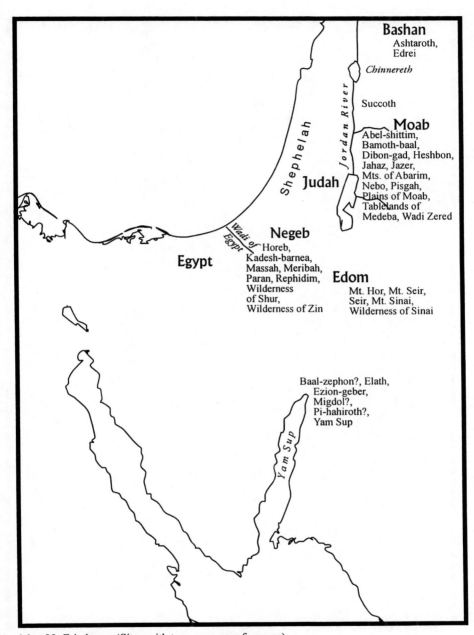

Map 33. Friedman: (Sites with two or more references)

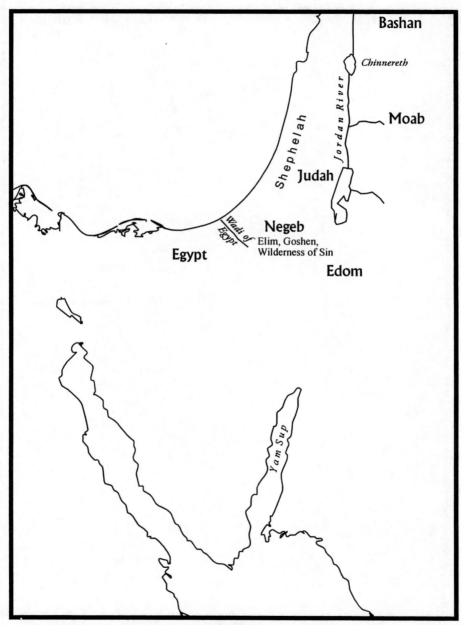

Map 34. Friedman: (One source—two or more references per site)

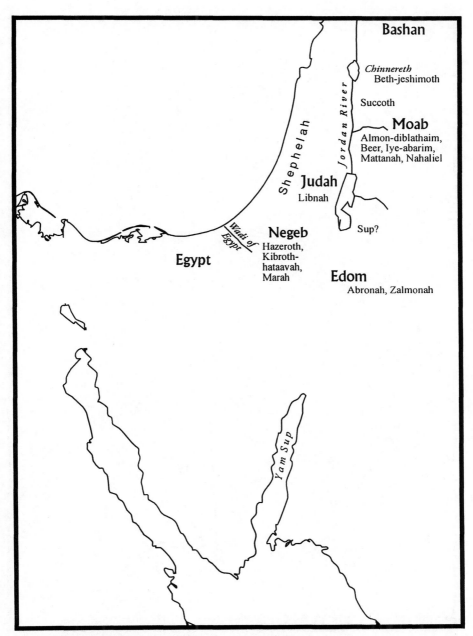

Map 35. Friedman: (One source—one reference per site)

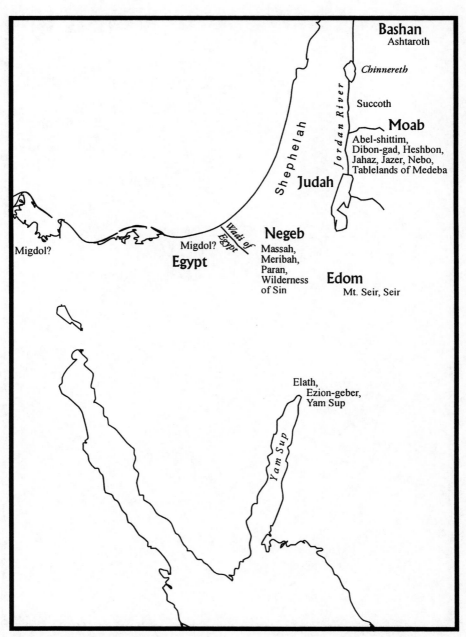

Map 36. Non-J, E, P, D

NOTES

Chapter One: Setting the Stage

1. In addition to the evidence presented here, scholars often point to two other aspects of archaeological research. First, the expansion of mostly unwalled villages in the highlands of Canaan, indicating a lack of need for defense in some areas. Second, the widespread destruction that affected nearly all the important urban centers of the region during the Late Bronze to Early Iron transition. These conditions helped set the stage for the emergence of Israel in Canaan.

2. N. H. Snaith, "סוּף יָם : The Sea of Reeds : The Red Sea," *VT* 15 (1965) 395–98; B. F. Batto, "The Reed Sea: Requiescat in Pace," *JBL* 102/1 (1983) 27–35; B. F. Batto, "Red Sea or Reed Sea?" *BAR* 10/4 (1984) 56–63; B. F. Batto, *Slaying the Dragon - Mythmaking in the Biblical Tradition* (Louisville: Westminster/John Knox, 1992); W. Wifall, "The Sea of Reeds as Sheol," *ZAW* 92/3 (1980) 325–32.

3. W. F. Albright, "A Revision of Early Hebrew Chronology," *JPOS* 1 (1920/21) 49–79; D. N. Freedman, *Pottery, Poetry, and Prophecy: Studies in Early Hebrew Poetry* (Winona Lake: Eisenbrauns, 1980).

4. Albright, "Chronology," 54–55.

5. Albright, "Chronology," 60.

6. Albright, "Chronology," 60–65.

7. Freedman, *Pottery, Poetry, and Prophecy*, 6.

8. Freedman, *Pottery, Poetry, and Prophecy*, 149.

9. Freedman, *Pottery, Poetry, and Prophecy*, 149.

10. G. A. Rendsburg, "The Date of the Exodus and the Conquest/Settlement: The Case for the 1100s," *VT* 42/4 (1992) 512.

11. Rendsburg, "1100s," 512, n. 5.

12. A. Malamat, "The Exodus: Egyptian Analogies," *Exodus: The Egyptian Evidence* (eds E. S. Frerichs and L. H. Lesko; Winona Lake: Eisenbrauns, 1997: 17–19.

13. Malamat, "The Exodus," 15.

14. Malamat, "The Exodus," 15–16. See also K. A. Kitchen for arguments concerning Merneptah as well as other criteria discussed here: K. A. Kitchen, *Ancient Orient and Old Testament* (London: The Tyndale Press, 1966) 57–72.

15. Albright, "Chronology," 64; W. F. Albright, *The Archaeology of Palestine and the Bible* (Cambridge, Massachusetts: American Schools of Oriental Research, 1974) 144.

16. Albright, "Chronology," 64.

17.   Albright, "Chronology," 65–66; W. F. Albright, "Archaeology and the Date of the Hebrew Conquest of Palestine," *BASOR* 58 (1935) 16; Albright, *Palestine and the Bible,* 143–47.

18.   See also J. J. Bimson for arguments supporting a Bronze Age date for the Exodus: J. J. Bimson, *Redating the Exodus and Conquest* (Sheffield: Almond, 1981); J. J. Bimson and D. Livingston, "Redating the Exodus," *BAR* 13/5 (1987) 40–53, 66–68; J. Bimson, "The Origins of Israel in Canaan: An Examination of Recent Theories," *Themelios* 15 (1989) 4–15.

19.   C. H. Gordon, "Vergil and the Near East," *Ugaritica* IV (1969) 285–86; S. Gevirtz, "Abram's 318," *IEJ* 19 (1969) 110–13; S. Gevirtz, "The Life Spans of Joseph and Enoch and the Parallelism šibʿātayim-šibʿîm wĕšibʿāh," *JBL* 96/4 (1977) 570–71; J. G. Williams, "Number Symbolism and Joseph as Symbol of Completion," *JBL* 98/1 (1979) 86–87.

20.   F. M. Cross and D. N. Freedman, "The Song of Miriam," *JNES* 14 (1955) 237–50; F. M. Cross, *Canaanite Myth and Hebrew Epic—Essays in the History of the Religion of Israel* (Cambridge: Harvard University Press, 1973); Freedman, *Pottery, Poetry, and Prophecy,* 179–86.

21.   Cross, *Canaanite Myth,* 121.

22.   Cross and Freedman, "Song of Miriam," 240, 248.

23.   Cross and Freedman, "Song of Miriam," 237.

24.   Cross and Freedman, "Song of Miriam," 239.

25.   Freedman, *Pottery, Poetry, and Prophecy,* 145.

26.   Cross and Freedman, "Song of Miriam," 239.

27.   Freedman, *Pottery, Poetry, and Prophecy,* 145.

28.   This is not an issue of casually rejecting Louis XIV's statement, "*L'État c'est moi.*" In the over 1,000 occurrences of פרעה and מצרים in the MT, they are never used in an identifying or equating parallelism, nor are they ever stated or implied to be equal entities. We cannot presume, based upon our own biases, that the same identification existed in ancient Israel's view of Egypt.

29.   A. Bender, "Das Lied Exodus 15," *ZAW* 23 (1903) 1–48. For discussion on this issue, the reader is directed to the following: B. A. Mastin, "Was the Šālîš the Third Man in the Chariot?" *VTSup* 30 (1979) 125–54; N. Naʾaman, "The List of David's Officers (*ŠĀLÎŠÎM*)," *VT* 38/1 (1988) 71; D. G. Schley, "The *ŠĀLÎŠÎM:*Officers or Special Three-Man Squads?" *VT* 40/3 (1990) 312–26. Although Mastin's detailed presentation is much appreciated, it is clear that he does not consider the possibility that שלש could refer to a grouping (in much the same sense that the English word "pair" refers to a grouping of two) of three. This point is made by Schley, and it is this sense that I accept.

30.   M. A. Littauer and J. H. Crouwel, "Chariots," *The Anchor Bible Dictionary* (ed. D. N. Freedman; New York: Doubleday, 1992) 888–92.

31.   Albright, "Chronology," 50–51.

32. Albright, "Chronology," 52–53.

33. This comment was suggested by Cohen as a respondent to Herrmann: S. Herrmann, "Basic Factors of Israelite Settlement in Canaan," *Biblical Archaeology Today - Proceedings of the International Congress on Biblical Archaeology, Jerusalem, April 1984* (ed. International Congress on Biblical Archaeology; Jerusalem: Israel Exploration Society, 1985) 79.

34. Albright, *Palestine and the Bible*, 147.

35. J. Bright, *A History of Israel, 3rd Edition* (Philadelphia: Westminster Press, 1981) 121.

36. N. K. Gottwald, "The Israelite Settlement as a Social Revolutionary Movement," *Biblical Archaeology Today—Proceedings of the International Congress on Biblical Archaeology, Jerusalem, April 1984* (ed. International Congress on Biblical Archaeology; Jerusalem: Israel Exploration Society, 1985) 36; Rendsburg, "1100s," 512–13.

37. I. Finkelstein and N. A. Silberman, *The Bible Unearthed* (New York: The Free Press, 2001) 54–56.

38. Albright, "Hebrew Conquest," 16; Y. Aharoni, *The Land of the Bible—a Historical Geography* (Philadelphia: Westminster Press, 1979) 176–77.

39. Albright, *Palestine and the Bible*, 143.

40. Albright, "Chronology," 65.

41. Bright, *History*, 121.

42. Bright, *History*, 139.

43. Albright, "Hebrew Conquest," 16.

44. D. B. Redford, "Zoan," *The Anchor Bible Dictionary, Vol 6* (ed. D. N. Freedman; New York: Doubleday, 1992) 1106.

45. F. M.-J. Lagrange, "L'Itinéraire des Israélites du Pays de Gessen aux bords du Jourdain," *RB* 9 (1900) 71–73; W. F. Albright, *The Biblical Period from Abraham to Ezra—an Historical Survey* (New York: Harper & Row, 1965) 11.

46. G. I. Davies, *The Way of the Wilderness—A Geographical Study of the Wilderness Itineraries in the Old Testament* (Society for Old Testament Study Monograph Series; Cambridge: Cambridge University Press, 1979) 79.

47. C. Houtman, *Exodus, Vol. 1* (Kampen: Kok Publishing House, 1993) 125–26.

48. Houtman, *Exodus*, 126–27.

49. For similar suggestions refer to the following: U. Cassuto, *A Commentary on the Book of Exodus* (Jerusalem: Hebrew University, 1967) 11; R. Giveon, "Archaeological Evidence for the Exodus," *Bulletin of the Anglo-Israel Archaeological Society* (1983/84) 42.

50. L. E. Axelsson, *The Lord Rose up from Seir—Studies in the History and Traditions of the Negev and Southern Judah* (Coniectanea Biblica—Old Testament Series; Stockholm: Almqvist & Wiksell International, 1987) 46.

51. E. Anati, "Has Mt. Sinai Been Found?" *BAR* 11/4 (1985) 42–56; E. Anati, *Har*

Karkom—the Mountain of God (New York: Rizzoli, 1986); I. Finkelstein, "Raider of the Lost Mountain—an Israeli Archaeologist Looks at the Most Recent Attempt to Locate Mt. Sinai," *BAR* 14/4 (1988) 46; G. I. Davies, "The Wilderness Itineraries and Recent Archaeological Research," *Supplements to Vetus Testamentum XLI: Studies in the Pentateuch* (ed. J. A. Emerton; Leiden: E. J. Brill, 1990) 161–76.

52.   D. Faiman, "From Horeb to Kadesh in Eleven Days," *Jewish Bible Quarterly* 22 (1994) 91–102 Wifall, "Sea of Reeds."

53.   Wifall, "Sea of Reeds," 325–27.

54.   Snaith, "The Sea of Reeds," 395.

55.   E. D. Oren, "The 'Way of Horus' in North Sinai," *Egypt, Israel, Sinai: Archaeological and Historical Relationships in the Biblical Period* (ed. A. F. Rainey; Tel Aviv: Tel Aviv University, 1987) 73 note 3; D. B. Redford, "An Egyptological Perspective on the Exodus Narrative," *Egypt, Israel, Sinai: Archaeological and Historical Relationships in the Biblical Period* (ed. A. F. Rainey; Tel Aviv: Tel Aviv University, 1987) 153.

56.   Meyer quoted in Albright: Albright, "Chronology," 50–51; Finkelstein and Silberman, *Bible Unearthed*, 48–71.

57.   N. P. Lemche, *Prelude to Israel's Past—Background and Beginnings of Israelite History and Identity* (Peabody: Hendrickson Publishers, 1998).

58.   Lemche, *Prelude*, 42.

59.   Lemche, *Prelude*, 43–47.

60.   D. B. Redford, *Egypt, Canaan and Israel in Ancient Times* (New Jersey: Princeton University, 1992) 412–13; H. Cazelles, "Les Localisations de L'Exode et la Critique Littéraire," *RB* 62 (1955) 364.

61.   Redford, "Egyptological Perspective," 138–44, in which he deals with attempting to situate Goshen, Succoth, Etham, Migdol and Rameses.

62.   Redford, "Egyptological Perspective," 148–50.

63.   Lagrange, "L'itinéraire," 71–73.

64.   A. Alt, *Essays on Old Testament History and Religion* (Garden City: Doubleday & Company, Inc., 1967) 182.

65.   A. Perevolotsky and I. Finkelstein, "The Southern Sinai Exodus Route in Ecological Perspective," *BAR* 11/4 (1985) 28.

66.   J. Van Seters, *The Life of Moses: The Yahwist as Historian in Exodus-Numbers* (Kampen: Kam Pharos Publishing, 1994) 24.

67.   J. K. Hoffmeier, *Israel in Egypt—the Evidence for the Authenticity of the Exodus Tradition* (New York: Oxford University Press, 1997) 117–22.

68.   Finkelstein and Silberman, *Bible Unearthed,* 70–71.

69.   Scholars indicating the Red Sea Presuppositions are listed in Chapter Two, note 1.

70.   A. Lucas, *The Route of the Exodus of the Israelites from Egypt* (London: Edward Arnold & Co., 1938); Davies, *Way of the Wilderness*; Aharoni, *Land of the Bible*; I. Beit-Arieh, "The Route Through Sinai: Why the Israelites Fleeing Egypt Went

South," *BAR* 14/3 (1988) 28–37; Bright, *History*.

71.   Batto, "Red Sea?"; Batto, "Reed Sea."; Batto, *The Dragon*.

72.   Batto, *The Dragon*, 102–27.

73.   Batto, *The Dragon*, 103.

74.   Batto, *The Dragon*, 103.

75.   Batto, *The Dragon*, 109, 115.

76.   Batto, *The Dragon*, 115.

77.   Batto, *The Dragon*, 115–16.

78.   Batto, *The Dragon*, 118–20.

79.   Batto, *The Dragon*, 116.

80.   Batto, "Red Sea?" 57; Batto, *The Dragon*, 115.

81.   Batto, *The Dragon*, 116.

82.   Batto also identifies YHWH's abode as Zion (Exod 15:17). This is not justified within the song itself, just as an exodus from Egypt is also a conclusion that may not be derived from the text in isolation from the surrounding material. The connections between YHWH and Zion appears to be made in the Hebrew Bible in material that may only be accurately dated to the 8th century B.C.E., at the earliest (Isa 8:18; 18:7; 24:23; 33:6; 52:8; Jer 31:6; Joel 3:16–17; Mic 4:7; Pss 9:12; 76:3). If the Song of the Sea is to be dated in the 10th–9th centuries B.C.E., or even earlier, there is no justification from the song itself that the place described in Exod 15:17 may be identified as Zion.

83.   Davies, *Way of the Wilderness*, 4.

84.   Davies, *Way of the Wilderness*, 58–59.

85.   Davies, *Way of the Wilderness*, 79.

86.   Davies, *Way of the Wilderness*, 79–83, in particular 83.

87.   Davies, *Way of the Wilderness*, 62.

88.   Davies, *Way of the Wilderness*, 79–84.

89.   Finkelstein and Silberman, *Bible Unearthed*, 68–71; Malamat, "The Exodus," 17, 19; T. B. Dozeman, "The Yam-Sûp in the Exodus and the Crossing of the Jordan River," *CBQ* 58/3 (July 1996) 409; R. Albertz, *A History of Israelite Religion in the Old Testament Period, Vol 1* (Louisville: Westminster/John Knox Press, 1994) 44; G. W. Ahlström, *The History of Ancient Palestine* (Minneapolis: Fortress Press, 1994) 369–70; Faiman, "Eleven Days."; Van Seters, *Moses*, 34; Houtman, *Exodus*, 109; D. N. Freedman, *The Anchor Bible Dictionary, Vol 2 & 5* (New York: Doubleday, 1992) 634; D. N. Freedman, "The Chronology of Israel in the Ancient Near East—Old Testament Chronology," *The Bible and the Ancient Near East—Essays in Honor of William Foxwell Albright* (ed. G. E. Wright; Garden City: Doubleday and Company, Inc., 1961) 207; Redford, *Egypt, Cannan.*, 412–13; Redford, "Egyptological Perspective," 140, 144; Rendsburg, "1100s," 512; Axelsson, *Lord from Seir*, 114; J. M. Miller and J. H. Hayes, *A History of Ancient Israel and Judah* (Philadelphia: Westminster Press, 1986) 67, 75; N. Na'aman,

Borders & Districts in Biblical Historiography (Jerusalem Biblical Studies; Jerusalem: Simor, 1986) 249; Gottwald, "Social Revolutionary," 36; N. K. Gottwald, *The Tribes of Yahweh—A Sociology of the Religion of Liberated Israel 1250–1050 B.C.E.* (Maryknoll: Orbis Books, 1981) 35–41, 453; Batto, "Red Sea?" 57; Giveon, "Evidence," 42; B. Halpern, *The Emergence of Israel in Canaan* (Society of Biblical Literature Monograph Series; Chico: Scholars Press, 1983) 25, 223–24; Wifall, "Sea of Reeds," 329; Davies, *Way of the Wilderness*, 41–42, 79–93; D. Patrick, "Traditio-History of the Reed Sea Account," *VT* 26 (1976) 248–49; D. Baly, *The Geography of the Bible* (New York: Harper & Row, 1974) 103, 251; W. A. Ward, "The Semitic Biconsonantal Root *SP* and the Common Origin of Egyptian *CWF* and Hebrew *SUP*: 'Marsh (-Plant)'," *VT* 24 (1974) 345; B. S. Childs, "A Traditio-Historical Study of the Reed Sea Tradition," *VT* 20 (1970) 406–18; R. Smend, *Yahweh War and Tribal Confederation—Reflections Upon Israel's Earliest History* (trans. M. G. Rogers; Nashville: Abingdon Press, 1970) 120; Snaith, "The Sea of Reeds," 396–98; W. Beyerlin, *Origins and History of the Oldest Sinaitic Traditions* (S. Rudman; Oxford: Basil Blackwell, 1961) 145–46; G. E. Mendenhall, "Biblical History in Transition," *The Bible and the Ancient Near East—Essays in Honor of William Foxwell Albright* (ed. G. E. Wright; Garden City: Doubleday and Company, Inc., 1961) 40, 43; M. Noth, *The History of Israel* (London: Adam & Charles Black, 1959) 112; J. Simons, *The Geographical and Topographical Texts of the Old Testament* (Leiden: E.J. Brill, 1959) 235–38; Cazelles, "Les Localisations," 364; Albright, "Chronology," 79; A. H. Sayce, *The "Higher Criticism" and the Verdict of the Monuments* (London: Richard Clay & Sons, Ltd., 1901) 257; H. L. Jones, trans, *The Geography of Strabo* (Cambridge: Harvard University Press, 1960); R. B. Coote, *Early Israel: A New Horizon* (Minneapolis: Fortress Press, 1990) 89–91; J. Bright, "Modern Studies of Old Testament Literature," *The Bible and the Ancient Near East—Essays in Honor of William Foxwell Albright* (ed. G. E. Wright; Garden City: Doubleday and Company, Inc., 1961) 13–31.

90.   Finkelstein and Silberman, *Bible Unearthed*, 69–70.

91.   Sayce also recognized that Yam Sûp is to be identified with the Gulf of Elath, but could not separate himself from the presupposition that the Israelites must have left from Egypt. Thus, the sea crossed by the Israelites is not the same as Yam Sûp. Sayce, *Higher Criticism*, 255–59.

Chapter Two: The More Things Change...

1.   B. A. Levine, *Numbers 21–36* (The Anchor Bible; New York: Doubleday, 2000) 518. Attention is drawn as well to the following scholars who also presuppose the identification in the ancient world of the Gulfs of Suez and Elath with the Red Sea: A. H. Sayce, *The "Higher Criticism" and the Verdict of the Monuments* (London:

Richard Clay & Sons, Ltd., 1901) 255–56; J. Simons, *The Geographical and Topographical Texts of the Old Testament* (Leiden: E.J. Brill, 1959) 238; D. Baly, *The Geography of the Bible* (New York: Harper & Row, 1974) 206–9; J. T. Walsh, "From Egypt to Moab: A Source Critical Analysis of the Wilderness Itinerary," *CBQ* xxxix/1 (1977) 32–33; Y. Aharoni, *The Land of the Bible—a Historical Geography* (Philadelphia: Westminster Press, 1979) 32, 36, 40; G. I. Davies, *The Way of the Wilderness—A Geographical Study of the Wilderness Itineraries in the Old Testament* (Society for Old Testament Study Monograph Series; Cambridge: Cambridge University Press, 1979) 41–42; J. Bright, *A History of Israel, 3rd Edition* (Philadelphia: Westminster Press, 1981) 122, 215; B. F. Batto, "Red Sea or Reed Sea?" *BAR* 10/4 (1984) 60; J. M. Miller and J. H. Hayes, *A History of Ancient Israel and Judah* (Philadelphia: Westminster Press, 1986) 36; B. F. Batto, *Slaying the Dragon—Mythmaking in the Biblical Tradition* (Louisville: Westminster/John Knox, 1992) 115; D. N. Freedman, *The Anchor Bible Dictionary, Vol 2 & 5* (New York: Doubleday, 1992) 634, 636; C. Houtman, *Exodus, Vol. 1* (Kampen: Kok Publishing House, 1993) 109; T. B. Dozeman, "The Yam-Sûp in the Exodus and the Crossing of the Jordan River," *CBQ* 58/3 (July 1996) 409.

2.   1B. Marzullo, *A Complete Concordance to the Iliad of Homer* (Hildesheim: Georg Olms Verlagsbuchhandlung, 1962); idem, *A Complete Concordance to the Odyssey of Homer* (Hildesheim: Georg Olms Verlagsbuchhandlung, 1962)

3.   W. Horowitz, *Mesopotamian Cosmic Geography* (Winona Lake: Eisenbrauns, 1998) 72–73, 325.

4.   H. L. Jones, trans, *The Geography of Strabo* (London: William Heinemann, Ltd., 1932); idem, trans, *The Geography of Strabo* (Cambridge: Harvard University Press, 1960).

5.   W. H. Race, *Pindar I—Olympian Odes, Pythian Odes* (The Loeb Classical Library; Cambridge: Harvard University Press, 1997).

6.   N. Dunbar, *Aristophanes—The Birds* (Oxford: Clarendon Press, 1995); A. H. Sommerstein, *Birds* (Wiltshire, England: Aris & Phillips, Ltd., 1987).

7.   A. D. Godley, *Herodotus* (Cambridge: Harvard University Press, 1981).

8.   W. Miller, *Xenophon Cyropaedia II* (The Loeb Classical Library; London: The MacMillan Company, 1914).

9.   C. Mullerus, *Geographi Graeci Minores* (Hildesheim: Georg Olms Verlag, 1990); S. M. Burstein, ed & trans, *Agatharchides of Cnidus—On the Erythraean Sea* (London: The Hakluyt Society, 1989).

10.   Burstein, *Agatharchides*, 150, n. 2; C. E. Bosworth, E. van Donzel, B. Lewis and C. Pellat, eds, *The Encyclopaedia of Islam V* (Leiden: E. J. Brill, 1983) 761–63; R. Stillwell, ed, *The Princeton Encyclopedia of Classical Sites* (Princeton: Princeton University Press, 1976) 12.

11.   H. Rackham, *Pliny—Natural History* (Cambridge: Harvard University Press, 1961).

12.   Jones, *Strabo*, 1932; idem, *Strabo*, 1960.

13. Burstein, *Agatharchides*, 150, n.2.

14. See J. Lewy, "The Old West Semitic Sun God Ḥammu," *HUCA* 18 (1944) 429–88; N. Avigad, "The Jothan Seal from Elath," *BASOR* 163 (1961) 18–22; S. T. Parker, "The Roman Aqaba Project: The Economy of Aila on the Red Sea," *BA* 59/3 (1996) 182. אילת is translated in the LXX on nearly all occasions with a final letter -θ (1 Kgs 9:26; 2 Kgs 14:22; 16:6; 2 Chr 8:17; 26:2). In Deut 2:8, however, it is rendered as *Aέλον*. Further examples of final -ν replacing final ת- are found in Josh 13:17 (במות = *βαιμών*), Josh 19:44 (בעלת = *βααλών*) and Josh 15:59 (בית-ענות = *βαιθανών*). As the ת- is non-consonantal in each case, it appears that the Greek transliteration readily substitutes a -ν for a final, non-consonantal letter. The most notable example of this practice would be the rendering of שלמה as *Σολομών*. Hence, it is appropriate to accept the naming of the city Aelana, as well as the Aelanite Gulf, as derived from Elath.

15. Müllerus, *GGM*.

16. M. Quatremère, "Mémoire sur les Nabatéens," *Journal Asiatique* 15 (Janvier 1835) 5–55; G. Booth, trans, *The Geographical Library of Diodorus the Sicilian* (London: Edward Jones, 1700); Book I, Chapter II, p. 8; Book V, Chapter II, pp. 95, 102; Book V, Chapter III, p. 102.

17. Booth, *Diodorus*, Book V, Chapter III, p. 102.

18. Booth, *Diodorus*, Book V, Chapter III, pp. 104–5.

19. C. Müllerus, *Fragmenta Historicorum Graecorum* (Parisiis: Fermin-Didot et Sociis, 1883) 479. 62; 480. 66; H. Rackham, *Pliny*, VI. xxxii. 156.

20. Jones, *Strabo, 1932; idem, Strabo*, 1960.

21. P. A. Brunt, *Arrian* (Cambridge: Harvard University Press, 1983).

22. P. Berry, trans, *Pomponius Mela—Geography/De Situ Orbis A.D. 43* (Studies in Classics; Lewiston: Edwin Mellen Press, 1997); F. E. Romer, *Pomponius Mela's Description of the World* (Ann Arbor: University of Michigan Press, 1998).

23. H. Rackham, Pliny; Müllerus, *FHG*.

24. Another version, sited by Müllerus (in *FHG*, p. 477), indicates that Pliny also referred to the Gulf of Aqaba as the Aelanite Gulf. The text reads, *A sinu Ælanitico alter sinus, quem Arabes Æant vocant...*Plinius VI, s. 33, p. 384.

25. W. M. Ellis, *Ptolemy of Egypt* (London: Routledge, 1994); W. Kubitschek, *Studien zur Geographie des Ptolemäus—I. Die Ländergrenzen* (Wien: Akademie der Wissenschaften); S. Ziegler, *Ptolemy—Geography, Book 6* (Wiesbaden: Dr. Ludwig Reichert Verlag, 1998); E. L. Stevenson, trans & ed, *Claudius Ptolemy—the Geography* (New York: Dover Publishers, 1991).

26. Stevenson's translation (pp. 107–9) continues with a description of the southern portion of Today's Red Sea, eventually arriving at what are likely the Bab el Mandeb Straits, which, "After the strait in the Red Sea" one arrives "then in Avalites Bay" (Gulf of Aden). The Avalites Bay contains a number of islands. Traveling "to the east of these islands" one eventually arrives in "the sea called Hip-

palum near which is the Indian Sea."

27.   Stevenson's translation (p. 128) continues, "The village Elana, which is located in the angle of a bay of this name, has this position 65 50   29 15...." The Pharan Promontory would appear to be the Sinai Peninsula.

28.   W. P. Wilson, *The Periplus of the Erythraean Sea* (Philadelphia: Philadelphia Museums, 1911); E. H. Bunbury, *A History of Ancient Geography Among the Greeks and Romans from the Earliest Ages Till the Fall of the Roman Empire* (New York: Dover Publications, Inc., 1959); S. Chattopadhyaya, *The Periplus of the Erythraean Sea & Ptolemy on Ancient Geography of India* (Prajñā: Asoke Ray, 1980); G. W. B. Huntingford, ed & trans, *The Periplus of the Erythraean Sea* (London: The Hakluyt Society, 1980).

29.   Huntingford notes (*Periplus,* pp. 67, 107–8) that Skuthia is the term by which the Greeks indicated the the northwest corner of India, on the coast. He also comments that "Sinthos is from Sanskrit *sindhu*, 'the sea', which became *hindu* in Old Persian, whence the Greek form *Indos* meaning the river...." Thus, Sinthos would refer to the Indus River.

30.   A. Golding, *The Excellent and Pleasant Worke—Collectanea Rerum Memorabilium of Caius Julius Solinus* (A. Golding; Gainesville: Scholars' Facsimiles and Reprints, 1587); T. Mommsen, *C. IVLII SOLINI—Collectanea Rervm Memorabilivm* (Berolini: Apud Weidmannos, 1895) Using Golding's designations the references are to be found in Chapters XLIV, XLV, XLVI, LXIV, LXVI, LXVII.

31.   M. Chiabò, *Index Verborum Ammiani Marcellini* (Hildesheim: Georg Olms Verlag, 1983), XXII, 15, 2; XXIII, 6, 13; XXIII, 6, 45; J. C. Rolfe, Ammianus Marcellinus, Vol I, *The Loeb Classical Library* (ed. E. H. Warmington; Cambridge: Harvard University Press, 1971; idem, Marcellinus, Vol II, 1972; idem, Marcellinus, Vol III, 1939

Chapter Three: ...the More They Remain the Same

1.   See, for example, A. H. Sayce, *The "Higher Criticism" and the Verdict of the Monuments* (London: Richard Clay & Sons, Ltd., 1901) 255–59; N. H. Snaith, "‏ים‎-‏סוף‎: The Sea of Reeds: The Red Sea," *VT* 15 (1965) 395; T. B. Dozeman, "The Yam-Sûp in the Exodus and the Crossing of the Jordan River," *CBQ* 58/3 (July 1996) 408; J. K. Hoffmeier, *Israel in Egypt—the Evidence for the Authenticity of the Exodus Tradition* (New York: Oxford University Press, 1997) 205.

2.   Exod 13:18; 15:4, 22; 23:31; Num 14:25; 21:4; 33:10, 11; Deut 1:1 (only ‏סוף‎) in HB; 1:40; 2:1; 11:4; Josh 2:10; 4:23; 24:6; Jer 49:21; Pss 106:7, 9, 22; 136:13, 15; Neh 9:9.

3.   J. A. Montgomery, "Hebraica," *JAOS* 58 (1938) 131.

4.   Hoffmeier, *Israel in Egypt*, 205.

5.   Montgomery, *"Hebraica,"* 132; B. Moritz, *Arabien—Studien zur Physikalischen und Historischen Geographie des Landes* (Hannover: Buchhandlung Heinz LaFaire, 1923) 71, and note 2; *Mikraoth Gedoloth—Shemot* (Jerusalem: Am Olam, 1961), Rashi's comment on 13:18; A. H. Sayce, *The "Higher Criticism" and the Verdict of the Monuments* (London: Richard Clay & Sons, Ltd., 1901) 256; J. R. Tower, "The Red Sea," *JNES* 18 (1959) 150–53; M. Copisarow, "The Ancient Egyptian, Greek and Hebrew Concept of the Red Sea," *VT* 12 (1962) 1–13; N. H. Snaith, "יַם סוּף : The Sea of Reeds : The Red Sea," *VT* 15 (1965) 397; M. Haran, "The Exodus Route in the Pentateuchal Sources (Hebrew)," *Tarbiz* 40 (1970/71) 129–30; W. A. Ward, "The Semitic Biconsonantal Root *SP* and the Common Origin of Egyptian *CWF* and Hebrew *SUP*: 'Marsh (-Plant)'," *VT* 24 (1974) 339–48; M. Lubetski, "New Light on Old Seas," *JQR* 68 (1978) 65–77;; Davies, *Way of the Wilderness*, 70–71, 79–80; W. Wifall, "The Sea of Reeds as Sheol," *ZAW* 92/3 (1980) 325–32; B. F. Batto, "The Reed Sea: Requiescat in Pace," *JBL* 102/1 (1983) 27–35; B. F. Batto, "Red Sea or Reed Sea?" *BAR* 10/4 (1984) 56–63; B. F. Batto, *Slaying the Dragon—Mythmaking in the Biblical Tradition* (Louisville: Westminster/John Knox, 1992) 115; C. Houtman, *Exodus, Vol. 1* (Kampen: Kok Publishing House, 1993) 109–10; Dozeman, "Yam-Sûp."; Hoffmeier, *Israel in Egypt*, 204–6. It is important to recognize that, although there is often much discussion concerning the meaning of סוּף, the concern in this investigation is rather with the location of the sea and not the meaning or derivation of the word.
6.   q.v., note 1, Chapter 2.
7.   Moritz (ibid.) suggests that the Gulf of Suez (his Reed Sea) may have extended farther north in those days, perhaps connecting with the bodies of water north of the gulf.
8.   Hoffmeier, *Israel in Egypt*, 206.
9.   N. Avigad and Y. Yadin, *A Genesis Apocryphon—a Scroll from the Wilderness of Judaea* (Jerusalem: The Magnes Press of the Hebrew University, 1956); J. A. Fitzmyer, *The Genesis Apocryphon of Qumran Cave 1—a Commentary* (Rome: Biblical Institute Press, 1971); P. Joüon and T. Muraoka, trans, *A Grammar of Biblical Hebrew, Part One* (Rome: Editrice Pontificio Instituto Biblico, 1996); F. G. Martínez, *The Dead Sea Scrolls Translated—The Qumran Texts in English* (Leiden: E. J. Brill, 1996); F. G. Martínez and E. J. C. Tigchelaar, *The Dead Sea Scrolls Study Edition* (Leiden: E. J. Brill, 1997); F. G. Martínez and E. J. C. Tigchelaar, *The Dead Sea Scrolls Study Edition* (Leiden: E. J. Brill, 1998).
10.   One would expect סמוקא. As noted by Joüon & Muraoka (Grammar...§5m), it is not uncommon for ס to be replaced by שׁ.
11.   N. Avigad and Y. Yadin, *A Genesis Apocryphon—a Scroll from the Wilderness of Judaea* (Jerusalem: The Magnes Press of the Hebrew University, 1956) 31–32.
12.   M. Jastrow, *A Dictionary of the Targumim, the Talmud Babli and Yerushalmi, and the Midrashic Literature* (New York: The Judaica Press, 1992) 321–22 The journey

continues with Abram returning to his home, portrayed as near the River Gihon. If he is returning to the central region of Canaan, it would suggest that the correct translation would be "I went around the southern region" as he headed north.

13.   M. Baillet, J. Milik and R. De Vaux, *Les 'Petites Grottes' de Qumran* (Discoveries in the Judean Desert—III; Oxford: Clarendon Press, 1962); R. De Vaux and J. T. Milik, *Qumrân Grotte 4 II—I Archéologie—II Tefillin, Mezuzot et Targums (4Q128-4Q157)* (Discoveries in the Judean Desert—VI; Oxford: Clarendon Press, 1977); P. W. Skehan, E. Ulrich and J. E. Sanderson, *Qumran Cave 4 IV—Paleo-Hebrew and Greek Biblical Manuscripts* (Discoveries in the Judean Desert—IX; Oxford: Clarendon Press, 1992); H. Attridge, T. Elgvin and J. Milik, *Qumran Cave 4 VIII—Parabiblical Texts, Part 1* (Discoveries in the Judean Desert—XIII; Oxford: Clarendon Press, 1994); E. Ulrich and F. Cross, *Qumran Cave IV—Deuteronomy, Joshua, Judges, Kings* (Discoveries in the Judean Desert—XIV; Oxford: Clarendon Press, 1995).

14.   D. L. Tiede, *The Charismatic Figure as Miracle Worker* (The Seminar on the Gospels, Dissertation Series, 1; Missoula: Society of Biblical Literature, 1972); J. H. Charlesworth, *The Old Testament Pseudepigrapha, Vol I & II* (Garden City: Doubleday & Co., Inc., 1983).

15.   Charlesworth, *Pseudepigrapha* J. C. VanderKam, *Textual and Historical Studies in the Book of Jubilees* (Harvard Semitic Monographs; Missoula: Scholars Press, 1977). For the Ethiopic text refer to the following: J. C. VanderKam, ed, *The Book of Jubilees—A Critical Text* (Corpus Scriptorum Christianorum Orientalium; Lovanii: Peeters, 1989) 52–53, 57–58.

16.   F. Brown, S. R. Driver and C. A. Briggs, *The Brown—Driver—Briggs Hebrew and English Lexicon* (Peabody, Massachusetts: Hendrickson Publishers, Inc., 1966) 815.

17.   R. G. Boling and G. E. Wright, *Joshua* (Garden City: Doubleday & Co., 1984) 365–66.

18.   Boling and Wright, *Joshua*, 366.

19.   Boling and Wright, *Joshua*, 430.

20.   G. B. Gray, A Critical and Exegetical Commentary on The Book of Isaiah, *International Critical Commentary* (eds. C. A. Briggs, S. R. Driver and A. Plummer; New York: Charles Scribner's Sons, 1912) 227; R. E. Clements, Isaiah 1-39, *New Century Bible Commentary* (ed. R. E. Clements; Grand Rapids: William B. Eerdmans Publishing Company, 1980) 127 G. R. Driver, "Studies in the Vocabulary of the Old Testament II," *JTS* 32 (1931) 251. Driver bases his suggestion that the root ח-ר-ם is to be retained upon support from the Akkadian *ḫarāmu* (to separate, to cut off). The Akkadian, however, would seem to support the LXX reading. The verb *ḫarābu* (to lay waste) is much more readily attested, especially in regard to geographical features (cf., A. L. Oppenheim, ed, *The Assyrian Dictionary Volume 6—Ḫ* (Chicago: Oriental Institute, 1956) 87–88 vs. 89–90).

21.   The reading is, however, supported in the DSS Isaiah Manuscript. See M. Burrows,

ed, *The Dead Sea Scrolls of St. Mark's Monastery, Vol I: The Isaiah Manuscript and the Habakkuk Commentary* (New Haven: ASOR, 1950), Plate 11.

22.   Gray, *Isaiah*, 227; Clements, *Isaiah*, 127; G. J. Botterweck, H. Ringgren and H.-J. Gabry, eds, *Theological Dictionary of the Old Testament* (Grand Rapids: Eerdmans Publishing Company, 1997) 28 P. Auvray, *Isaïe 1–39* (Paris: Gabalda, 1972) 148.

23.   S. Tedesche, *The First Book of the Maccabees* (New York: Harper & Brothers, 1950).

24.   J. T. Milik, "Henoch au pays des aromates—Ch Xxvii à Xxxii," *Revue Biblique* 65 (1958) 70–77; J. T. Milik, ed, *The Books of Enoch—Aramaic Fragments of Qumrân Cave 4* (Oxford: Oxford University Press, 1976); M. A. Knibb, *The Ethiopic Book of Enoch* (Oxford: Oxford University Press, 1978); Charlesworth, *Pseudepigrapha*; M. Black, *The Book of Enoch—or—I Enoch* (Leiden: E. J. Brill, 1985).

25.   From the "Astronomical Chapters" of the Ethiopic Book of Enoch, Chapter 77, in M. Black, *The Book of Enoch—or—I Enoch* (Leiden: E. J. Brill, 1985) 407.

26.   A. Sperber, *The Bible in Aramaic: Vol II, The Former Prophets According to Targum Jonathan* (Leiden: E. J. Brill, 1959); M. Rosenbaum and A. M. Silbermann, trans, *Pentateuch with Targum Onkelos, Haphtaroth and Rashi's Commentary* (Jerusalem: Silbermann Family, 1973).

27.   J. Tromp, *Studia in Veteris Testamenti Pseudepigrapha 10: The Assumption of Moses—a Critical Edition with Commentary* (eds A.-M. Denis and M. de Jonge; Leiden: E. J. Brill, 1993).

28.   Benedictus Niese Theodoro Noeldeke, ed, *Flavii Iosephi Opera* (Berolini: Apud Weidmannos, 1887); W. Whiston, trans, *The Life and Works of Flavius Josephus* (New York: Holt, Rinehart and Winston); H. S. J. Thackeray and R. Marcus, trans, *Josephus V—Jewish Antiquities, Books V–VIII* (Cambridge: Harvard University Press, 1977).

29.   P. Berry, trans, *Pomponius Mela—Geography/De Situ Orbis A.D. 43* (Studies in Classics; Lewiston: Edwin Mellen Press, 1997) (p. 135) Book III, p. 18; F. E. Romer, *Pomponius Mela's Description of the World* (Ann Arbor: University of Michigan Press, 1998) (p. 124) III: 80.

30.   M. Ginsburger, *Pseudo-Jonathan (Thargum Jonathan ben Usiël zum Pentateuch)* (Hildesheim: Georg Olms Verlag, 1971); E. G. Clark, *Targum Pseudo-Jonathan of the Pentateuch: Text and Concordance* (Hoboken: KTAV Publishing House, Inc., 1984).

31.   A. Sperber, *The Bible in Aramaic: Vol I, the Pentateuch According to Targum Onkelos* (Leiden: E. J. Brill, 1959); G. J. Kuiper, *The Pseudo-Jonathan Targum and Its Relationship to Targum Onkelos* (Studia Ephemeridis "Augustinianum"; Rome: Institutum Patristicum Augustinianum, 1972); *Mikraoth*.

32.   C. C. McCown, "The Testament of Solomon," Dissertation, University of ChicagoLeipzig: J. C. Hinrichs'sche Buchhandlung, 1922).

33.   B. Fischer, I. Gribomont and H. F. D. Sparks, eds, *Biblia Sacra—Iuxta Vulgatam*

Versionem (Stuttgart: Deutsche Bibelgesellschaft, 1994).

34.   P. G. Borbons and K. D. Jenner, eds, *The Old Testament in Syriac According to the Peshiṭta Version, Part V Concordance, Vol I The Pentateuch* (Leiden: E. J. Brill, 1997); The Peshiṭta Institute, ed, *The Old Testament in Syriac According to the Peshiṭta Version, Kings* (Leiden: E. J. Brill, 1976); The Peshiṭta Institute, ed, *The Old Testament in Syriac According to the Peshiṭta Version, Genesis-Exodus* (Leiden: E. J. Brill, 1977).

35.   B. B. Levy, *Targum Neophyti I—a Textual Study, Vol 1* (New York: University Press of America, 1986); M. Sokoloff, *A Dictionary of Jewish Palestinian Aramaic of the Byzantine Period* (Ramat-Gan: Bar Ilan University Press, 1990).

36.   A. Tal, *The Samaritan Targum of the Pentateuch, Parts I & II* (Tel Aviv: Tel Aviv University, 1981); A. Tal, *A Dictionary of Samaritan Aramaic* (Handbook of Oriental Studies: Abt. I. The Near and Middle East; Leiden: E. J. Brill, 2000).

37.   M. L. Klein, *The Fragment-Targums of the Pentateuch According to Their Extant Sources, Vol 1* (Analecta Biblica; Rome: Biblical Institute Press, 1980).

38.   *Mikraoth*; H. N. Strickman and A. M. Silver, trans, *Ibn Ezra's Commentary on the Pentateuch: Exodus (Shemot)* (New York: Menorah Publishing, 1996).

Chapter Four: The Journey

1.   S. R. Driver, *An Introduction to the Literature of the Old Testament* (Edinburgh: T. & T. Clark, 1950); M. Noth, *A History of Pentateuchal Traditions* (B. W. Anderson; Englewood Cliffs, NJ: Prentice Hall, 1972); M. Noth, *The Deuteronomistic History* (JSOTSup; Sheffield: JSOT, 1981); R. E. Friedman, *Who Wrote the Bible?* (New York: Summit Books, 1987).

2.   N. Na'aman, *Borders & Districts in Biblical Historiography* (Jerusalem Biblical Studies; Jerusalem: Simor, 1986) 249.

3.   T. O. Lambdin, "Shihor," *The Interpreter's Dictionary of the Bible 4* (Nashville: Abingdon Press, 1962) 328; P. Montet, *Egypt and the Bible* (trans. L. R. Keylock; Philadelphia: Fortress Press, 1968); J. Simons, *The Geographical and Topographical Texts of the Old Testament* (Leiden: E.J. Brill, 1959); N. Na'aman, "The Brook of Egypt and Assyrian Policy on the Border of Egypt," *Tel Aviv* 6/1–2 (1979) 68–90; A. H. Gardiner, "The Ancient Military Road Between Egypt and Palestine," *JEA* 6 (1920) 99–116; H. Kees, *Ancient Egypt—a Cultural Topography* (Chicago: University of Chicago Press, 1961); Z. Kallai, "The Boundaries of Canaan and the Land of Israel in the Bible (Hebrew)," *Eretz Israel* 12 (1975) 27–34; N. Na'aman, "The Shihor of Egypt and Shur That is Before Egypt," *Tel Aviv* 7/1–2 (1980) 95–109; Na'aman, *Borders*; M. Garsiel and I. Finkelstein, "The Westward Expansion of the House of Joseph in the Light of the 'Izbet Ṣarṭah Excavations," *Tel Aviv* 5/3–4 (1978) 192–98 P. K. Hooker, "The Location of the Brook of Egypt,"

History and Interpretation: Essays in Honour of John H. Hayes (eds. M. P. Graham, W. P. Brown and J. K. Kuan; Sheffield: Sheffield Academic Press, 1993) 203–14.

4.   Lambdin, "Shihor," 328.

5.   It is not necessary to translate שׁיחור (here שׁחר) as parallel with Nile. They may both be understood as designations for Egypt, with their separate produce as revenue destined for Sidon. As noted in Gen 47:24; Lev 25:15–16; Deut 33:14; 2 Kgs 8:6; Jer 12:13; Prov 14:4; 16:8, תבואת occurs in the plural without the *vav* plural indicator. Thus it is possible to translate as, "your revenues were the grain of Shihor and the harvest of the Nile."

6.   The Euphrates may be designated by נהר both with the definite article (as in Gen 31:21; Exod 23:31; Num 22:5; Jos 24:2–3, 14–15) and without (Isa 7:20; Mic 7:12; Zech 9:10; Ps 72:8).

7.   B. Gemser, "Be'Eber Hajjarden: In Jordan's Borderland," *VT* 2 (1952) 349–55.

8.   B. K. Waltke and M. O'Connor, *An Introduction to Biblical Hebrew Syntax* (Winona Lake: Eisenbrauns, 1990) sect. 10.5 See also Gen 43:17.

9.   Simons, *Geographical and Topographical*, section 70; Na'aman, "Brook," 77; Na'aman, *Borders*, 246–47; Hooker, "Brook of Egypt."; D. Baly, *The Geography of the Bible* (New York: Harper & Row, 1974) 250.

10.   M. Haran, "The Exodus Route in the Pentateuchal Sources (Hebrew)," *Tarbiz* 40 (1970/71) 126.

11.   Num 22:1; 26:3, 63; 31:12; 33:48–50; 35:1; 36:13; Deut 1:1, 7; 2:8; 3:17; 4:49; 11:30; 34:1, 8; Josh 3:16; 4:13; 5:10; 8:14; 11:2, 16; 12:1, 3; 13:32; 18:18; 1 Sam 23:24; 2 Sam 2:29; 2 Kgs 25:4–5; Jer 39:4–5; 52:7–8; Ezek 47:8.

12.   For discussion concerning the post-exilic dating of P, the reader is directed to the following works: J. Wellhausen, *Prolegomena to the History of Ancient Israel* (New York: Meridian Books, 1957); R. N. Whybray, *The Making of the Pentateuch* (Sheffield: JSOT Press, 1987); J. G. Vink, *The Priestly Code and Seven Other Studies* (Leiden: E. J. Brill, 1969); B. A. Levine, "Late Language in the Priestly Source: Some Literarty and Historical Observations," *Proceedings of the Eighth World Congress of Jewish Studies (1981)* (Jerusalem: World Union of Jewish Studies, 1983) 69–82; N. K. Gottwald, *The Hebrew Bible—A Socio-Literary Introduction* (Philadelphia: Fortress Press, 1987); R. B. Coote and D. R. Ord, *In the Beginning: Creation and the Priestly History* (Minneapolis: Fortress Press, 1991). Exilic dating of P may be found supported in the following: Noth, *Traditions*; F. M. Cross, *Canaanite Myth and Hebrew Epic—Essays in the History of the Religion of Israel* (Cambridge: Harvard University Press, 1973); R. Polzin, *Late Biblical Hebrew: Toward an Historical Typology of Biblical Hebrew Prose* (Missoula: Scholars Press, 1976).

13.   Y. Kaufmann, *The Religion of Israel: From Its Beginnings to the Babylonian Exile* (Chicago: University of Chicago Press, 1960); J. Milgrom, *Studies in Cultic Theology and Terminology* (Leiden: E.J. Brill, 1983); J. Milgrom, *Studies in*

Levitical Terminology (Berkeley: University of California, 1970); J. Milgrom, "Priestly ('P') Source" (ed. D. Freedman), *The Anchor Bible Dictionary* (New York: Doubleday, 1991) 454–61; A. Hurvitz, "The Evidence of Language in Dating the Priestly Code," *RB* 81 (1974) 24–56; A. Hurvitz, "The Language of the Priestly Source and Its Historical Setting—The Case for an Early Date," *Proceedings of the Eighth World Congress of Jewish Studies (1981)* (Jerusalem: World Union of Jewish Studies, 1983) 83–94; A. Hurvitz, "Dating the Priestly Source in Light of the Historical Study of Biblical Hebrew a Century After Wellhausen," *ZAW* 100/supplement (1988) 88–100; G. A. Rendsburg, "Late Biblical Hebrew and the Date of 'P.'," *JANES* 12 (1980) 65–80; T. J. King, "The Priestly Literature and Its Northern Component," Ph. D. Dissertation (Berkeley: Graduate Theological Union, 1996).

14. King, "Priestly Literature," 122–58.
15. O. Procksch, *Das Nordhebräische Sagenbuch, Die Elohimquelle* (Leipzig: J. C. Hinrichs, 1906) 307–8; H.-J. Kraus, *Gottesdienst in Israel* (München: Chr. Kaiser Verlag, 1962) 32–37; J. Muilenberg, "The Form and Structure of the Covenantal Formulations," *VT* 39 (1959) 350–51; R. P. Carroll, "Psalm LXXVIII: Vestiges of a Tribal Polemic," *VT* 21 (1971) 133–50; Y. Hoffman, יציאת מצרים באמונת המקרה (Tel Aviv: Tel Aviv University, 1983) 25–75; Y. Hoffman, "A North Israelite Typological Myth and a Judaean Historical Tradition: The Exodus in Hosea and Amos," *VT* 39 (1989) 169–82. My current research (and an article in progress), which was presented orally at the Society of Biblical Literature meeting in Toronto, Ontario ("The Exodus from Egypt in the Prophets: Evidence for a Judean Appropriation of Israelite Tradition," Nov. 25, 2002), indicates that the earliest written prophetic material (Amos, Hosea, Micah and First Isaiah) differs significantly in this regard from the 7th and 6th century material. The earliest writing prophets clearly distinguish between northern Israel and Judah to the south. This distinction is evident in the synonyms employed to refer to each nation, as these prophets never refer to one nation utilizing the synonyms for the other. Furthermore, the use of the name YHWH follows a related pattern, from the earliest being identified as Israel's god (as distinct from "Judah's" god). Most importantly, while differentiating between Israel and Judah, the early prophets clearly identify the exodus with northern Israel. There is no evidence of the existence of "Ideological Israel" in these early prophets. It is only within the late 7th through the entire 6th centuries that the prophetic material gives evidence of Judean acquisition of YHWH as the God of Jerusalem, of Judah being a part of the Israelite "Family," and of the exodus holding any position of importance within Judean history.

16. D. Zohary, "Notes on Ancient Agriculture in the Central Negev," *IEJ* 4/1 (1954) 17–25; M. Evenari, Y. Aharoni, L. Shanan and N. H. Tadmor, "The Ancient Desert Agriculture of the Negev—III. Early Beginnings," *IEJ* 8 (1958) 231–68; L. Shanan, N. H. Tadmor and M. Evenari, "The Ancient Desert Agriculture of the Negev, II:

Utilization of the Runoff from Small Watersheds in the 'Avdat Region," *Ktavim* 9 (1958); H. H. Tadmor, M. Evenari, L. Shanan and D. Hillel, "The Ancient Desert Agriculture of the Negev, I: Gravel Mounds and Strips of the Shivta Area," *Ktavim* 8 (1958) 127–36; Y. Aharoni, M. Evenari, L. Shanan and N. H. Tadmor, "The Ancient Desert Agriculture of the Negev: V. An Israelite Agricultural Settlement at Ramat Maṭred," *IEJ* 10/1 (1960) 23–36; Y. Aharoni, M. Evenari, L. Shanan and N. H. Tadmor, "The Ancient Desert Agriculture of the Negev: V. An Israelite Agricultural Settlement at Ramat Maṭred," *IEJ* 10/2 (1960) 97–111; J. E. Spencer and G. A. Hale, "The Origin, Nature and Distribution of Agricultural Terracing," *Pacific Viewpoint* 2/1 (1961) 1–40; R. Amiran, Y. Beit-Arieh and J. Glass, "The Interrelationship Between Arad and Sites in Southern Sinai in the Early Bronze Age II (Preliminary Report)," *IEJ* 23/4 (1973) 193–97; J. M. Treacy, "The Creation of Cultivable Land Through Terracing," *The Archaeology of Garden and Field* (eds. N. F. Miller and K. L. Gleason; Philadelphia: University of Pennsylvania Press, 1994) 91–110; N. H. Greenwood, *The Sinai—A Physical Geography* (Austin: University of Texas, 1997).

17. E. Ben Zvi, *A Historical-Critical Study of the Book of Zephaniah* (BZAW 198; Berlin: Walter de Gruyter, 1991) 234.

18. M. D. Oblath, "Of Pharaohs and Kings—Whence the Exodus?" *JSOT* 87 (2000) 39–40.

19. C. Houtman, *Exodus, Vol. 1* (Kampen: Kok Publishing House, 1993) 109; C. Houtman, *Exodus, Vol. 2* (Kampen: Kok Publishing House, 1996) 113–14; W. H. C. Propp, *Exodus 1–18* (The Anchor Bible; New York: Doubleday, 1999) 339.

20. E. Kautzsch, ed, *Gesenius' Hebrew Grammar* (Oxford: Clarendon Press, 1910) sect. 127f; Propp, *Exodus*, 486, as he states, "This analysis entails a minor anomaly, the definite article on a noun in construct, but this is permitted when the genitive is a geographical name."

21. Gardiner, "Military Road."; J. K. Hoffmeier, *Israel in Egypt—the Evidence for the Authenticity of the Exodus Tradition* (New York: Oxford University Press, 1997) 183–87; Houtman, *Exodus, 2*, 249–50; Propp, *Exodus*, 485–86.

22. L. E. Axelsson, *The Lord Rose up from Seir—Studies in the History and Traditions of the Negev and Southern Judah* (Coniectanea Biblica - Old Testament Series; Stockholm: Almqvist & Wiksell International, 1987) 44–46.

23. B. A. Levine, *Numbers 1–20* (The Anchor Bible; New York: Doubleday, 1993) 368.

24. D. L. Christensen, "Numbers 21:14–15 and the Book of the Wars of Yahweh," *CBQ* 36 (1974) 359–60; M. Weippert, "The Israelite 'Conquest' and Evidence from Transjordan," *Symposia Celebrating the 75th Anniversary of the ASOR (1900–1975)* (ed. D. N. Freedman; Cambridge, MA: ASOR Press, 1979) 15–34.

25. B. A. Levine, *Numbers 21–36* (The Anchor Bible; New York: Doubleday, 2000) 93–94.

26. Gemser, "Be'Eber Hajjarden."

27.   G. I. Davies, *The Way of the Wilderness—A Geographical Study of the Wilderness Itineraries in the Old Testament* (Society for Old Testament Study Monograph Series; Cambridge: Cambridge University Press, 1979) 81–82; D. B. Redford, *Egypt, Canaan and Israel in Ancient Times* (New Jersey: Princeton University, 1992) 360, note 199; Hoffmeier, *Israel in Egypt*, 181–83, 188–91; I. Finkelstein and N. A. Silberman, *The Bible Unearthed* (New York: The Free Press, 2001) 66.

28.   D. W. Baker, "Pathros," *The Anchor Bible Dictionary* (ed. D. N. Freedman; New York: Doubleday, 1992) 178; D. N. Freedman, *Eerdmans Dictionary of the Bible* (Grand Rapids: Wm. B. Eerdmans Publishing Co., 2000) 1015.

29.   Gardiner, "Military Road."; Finkelstein and Silberman, *Bible Unearthed*, 58–60.

30.   G. B. Gray, A Critical and Exegetical Commentary on The Book of Isaiah, *International Critical Commentary* (eds. C. A. Briggs, S. R. Driver and A. Plummer; New York: Charles Scribner's Sons, 1912) 311; O. Kaiser, *Isaiah 13–39* (Philadelphia: The Westminster Press, 1974) 93.

31.   R. E. Clements, Isaiah 1–39, *New Century Bible Commentary* (ed. R. E. Clements; Grand Rapids: William B. Eerdmans Publishing Company, 1980) 164.

32.   Gen 14:7; 36:12, 16; Num 13:29; Judg 12:15; 1 Sam 15:7; 27:8; 1 Chr 1:36.

33.   R. G. Boling, *Judges* (The Anchor Bible; New York: Doubleday & Company, Inc, 1975) 216.

34.   S. Gevirtz, "Of Patriarchs and Puns: Joseph at the Fountain, Jacob at the Ford," *HUCA* 46 (1975) 42–49; M. D. Oblath, "Of Pharaohs and Kings," 24–25. As noted, 1 Sam 27:8 has an alternate reading from the LXX, locating the Amalekites in and around the region of T/Gelam. From Josh 15:24 Telem (assuming the possibility, from the LXX, that the sites are the same) is located south of Judah, near Edom.

35.   Finkelstein and Silberman, *Bible Unearthed*, 64, 66–70.

36.   F. Brown, S. R. Driver and C. A. Briggs, *The Brown - Driver - Briggs Hebrew and English Lexicon* (Peabody, Massachusetts: Hendrickson Publishers, Inc., 1966) 206.

37.   Waltke and O'Connor, *Biblical Hebrew*, section 11.1.2d. This form is found only in Job (27:14; 29:21; 38:40; 40:4), implying, even beyond the contextual translation difficulties, an unacceptably late date for this poem.

38.   This emendation has previously been suggested, but only in the first instance of למו, by I. L. Seeligman; I. L. Seeligman, "A Psalm from Pre-Regal Times," *VT* 14 (1964) 76–77. He suggests a similar phenomenon is to be noted in 1 Kgs 12:28 (as translated in the Septuagint) and Ps 28:8. I would maintain that לעמו be read in both of its occurrences here. An intriguing possibility for translating this passage has been discussed by M. Weinfeld ("Kuntillet 'Ajrud Inscriptions and Their Significance," *SEL* 1 (1984) 124): "At His right hand, Asherah" (Deut 33:2). Even if correct, the relevant geographical reference remains unaffected.

39.   Cross, *Canaanite Myth*, 164; Boling, *Judges*, 108; Waltke and O'Connor, *Biblical Hebrew*, section 19.5d.

40.   Brown, Driver and Briggs, *BDB*, 18.

41.   Levine, *Numbers 21–36*, 202–3.

42.   M. Cogan and H. Tadmor, *II Kings* (The Anchor Bible; New York: Doubleday & Company, Inc., 1988) 186–87.

43.   J. K. Kuan, *Neo-Assyrian Historical Inscriptions and Syria-Palestine* (Jian Dao Dissertation Series 1; Hong Kong: Alliance Bible Seminary, 1995) 102–3.

44.   See also: J. R. Bartlett, *Edom and the Edomites* (JSOTSupp; Sheffield: Sheffield Academic Press, 1989).

45.   Kautzsch, *Gesenius*, section 75bb1; Levine, *Numbers 21–36*, 534.

46.   Oblath, "Of Pharaohs and Kings."

47.   Levine, *Numbers 21–36*, 83, plus his discussion on 108–9.

48.   Brown, Driver and Briggs, *BDB*, 854.

49.   P. K. McCarter, *II Samuel* (The Anchor Bible; Garden City: Doubleday & Company, Inc., 1984) 504.

Chapter Five: Summary and Conclusions

1.   R. D. Nelson, "Josiah in the Book of Joshua," *JBL* 100/4 (1981) 531–40; R. B. Coote, "The Book of Joshua," *The New Interpreter's Bible* (Nashville: Abingdon Press, 1998) 555–81; I. Finkelstein and N. A. Silberman, *The Bible Unearthed* (New York: The Free Press, 2001) 68–71.

2.   S. Gevirtz, "Of Patriarchs and Puns: Joseph at the Fountain, Jacob at the Ford," *HUCA* 46 (1975) 33–54; S. Gevirtz, "Adumbrations of Dan in Jacob's Blessing on Judah," *ZAW* 93/1 (1981) 21–37; M. D. Oblath, "Of Pharaohs and Kings—Whence the Exodus?" *JSOT* 87 (2000) 23–42.

3.   A. H. Gardiner, *Egypt of the Pharaohs* (London: Oxford University Press, 1964) 529–33; K. A. Kitchen, *The Third Intermediate Period in Egypt (1100–650 BC)* (Warminster: Aris & Phillips, Ltd, 1986) 432–47; D. B. Redford, *Egypt, Canaan and Israel in Ancient Times* (New Jersey: Princeton University, 1992) 312–15; G. W. Ahlström, *The History of Ancient Palestine* (Minneapolis: Fortress Press, 1994) 549, 554–58.

4.   M. Dothan, "The Fortress at Kadesh-Barnea," *IEJ* 15 (1965) 134–51; R. Cohen, "Kadesh-Barnea, 1976," *IEJ* 26 (1976) 201–2; R. Cohen, "Kadesh-Barnea, 1978," *IEJ* 28 (1978) 197; R. Cohen, "The Iron Age Fortresses in the Central Negev," *BASOR* 236 (1979) 61–79; R. Cohen, "Kadesh-Barnea, 1979," *IEJ* 30 (1980) 235–36; R. Cohen, "The Excavations at Kadesh-Barnea (1976–1978)," *BA* 44/2 (1981) 93–107; R. Cohen, "Did I Excavate Kadesh-Barnea?" *BAR* 7/3 (1981) 21–33; R. Cohen, "Kadesh-Barnea, 1980," *IEJ* 32 (1982) 70–71; R. Cohen, "Kadesh-Barnea, 1981–82," *IEJ* 32 (1982) 266–67; R. Cohen, "Excavations at Kadesh-Barnea, 1976–1982," *(Hebrew) Qadmoniot* 16/61 (1983) 2–14; Z. Herzog, "Enclosed Settlements in the Negeb and the Wilderness of Beer-Sheba," *BASOR*

250 (1983) 41–49; R. Cohen, "Les fouilles de Qadesh-Barnea et les forteresses du Néguev," *Archéologie Art et Histoire de la Palestine* (ed. E. H. Laperrousaz; Paris: Les Éditions du Cerf, 1988) 85–98.

BIBLIOGRAPHY

Aharoni, Y. *The Land of the Bible—a Historical Geography*. Philadelphia: Westminster Press, 1979.

Aharoni, Y., M. Evenari, L. Shanan, and N. H. Tadmor. "The Ancient Desert Agriculture of the Negev: V. An Israelite Agricultural Settlement at Ramat Maṭred." *IEJ* 10/1 (1960): 23–36.

———. "The Ancient Desert Agriculture of the Negev: V. An Israelite Agricultural Settlement at Ramat Maṭred." *IEJ* 10/2 (1960): 97–111.

Ahlström, G. W. "Where Did the Israelites Live?" *JNES* 41 (1982): 133–38.

———. *The History of Ancient Palestine*. Minneapolis: Fortress Press, 1994.

Albertz, R. *A History of Israelite Religion in the Old Testament Period, Vol 1*. Louisville: Westminster/John Knox Press, 1994.

Albright, W. F. "A Revision of Early Hebrew Chronology." *JPOS* 1 (1920/21): 49–79.

———. "Archaeology and the Date of the Hebrew Conquest of Palestine." *BASOR* 58 (1935): 10–18.

———. "The Israelite Conquest of Canaan in Light of Archaeology." *BASOR* 74 (1939): 11–23.

———. *The Biblical Period from Abraham to Ezra—an Historical Survey*. New York: Harper & Row, 1965.

———. *The Archaeology of Palestine and the Bible*. Cambridge, Massachusetts: American Schools of Oriental Research, 1974.

Alt, A. *Essays on Old Testament History and Religion*. Garden City: Doubleday & Company, Inc., 1967.

Amiran, R., Y. Beit-Arieh, and J. Glass. "The Interrelationship Between Arad and Sites in Southern Sinai in the Early Bronze Age II (Preliminary Report)." *IEJ* 23/4 (1973): 193–97.

Anati, E. "Has Mt. Sinai Been Found?" *BAR* 11/4 (1985): 42–56.

———. *Har Karkom—the Mountain of God*. New York: Rizzoli, 1986.

Attridge, H., T. Elgvin, and J. Milik *Qumran Cave 4 VIII—Parabiblical Texts, Part 1*. Vol. XIII of *Discoveries in the Judean Desert*. Oxford: Clarendon Press, 1994.

Auvray, P., *Isaïe 1–39*. Paris: Gabalda, 1972.

Avigad, N. "The Jothan Seal from Elath." *BASOR* 163 (1961): 18–22.

Avigad, N., and Y. Yadin. *A Genesis Apocryphon—a Scroll from the Wilderness of Judaea*. Jerusalem: The Magnes Press of the Hebrew University, 1956.

Axelsson, L. E. *The Lord Rose up from Seir—Studies in the History and Traditions of the Negev and Southern Judah.* Coniectanea Biblica—Old Testament Series 25. Stockholm: Almqvist & Wiksell International, 1987.

Baillet, M., J. Milik, and R. De Vaux. *Les 'Petites Grottes' de Qumran.* Vol. III of *Discoveries in the Judean Desert.* Oxford: Clarendon Press, 1962.

Baker, D. W. "Pathros." Page 178 in *The Anchor Bible Dictionary Vol. 5.* Edited by D. N. Freedman. New York: Doubleday, 1992.

Baly, D. *The Geography of the Bible.* New York: Harper & Row, 1974.

Bartlett, J. R. *Edom and the Edomites.* JSOTSupp 77. Sheffield: Sheffield Academic Press, 1989.

Batto, B. F. "The Reed Sea: Requiescat in Pace." *JBL* 102/1 (1983): 27–35.

———. "Red Sea or Reed Sea?" *BAR* 10/4 (1984): 56–63.

———. *Slaying the Dragon—Mythmaking in the Biblical Tradition.* Louisville: Westminster/John Knox, 1992.

Beit–Arieh, I. "Fifteen Years in Sinai—Israeli Archaeologists Discover a New World." *BAR* 10/4 (1984): 26–54.

———. "The Route Through Sinai: Why the Israelites Fleeing Egypt Went South." *BAR* 14/3 (1988): 28–37.

Bender, A. "Das Lied Exodus 15." *ZAW* 23 (1903): 1–48.

Benedictus Niese Theodoro Noeldeke, ed. *Flavii Iosephi Opera.* Berolini: Apud Weidmannos, 1887.

Ben Zvi, E. *A Historical-Critical Study of the Book of Zephaniah.* BZAW 198. Berlin: Walter de Gruyter, 1991.

Berry, P. *Pomponius Mela—Geography/De Situ Orbis A.D. 43.* Studies in Classics 3. Lewiston: Edwin Mellen Press, 1997.

Beyerlin, W. *Origins and History of the Oldest Sinaitic Traditions.* Translated by S. Rudman. Oxford: Basil Blackwell, 1961.

Bietak, M. "Comments on the Exodus." Pages 163–71 in *Egypt, Israel, Sinai—Archaeological and Historical Relationships in the Biblical Period.* Edited by A. F. Rainey. Tel Aviv: Tel Aviv University, 1987.

Bimson, J. J. *Redating the Exodus and Conquest.* Sheffield: Almond, 1981.

———. "The Origins of Israel in Canaan: An Examination of Recent Theories." *Themelios* 15 (1989): 4–15.

———. "Merneptah's Israel and Recent Theories of Israelite Origins." *JSOT* 49 (1991): 3–29.

Bimson, J. J., and D. Livingston. "Redating the Exodus." *BAR* 13/5 (1987): 40–53, 66–68.

Black, M. *The Book of Enoch –or– I Enoch.* Leiden: E. J. Brill, 1985.

Black, M., A. –M. Denis, and M. de Jonge, eds. *Pseudepigrapha Veteris Testamenti Graece Volumen Tertium: Apocalypsis Henochi Graece.* Leiden: E. J. Brill, 1970.

Boling, R. G. *Judges.* The Anchor Bible 6A. Garden City: Doubleday & Co., 1975.

Booth, G. *The Geographical Library of Diodorus the Sicilian.* London: Edward Jones, 1700.

Borbons, P. G., and K. D. Jenner, eds. *The Old Testament in Syriac According to the Peshiṭta Version, Part V Concordance, Vol I The Pentateuch*. Leiden: E. J. Brill, 1997.

Bosworth, C. E., E. van Donzel, B. Lewis, and C. Pellat, eds. Pages 761–63 (Liḥyan) in *The Encyclopaedia of Islam V*. Leiden: E. J. Brill, 1983.

Botterweck, G. J., H. Ringgren, and H.-J. Fabry, eds. *Theological Dictionary of the Old Testament*. Translated by D. E. Green, and D. W. Stott. Grand Rapids: William B. Eerdmans Publishing Co.,1974–2001.

Bright, J. "Modern Studies of Old Testament Literature." Pages 13–31 in *The Bible and the Ancient Near East—Essays in Honor of William Foxwell Albright*. Edited by G. E. Wright. Garden City: Doubleday and Company, Inc., 1961.

————. *A History of Israel, 3rd Edition*. Philadelphia: Westminster Press, 1981.

Brown, F., S. R. Driver, and C. A. Briggs, eds. *The Brown—Driver—Briggs Hebrew and English Lexicon*. Peabody, Massachusetts: Hendrickson Publishers, Inc., 1966.

Brunt, P. A. *Arrian*. Cambridge: Harvard University Press, 1983.

Bunbury, E. H. *A History of Ancient Geography Among the Greeks and Romans from the Earliest Ages Till the Fall of the Roman Empire*. New York: Dover Publications, Inc., 1959.

Burrows, M., ed. *The Dead Sea Scrolls of St. Mark's Monastery, Vol I: The Isaiah Manuscript and the Habakkuk Commentary*. New Haven: ASOR, 1950.

Burstein, S. M. *Agatharchides of Cnidus—On the Erythraean Sea*. London: The Hakluyt Society, 1989.

Carroll, R. P. "Psalm LXXVIII: Vestiges of a Tribal Polemic." *VT* 21 (1971): 133–50.

Cassuto, U. *A Commentary on the Book of Exodus*. Jerusalem: Hebrew University, 1967.

Cazelles, H. "Les Localisations de L'Exode et la Critique Littéraire." *RB* 62 (1955): 321– 64.

Charles, R. H. *The Assumption of Moses*. London: Adam & Charles Black, 1897.

Charlesworth, J. H. *The Old Testament Pseudepigrapha, Vol I & II*. Garden City: Doubleday & Co., Inc., 1983.

Graphic Concordance to the Dead Sea Scrolls. Louisville: Westminster/John Knox Press, 1991.

Chattopadhyaya, S. *The Periplus of the Erythraean Sea & Ptolemy on Ancient Geography of India*. Prajñā: Asoke Ray, 1980.

Chiabò, M. *Index Verborum Ammiani Marcellini*. Hildesheim: Georg Olms Verlag, 1983.

Childs, B. S. "A Traditio-Historical Study of the Reed Sea Tradition." *VT* 20 (1970): 406–18.

————. *The Book of Exodus—A Critical, Theological Commentary*. Philadelphia: Westminster, 1974.

Christensen, D. L. "Numbers 21:14–15 and the Book of the Wars of Yahweh." *CBQ* 36 (1974): 359–60.

Clark, E. G. *Targum Pseudo-Jonathan of the Pentateuch: Text and Concordance*. Hoboken: KTAV Publishing House, Inc., 1984.

Clements, R. E. *Isaiah 1–39*. New Century Bible Commentary. Grand Rapids: William B. Eerdmans Publishing Company, 1980.

Cogan, M., and H. Tadmor. *II Kings*. The Anchor Bible 11. New York: Doubleday & Company, Inc., 1988.

Cohen, R. "Kadesh-Barnea, 1976." *IEJ* 26 (1976): 201–2.

———. "Kadesh-Barnea, 1978." *IEJ* 28 (1978): 197.

———. "The Iron Age Fortresses in the Central Negev." *BASOR* 236 (1979): 61–79.

———. "Kadesh-Barnea, 1979." *IEJ* 30 (1980): 235–36.

———. "Did I Excavate Kadesh-Barnea?" *BAR* 7/3 (1981): 21–33.

———. "The Excavations at Kadesh-Barnea (1976–1978)." *BA* 44/2 (1981): 93–107.

———. "Kadesh-Barnea, 1980." *IEJ* 32 (1982): 70–71.

———. "Kadesh-Barnea, 1981–82." *IEJ* 32 (1982): 266–67.

———. "Excavations at Kadesh-Barnea, 1976–1982 (Hebrew)." *Qadmoniot* 16/61 (1983): 2–14.

———. "Les fouilles de Qadesh-Barnea et les forteresses du Néguev." Pages 85–98 in *Archéologie Art et Histoire de la Palestine*. Edited by E. H. Laperrousaz. Paris: Les Éditions du Cerf, 1988.

Coote, R. B. *Early Israel: A New Horizon*. Minneapolis: Fortress Press, 1990.

———. "The Book of Joshua." Pages 555–81 in *The New Interpreter's Bible, Vol. II*. Nashville: Abingdon Press, 1998.

Coote, R. B., and K. W. Whitelam. *The Emergence of Early Israel in Historical Perspective*. Sheffield: Almond, 1987.

Coote, R. B., and D. R. Ord. *In the Beginning: Creation and the Priestly History*. Minneapolis: Fortress Press, 1991.

Copisarow, M. "The Ancient Egyptian, Greek and Hebrew Concept of the Red Sea." *VT* 12 (1962): 1–13.

Cross, F. M. *Canaanite Myth and Hebrew Epic—Essays in the History of the Religion of Israel*. Cambridge: Harvard University Press, 1973.

Cross, F. M., and D. N. Freedman. "The Song of Miriam." *JNES* 14 (1955): 237–50.

Davies, G. I. *The Way of the Wilderness—A Geographical Study of the Wilderness Itineraries in the Old Testament*. Society for Old Testament Study Monograph Series 5. Cambridge: Cambridge University Press, 1979.

———. "The Wilderness Itineraries and Recent Archaeological Research." Pages 161–76 in *Supplements to Vetus Testamentum XLI: Studies in the Pentateuch*. Edited by J. A. Emerton. Leiden: E. J. Brill, 1990.

Denis, A. –M. *Pseudepigrapha Veteris Testamenti Graece Volumen Tertium: Fragmenta Pseudepigraphorum Quae Supersunt Graeca*. Edited by A. -M. Denis and M. de Jonge. Leiden: E. J. Brill, 1970.

De Vaux, R., and J. T. Milik. *Qumrân Grotte 4 II—I Archéologie—II Tefillin, Mezuzot et Targums (4Q128–4Q157)*. Vol. VI of *Discoveries in the Judean Desert*. Oxford: Clarendon Press, 1977.

Dever, W. G. "Is There any Archaeological Evidence for the Exodus?" Pages 67–86 in *Exodus: The Egyptian Evidence*. Edited by E. S. Frerichs and L. H. Lesko. Winona

Lake: Eisenbrauns, 1997.

Dothan, M. "The Fortress at Kadesh-Barnea." *IEJ* 15 (1965): 134–51.

Dozeman, T. B. "The Yam-Sûp in the Exodus and the Crossing of the Jordan River." *CBQ* 58/3 (July 1996): 407–16.

Driver, G. R. "Studies in the Vocabulary of the Old Testament II." *JTS* 32 (1931): 250–57.

Driver, S. R. *An Introduction to the Literature of the Old Testament*. Edinburgh: T. & T. Clark, 1950.

Dunbar, N. *Aristophanes—The Birds*. Oxford: Clarendon Press, 1995.

Ellis, W. M. *Ptolemy of Egypt*. London: Routledge, 1994.

Evenari, M., Y. Aharoni, L. Shanan, and N. H. Tadmor. "The Ancient Desert Agriculture of the Negev—III. Early Beginnings." *IEJ* 8 (1958): 231–68.

Faiman, D. "From Horeb to Kadesh in Eleven Days." *Jewish Bible Quarterly* 22 (1994): 91–102.

Finkelstein, I. "Raider of the Lost Mountain—an Israeli Archaeologist Looks at the Most Recent Attempt to Locate Mt. Sinai." *BAR* 14/4 (1988): 46–50.

———. "The Emergence of Early Israel: Anthropology, Environment and Archaeology." *JAOS* 110 (1990): 677–86.

Finkelstein, I., and N. A. Silberman. *The Bible Unearthed*. New York: The Free Press, 2001.

Fischer, B., I. Gribomont, and H. F. D. Sparks, eds. *Biblia Sacra—Iuxta Vulgatam Versionem*. Stuttgart: Deutsche Bibelgesellschaft, 1994.

Fitzmyer, J. A. *The Genesis Apocryphon of Qumran Cave 1—a Commentary*. Rome: Biblical Institute Press, 1971.

Freedman, D. N. "The Chronology of Israel in the Ancient Near East—Old Testament Chronology." Pages 203–13 in *The Bible and the Ancient Near East—Essays in Honor of William Foxwell Albright*. Edited by G. E. Wright. Garden City: Doubleday and Company, Inc., 1961.

———. *Pottery, Poetry, and Prophecy: Studies in Early Hebrew Poetry*. Winona Lake: Eisenbrauns, 1980.

———. *The Anchor Bible Dictionary, Vol 2 & 5*. New York: Doubleday, 1992.

———. *Eerdmans Dictionary of the Bible*. Grand Rapids: Wm. B. Eerdmans Publishing Co., 2000.

Frerichs, E. S., and L. H. Lesko, eds. *Exodus: The Egyptian Evidence*. Winona Lake: Eisenbrauns, 1997.

Friedman, R. E. *Who Wrote the Bible?* New York: Summit Books, 1987.

Gardiner, A. H. "The Delta Residence of the Ramessides." *JEA* 5 (1918): 179–200.

———. "The Ancient Military Road Between Egypt and Palestine." *JEA* 6 (1920): 99–116.

———. *Egypt of the Pharaohs*. London: Oxford University Press, 1964.

Garsiel, M., and I. Finkelstein. "The Westward Expansion of the House of Joseph in the Light of the 'Izbet Ṣarṭah Excavations." *Tel Aviv* 5/3–4 (1978): 192–98.

Gemser, B. "Be'Eber Hajjarden: In Jordan's Borderland." *VT* 2 (1952): 349–55.

Gevirtz, S. "Abram's 318." *IEJ* 19 (1969): 110–13.

————. "Of Patriarchs and Puns: Joseph at the Fountain, Jacob at the Ford." *HUCA* 46 (1975): 33–54.

————. "The Life Spans of Joseph and Enoch and the Parallelism šib'ātayim–šib'îm wĕšib'āh." *JBL* 96/4 (1977): 570–71.

————. "Adumbrations of Dan in Jacob's Blessing on Judah." *ZAW* 93/1 (1981): 21–37.

Ginsburger, M. *Pseudo-Jonathan (Thargum Jonathan Ben Usiël Zum Pentateuch).* Hildesheim: Georg Olms Verlag, 1971.

Giveon, R. "Archaeological Evidence for the Exodus." *Bulletin of the Anglo-Israel Archaeological Society.* (1983/84): 42–44.

Gnuse, R. K. *No Other Gods—Emergent Monotheism in Israel.* JSOTSupp 241. Sheffield: Sheffield Academic Press, 1997.

Godley, A. D. *Herodotus.* Cambridge: Harvard University Press, 1981.

Golding, A. *The Excellent and Pleasant Worke—Collectanea Rerum Memorabilium of Caius Julius Solinus.* Gainesville: Scholars' Facsimiles and Reprints, 1587.

Gordon, C. H. "Vergil and the Near East." *Ugaritica* IV (1969): 285–86.

Gottwald, N. K. *The Tribes of Yahweh—A Sociology of the Religion of Liberated Israel 1250–1050 B.C.E.* Maryknoll: Orbis Books, 1981.

————. "The Israelite Settlement as a Social Revolutionary Movement." Pages 34–46 in *Biblical Archaeology Today—Proceedings of the International Congress on Biblical Archaeology, Jerusalem, April 1984.* Edited by the International Congress on Biblical Archaeology. Jerusalem: Israel Exploration Society, 1985.

————. *The Hebrew Bible—A Socio-Literary Introduction.* Philadelphia: Fortress Press, 1987.

Gray, G. B. *A Critical and Exegetical Commentary on The Book of Isaiah.* International Critical Commentary. Edited by C. A. Briggs, S. R. Driver and A. Plummer. New York: Charles Scribner's Sons, 1912.

Greenwood, N. H. *The Sinai—A Physical Geography.* Austin: University of Texas, 1997.

Halpern, B. *The Emergence of Israel in Canaan.* Society of Biblical Literature Monograph Series 29. Chico: Scholars Press, 1983.

Hamilton, V. *The Book of Genesis—Chapters 18–50.* The New International Commentary on the Old Testament. Edited by R. Harrison and R. Hubbard. Grand Rapids: Wm. B. Eerdmans Publishing Co., 1995.

Haran, M. "The Exodus Route in the Pentateuchal Sources (Hebrew)." *Tarbiz* 40 (1970/71): 113–43.

Helck, W. "TKW und die Ramses-Stadt." *VT* 15 (1965): 35–48.

Herrmann, S. "Basic Factors of Israelite Settlement in Canaan." Pages 47–53 in *Biblical Archaeology Today—Proceedings of the International Congress on Biblical Archaeology, Jerusalem, April 1984.* Edited by the International Congress on Biblical Archaeology; Jerusalem: Israel Exploration Society, 1985.

Herzog, Z. "Enclosed Settlements in the Negeb and the Wilderness of Beer-Sheba." *BASOR* 250 (1983): 41–49.

Hoffman, Y. יציאת מצרים באמונת המקרה. Tel Aviv: Tel Aviv University, 1983.

———. "Concerning the Language of P and the Date of Its Composition (Hebrew)." *Te'udah* 4 (1986): 13–22.

———. "A North Israelite Typological Myth and a Judaean Historical Tradition: The Exodus in Hosea and Amos." *VT* 39 (1989): 169–82.

Hoffmeier, J. K. *Israel in Egypt—the Evidence for the Authenticity of the Exodus Tradition.* New York: Oxford University Press, 1997.

Hooker, P. K. "The Location of the Brook of Egypt." Pages 203–14 in *History and Interpretation: Essays in Honour of John H. Hayes.* Edited by M. P. Graham, W. P. Brown and J. K. Kuan. Sheffield: Sheffield Academic Press, 1993.

Horowitz, W. *Mesopotamian Cosmic Geography.* Winona Lake: Eisenbrauns, 1998.

Houtman, C. *Exodus, Vol. 1.* Kampen: Kok Publishing House, 1993.

———. *Exodus, Vol. 2.* Kampen: Kok Publishing House, 1996.

Huntingford, G. W. B.*The Periplus of the Erythraean Sea.* London: The Hakluyt Society, 1980.

Hurvitz, A. "The Evidence of Language in Dating the Priestly Code." *RB* 81 (1974): 24–56.

———. "The Language of the Priestly Source and Its Historical Setting—The Case for an Early Date." Pages 83–94 in *Proceedings of the Eighth World Congress of Jewish Studies (1981).* Jerusalem: World Union of Jewish Studies, 1983.

———. "Dating the Priestly Source in Light of the Historical Study of Biblical Hebrew a Century After Wellhausen." *ZAW* 100/supplement (1988): 88–100.

Jastrow, M. *A Dictionary of the Targumim, the Talmud Babli and Yerushalmi, and the Midrashic Literature.* New York: The Judaica Press, 1992.

Jenks, A. W. *The Elohist and North Israelite Traditions.* JBL MonSer 22. Missoula: Scholars Press, 1977.

Jones, H. L. *The Geography of Strabo, Vol. VII.* London: William Heinemann, Ltd., 1930.

———. *The Geography of Strabo.* London: William Heinemann, Ltd., 1932.

———. *The Geography of Strabo.* Cambridge: Harvard University Press, 1960.

Joüon, P., and T. Muraoka. *A Grammar of Biblical Hebrew, Part One.* Translated by T. Muraoka. Rome: Editrice Pontificio Instituto Biblico, 1996.

Kaiser, O. *Isaiah 13–39.* Philadelphia: The Westminster Press, 1974.

Kallai, Z. "The Boundaries of Canaan and the Land of Israel in the Bible (Hebrew)." *Eretz Israel* 12 (1975): 27–34.

———. "Territorial Patterns, Biblical Historiography and Scribal Tradition—a Programmatic Survey." *ZAW* 93 (1991): 427–32.

———. "Biblical Historiography and Literary History: A Programmatic Survey." *VT* 49/3 (1999): 338–50.

Kaufmann, Y. *The Religion of Israel: From Its Beginnings to the Babylonian Exile.* Chicago: University of Chicago Press, 1960.

Kees, H. *Ancient Egypt—a Cultural Topography.* Chicago: University of Chicago Press, 1961.

King, T. J. "The Priestly Literature and Its Northern Component." Ph. D. Dissertation. Berkeley: Graduate Theological Union, 1996.

Kitchen, K. A. *Ancient Orient and Old Testament*. London: The Tyndale Press, 1966.

———. *The Third Intermediate Period in Egypt (1100–650 BC)*. Warminster: Aris & Phillips Ltd, 1986.

Klein, M. L. *The Fragment-Targums of the Pentateuch According to Their Extant Sources, Vol 1*. Analecta Biblica 76. Rome: Biblical Institute Press, 1980.

Knibb, M. A. *The Ethiopic Book of Enoch*. Oxford: Oxford University Press, 1978.

Kornemann, E. *Die Alexandergeschichte Des Königs Ptolemaios I. Von Aegypten*. Groningen: Verlag Bouma's Boekhuis N.V., 1969.

Krahmalkov, C. R. "Exodus Itinerary Confirmed by Egyptian Evidence." *BAR* 20/5 (1994): 55–62.

Kraus, H. -J. *Gottesdienst in Israel*. München: Chr. Kaiser Verlag, 1962.

Krüger, T. "Erwägungen zur Redaktion der Meerwundererzählung (Exodus 13,17–14,31)." *ZAW* 108 (1966): 519–33.

Kuan, J. K. *Neo–Assyrian Historical Inscriptions and Syria-Palestine*. Jian Dao Dissertation Series 1. Hong Kong: Alliance Bible Seminary, 1995.

Kubitschek, W. "Studien zur Geographie des Ptolemäus—I. Die Ländergrenzen." Akademie der Wissenschaften in Wien Sitzungsberichte 215/5. Wien: Hölder, Pichler, Tempsky A.–G., 1935.

Kuiper, G. J. *The Pseudo-Jonathan Targum and Its Relationship to Targum Onkelos*. Studia Ephemeridis "Augustinianum" 9. Rome: Institutum Patristicum Augustinianum, 1972.

Lagrange, F. M. –J. "L'itinéraire des Israélites du Pays de Gessen aux bords du Jourdain." *RB* 9 (1900): 63–86.

Lambdin, T. O. "Shihor." Page 328 in *The Interpreter's Dictionary of the Bible 4*. Nashville: Abingdon Press, 1962.

Landsberger, B. "Über Farben im Sumerisch-Akkadischen." *JCS* 21 (1967): 139–73.

Lemche, N. P. *Early Israel: Anthropological and Historical Studies on the Israelite Society Before the Monarchy*. Leiden: E. J. Brill, 1985.

———. *Prelude to Israel's Past—Background and Beginnings of Israelite History and Identity*. Peabody: Hendrickson Publishers, 1998.

Levine, B. A. "Late Language in the Priestly Source: Some Literary and Historical Observations" Pages 69–82 in *Proceedings of the Eighth World Congress of Jewish Studies (1981)*. Jerusalem: World Union of Jewish Studies, 1983.

———. *Numbers 1–20*. The Anchor Bible 4. New York: Doubleday, 1993.

———. *Numbers 21–36*. The Anchor Bible 4A. New York: Doubleday, 2000.

Levy, B. B. *Targum Neophyti I—a Textual Study, Vol 1*. New York: University Press of America, 1986.

Lewy, J. "The Old West Semitic Sun God Ḥammu." *HUCA* 18 (1944): 429–88.

Liddell, H. G., and R. Scott. *A Greek-English Lexicon*. Oxford: University Press, 1961.

Littauer, M. A., and J. H. Crouwel. "Chariots." Pages 888–92 in *The Anchor Bible Dictionary, Vol. 1*. Edited by D. N. Freedman. New York: Doubleday, 1992.

Lloyd, A. B. *Herodotus Book II—Introduction*. Leiden: E. J. Brill, 1975.

———. *Herodotus Book II—Commentary 1–98*. Leiden: E. J. Brill, 1976.

———. *Herodotus Book II—Commentary 99–182*. Leiden: E. J. Brill, 1993.

Lubetski, M. "New Light on Old Seas." *JQR* 68 (1978): 65–77.

Lucas, A. *The Route of the Exodus of the Israelites from Egypt*. London: Edward Arnold & Co., 1938.

Malamat, A. "The Exodus: Egyptian Analogies." Pages 15–26 in *Exodus: The Egyptian Evidence*. Edited by E. S. Frerichs and L. H. Lesko. Winona Lake: Eisenbrauns, 1997.

Martínez, F. G. *The Dead Sea Scrolls Translated—The Qumran Texts in English*. Leiden: E. J. Brill, 1996.

Martínez, F. G., and E. J. C. Tigchelaar. *The Dead Sea Scrolls Study Edition*. Leiden: E. J. Brill, 1997.

———. *The Dead Sea Scrolls Study Edition*. Leiden: E. J. Brill, 1998.

Marzullo, B. *A Complete Concordance to the Odyssey of Homer*. Hildesheim: Georg Olms Verlagsbuchhandlung, 1962.

———. *A Complete Concordance to the Iliad of Homer*. Hildesheim: Georg Olms Verlagsbuchhandlung, 1962.

Mastin, B. A. "Was the *šālîš* the third man in the chariot?" *VTSup* 30 (1979): 125–54.

McCarter, P. K. *II Samuel*. The Anchor Bible 9. Garden City: Doubleday & Company, Inc., 1984.

McCown, C. C. "The Testament of Solomon." Dissertation, University of Chicago. Leipzig: J. C. Hinrichs'sche Buchhandlung, 1922.

Mendenhall, G. E. "Biblical History in Transition." Pages 32–53 in *The Bible and the Ancient Near East—Essays in Honor of William Foxwell Albright*. Edited by G. E. Wright. Garden City: Doubleday and Company, Inc., 1961.

Mikraoth Gedoloth—Shemot. Jerusalem: Am Olam, 1961.

Milgrom, J. *Studies in Levitical Terminology*. Berkeley: University of California, 1970.

———. *Studies in Cultic Theology and Terminology*. Leiden: E.J. Brill, 1983.

———. "Priestly ('P') Source." Pages 454–61 in *The Anchor Bible Dictionary Vol. 5*. Edited by D. N. Freedman. New York: Doubleday, 1991.

Milik, J. T., ed. *The Books of Enoch—Aramaic Fragments of Qumrân Cave 4*. Oxford: Oxford University Press, 1976.

———. "Henoch au pays des aromates—Ch xxvii à xxxii." *Revue Biblique* 65 (1958): 70–77.

Miller, J. M. "Biblical Maps—How Reliable Are They?" *Bible Review* 3/4 (1987): 32–41.

Miller, J. M., and J. H. Hayes. *A History of Ancient Israel and Judah*. Philadelphia: Westminster Press, 1986.

Miller, W. *Xenophon Cyropaedia II*. The Loeb Classical Library. London: The MacMillan Company, 1914.

Mommsen, T. *C. IVLII SOLINI—Collectanea Rervm Memorabilivm*. Berolini: Apud Weidmannos, 1895.

Montet, P. *Egypt and the Bible*. Translated by L. R. Keylock. Philadelphia: Fortress Press, 1968.

Montgomery, J. A. "Hebraica." *JAOS* 58 (1938): 130–39.

Moritz, B. *Arabien-Studien zur Physikalischen und Historischen Geographie des Landes.* Hannover: Buchhandlung Heinz LaFaire, 1923.

Muilenberg, J. "The Form and Structure of the Covenantal Formulations." *VT* 39 (1959).

M'Crindle, J. W. *The Invasion of India by Alexander the Great as Described by Arrian, q. Curtius, Diodorus, Plutarch and Justin*. New Delhi: Today & Tomorrow's Printers & Publishers, 1974.

Müllerus, C. *Fragmenta Historicorum Graecorum*. Parisiis: Fermin–Didot et Sociis, 1883.

———. *Geographi Graeci Minores*. Hildesheim: Georg Olms Verlag, 1990.

Na'aman, N. "The Brook of Egypt and Assyrian Policy on the Border of Egypt." *Tel Aviv* 6/1–2 (1979): 68–90.

———. "The Shihor of Egypt and Shur That is Before Egypt." *Tel Aviv* 7/1–2 (1980): 95–109.

———. *Borders & Districts in Biblical Historiography*. Jerusalem Biblical Studies; Jerusalem: Simor, 1986.

———. "The List of David's Officers *(ŠĀLÎŠÎM)*." *VT* 38 (1988): 71–79.

Nelson, R. D. "Josiah in the Book of Joshua." *JBL* 100/4 (1981): 531–40.

———. *Joshua—A Commentary*. Louisville: Westminster John Knox Press, 1997.

Noth, M. "Der Schauplatz der Meereswunders." Pages 181–90 in *Festschrift Otto Eissfeldt*. Edited by J. Fück. Halle: Niemeyer, 1947.

———. *The History of Israel*. London: Adam & Charles Black, 1959.

———. *Überlieferungsgeschichtliche Studien*. Tübingen: Max Niemeyer Verlag, 1943.

———. *A History of Pentateuchal Traditions*. Translated by B. W. Anderson. Englewood Cliffs, NJ: Prentice Hall, 1972.

———. *The Deuteronomistic History*. JSOTSupp 15. Sheffield: JSOT, 1981.

Oblath, M. D. "Of Pharaohs and Kings—Whence the Exodus?" *JSOT* 87 (2000): 23–42.

———. "The Exodus from Egypt in the Prophets: Evidence for a Judean Appropriation of Israelite Tradition." Paper presented at the annual meeting of the Society of Biblical Literature, Toronto, ON, Nov. 25, 2002.

Oppenheim, A. L., ed. *The Assyrian Dictionary Volume 6—Ḫ*. Chicago: Oriental Institute, 1956.

Oren, E. D. "The 'Way of Horus' in North Sinai." Pages 69–119 in *Egypt, Israel, Sinai: Archaeological and Historical Relationships in the Biblical Period*. Edited by A. F. Rainey. Tel Aviv: Tel Aviv University, 1987.

———. *The Hyksos: New Historical and Archaeological Perspectives*. University Museum Symposium Series 8. Philadelphia: The University Museum, 1997.

Parker, S. T. "The Roman Aqaba Project: The Economy of Aila on the Red Sea." *BA* 59/3 (1996): 182.

Patrick, D. "Traditio-History of the Reed Sea Account." *VT* 26 (1976): 248–49.

Perevolotsky, A., and I. Finkelstein. "The Southern Sinai Exodus Route in Ecological Perspective." *BAR* 11/4 (1985): 26–41.

Polzin, R. *Late Biblical Hebrew: Toward an Historical Typology of Biblical Hebrew Prose.* Missoula: Scholars Press, 1976.

Preisendanz, K. *Papyri Graecae Magicae—Die Griechischen Zauberpapyri.* Leipzig: Verlag und Druck von B.G. Teubner, 1928.

Procksch, O. *Das Nordhebräische Sagenbuch, Die Elohimquelle.* Leipzig: J. C. Hinrichs, 1906.

Propp, W. H. C. *Exodus 1–18.* The Anchor Bible 2. New York: Doubleday, 1999.

Quatremère, M. "Mémoire sur les Nabatéens." *Journal Asiatique* 15 (Janvier 1835): 5–55.

Race, W. H. *Pindar I—Olympian Odes, Pythian Odes.* The Loeb Classical Library. Cambridge: Harvard University Press, 1997.

Rackham, H. *Pliny—Natural History.* Cambridge: Harvard University Press, 1961.

Rainey, A. F., ed. *Egypt, Israel, Sinai—Archaeological and Historical Relationships in the Biblical Period.* Tel Aviv: Tel Aviv University, 1987.

Redford, D. B. "An Egyptological Perspective on the Exodus Narrative." Pages 137–61 in *Egypt, Israel, Sinai: Archaeological and Historical Relationships in the Biblical Period.* Edited by A. F. Rainey. Tel Aviv: Tel Aviv University, 1987.

———. *Egypt, Canaan and Israel in Ancient Times.* New Jersey: Princeton University, 1992.

Reiner, E., ed. *The Assyrian Dictionary, Vol 15—S.* Chicago: University of Chicago, 1984.

Rendsburg, G. A. "Late Biblical Hebrew and the Date of 'P'." *JANES* 12 (1980): 65–80.

———. "The Date of the Exodus and the Conquest/Settlement: The Case for the 1100s." *VT* 42/4 (1992): 510–27.

Robson, E. I. *Arrian II.* The Loeb Classical Library. Edited by T. E. Page. Cambridge: Harvard University Press, 1958.

Rolfe, J. C. *Ammianus Marcellinus, Vol III.* The Loeb Classical Library. Edited by E. H. Warmington. Cambridge: Harvard University Press, 1939.

———. *Ammianus Marcellinus, Vol I.* The Loeb Classical Library. Edited by E. H. Warmington; Cambridge: Harvard University Press, 1971.

———. *Ammianus Marcellinus, Vol II.* The Loeb Classical Library. Edited by E. H. Warmington; 1972.

Romer, F. E. *Pomponius Mela's Description of the World.* Ann Arbor: University of Michigan Press, 1998.

Rosenbaum, M., and A. M. Silbermann. *Pentateuch with Targum Onkelos, Haphtaroth and Rashi's Commentary.* Jerusalem: Silbermann Family, 1973.

Rothenberg, B. "An Archaeological Survey of South Sinai: First Season 1967/1968, Preliminary Report." *PEQ* 102 (1970): 18–19.

Sayce, A. H. *The "Higher Criticism" and the Verdict of the Monuments.* London: Richard Clay & Sons, Ltd., 1901.

Schley, D. G. "The ŠĀLĪŠÎM: Officers or Special Three-Man Squads?" *VT* 40 (1990): 312–26.

Seeligman, I. L. "A Psalm from Pre-Regal Times." *VT* 14 (1964): 75–92.

Shanan, L., N. H. Tadmor, and M. Evenari. "The Ancient Desert Agriculture of the Negev, II: Utilization of the Runoff from Small Watersheds in the 'Avdat Region." *Ktavim* 9 (1958).

Simons, J. *The Geographical and Topographical Texts of the Old Testament.* Leiden: E.J. Brill, 1959.

Skehan, P. W., E. Ulrich, and J. E. Sanderson. *Qumran Cave 4 IV—Paleo–Hebrew and Greek Biblical Manuscripts.* Vol. IX of *Discoveries in the Judean Desert.* Oxford: Clarendon Press, 1992.

Smend, R. *Yahweh War and Tribal Confederation—Reflections Upon Israel's Earliest History.* Translated by M. G. Rogers. Nashville: Abingdon Press, 1970.

Snaith, N. H. "יָם סוּף : The Sea of Reeds : The Red Sea." *VT* 15 (1965): 395–98.

Sokoloff, M. *A Dictionary of Jewish Palestinian Aramaic of the Byzantine Period.* Ramat–Gan: Bar Ilan University Press, 1990.

Sommerstein, A. H. *Birds.* Wiltshire, England: Aris & Phillips, Ltd., 1987.

Spencer, J. E., and G. A. Hale. "The Origin, Nature and Distribution of Agricultural Terracing." *Pacific Viewpoint* 2/1 (1961): 1–40.

Sperber, A. *The Bible in Aramaic: Vol I, the Pentateuch According to Targum Onkelos.* Leiden: E. J. Brill, 1959.

———. *The Bible in Aramaic: Vol II, The Former Prophets According to Targum Jonathan.* Leiden: E. J. Brill, 1959.

———. *The Bible in Aramaic: Vol IVA, The Hagiographa.* Leiden: E. J. Brill, 1968.

Stevenson, E. L. *Claudius Ptolemy—the Geography.* New York: Dover Publishers, 1991.

Stiebing Jr., W. H. "Should the Exodus and the Israelite Settlement Be Redated?" *BAR* 11/4 (1985): 58–69.

Stillwell, R., ed. *The Princeton Encyclopedia of Classical Sites.* Princeton: Princeton University Press, 1976.

Strickman, H. N., and A. M. Silver. *Ibn Ezra's Commentary on the Pentateuch: Exodus (Shemot).* New York: Menorah Publishing, 1996.

Tadmor, H., M. Evenari, L. Shanan, and D. Hillel. "The Ancient Desert Agriculture of the Negev, I: Gravel Mounds and Strips of the Shivta Area." *Ktavim* 8 (1958): 127–36.

Tal, A. *The Samaritan Targum of the Pentateuch, Parts I & II.* Tel Aviv: Tel Aviv University, 1981.

———. *A Dictionary of Samaritan Aramaic.* Handbook of Oriental Studies: Abt. I. The Near and Middle East; Leiden: E. J. Brill, 2000.

Tedesche, S. *The First Book of the Maccabees.* New York: Harper & Brothers, 1950.

Thackeray, F. S. J. *Anthologia Graeca—Passages from the Greek Poets.* London: G. Bell and Sons, Ltd., 1911.

Thackeray, H. S. J., and R. Marcus. *Josephus V—Jewish Antiquities, Books V–VIII.* Cambridge: Harvard University Press, 1977.

The Peshiṭta Institute, ed. *The Old Testament in Syriac According to the Peshiṭta Version, Kings.* Leiden: E. J. Brill, 1976.

————. *The Old Testament in Syriac According to the Peshiṭṭa Version, Genesis–Exodus*. Leiden: E. J. Brill, 1977.

Tiede, D. L. *The Charismatic Figure as Miracle Worker*. The Seminar on the Gospels, Dissertation Series 1. Missoula: Society of Biblical Literature, 1972.

Tower, J. R. "The Red Sea." *JNES* 18 (1959): 150–53.

Treacy, J. M. "The Creation of Cultivable Land Through Terracing." Pages 91–110 in *The Archaeology of Garden and Field*. Edited by N. F. Miller and K. L. Gleason. Philadelphia: University of Pennsylvania Press, 1994.

Tromp, J. *Studia in Veteris Testamenti Pseudepigrapha 10: The Assumption of Moses—a Critical Edition with Commentary*. Edited by A.-M. Denis and M. de Jonge; Leiden: E. J. Brill, 1993.

Ulrich, E., and F. Cross. *Qumran Cave IV—Deuteronomy, Joshua, Judges, Kings*. Vol. XIV of *Discoveries in the Judean Desert*. Oxford: Clarendon Press, 1995.

Uphill, E. "Pithom and Raamses: Their Location and Significance I." *JNES* 27 (1968): 291–316.

————. "Pithom and Raamses: Their Location and Significance II." *JNES* 28 (1969): 15–39.

VanderKam, J. C., ed. *The Book of Jubilees—A Critical Text*. Corpus Scriptorum Christianorum Orientalium; Lovanii: Peeters, 1989.

————. *Textual and Historical Studies in the Book of Jubilees*. Harvard Semitic Monographs 510. Missoula: Scholars Press, 1977.

Van Seters, J. *The Life of Moses: The Yahwist as Historian in Exodus-Numbers*. Kampen: Kam Pharos Publishing, 1994.

Vink, J. G. *The Priestly Code and Seven Other Studies*. Leiden: E. J. Brill, 1969.

Waddell, W. G. *Manetho*. London: William Heinemann Ltd., 1940.

Walsh, J. T. "From Egypt to Moab: A Source Critical Analysis of the Wilderness Itinerary." *CBQ* xxxix/1 (1977): 20–33.

Walter, H. *Die "Collectanea Rerum Memorabilium" Des C. Iulius Solinus*. Hermes—Zeitschrift Für Klassische Philologie 22. Wiesbaden: Franz Steiner Verlag GMBH, 1969.

Waltke, B. K., and M. O'Connor. *An Introduction to Biblical Hebrew Syntax*. Winona Lake: Eisenbrauns, 1990.

Ward, W. A. "The Semitic Biconsonantal Root *SP* and the Common Origin of Egyptian *CWF* and Hebrew *SUP*: 'Marsh (-Plant)'." *VT* 24 (1974): 339–49.

Weippert, M. *The Settlement of Israelite Tribes in Palestine*. London: SCM, 1971.

————. "The Israelite 'Conquest' and Evidence from Transjordan." Pages 15–34 in *Symposia Celebrating the 75th Anniversary of TheASOR (1900–1975)*. Edited by D. N. Freedman. Cambridge, MA: ASOR Press, 1979.

Weippert, M., and M. Edom. "Studien und Materialen zur Geschichte der Edomiter auf Grund Schriftlicher und Archäologischer Quellen." Tübingen: Tübingen, 1971.

Wellhausen, J. *Prolegomena to the History of Ancient Israel*. New York: Meridian Books, 1957.

Whiston, W., trans. *The Life and Works of Flavius Josephus*. New York: Holt, Rinehart and Winston.

Whybray, R. N. *The Making of the Pentateuch*. Sheffield: JSOT Press, 1987.

Wifall, W. "The Sea of Reeds as Sheol." *ZAW* 92/3 (1980): 325–32.

Williams, J. G. "Number Symbolism and Joseph as Symbol of Completion." *JBL* 98/1 (1979): 86–87.

Wilson, W. P. *The Periplus of the Erythraean Sea*. Philadelphia: Philadelphia Museums, 1911.

Winnett, F. V., and W. L. Reed. *Ancient Records from North Arabia*. Toronto: University of Toronto Press, 1970.

Wissowa, G. *Paulys Real-Encyclopädie der Classischen Altertumswissenschaft*. Stuttgart: J. B. Metzler, 1907.

Yurco, F. "Merenptah's Canaanite Campaign and Israel's Origins." Pages 27–55 in *Exodus: The Egyptian Evidence*. Edited by E. S. Frerichs and L. H. Lesko. Winona Lake: Eisenbrauns, 1997.

Ziegler, K., and W. Sontheimer. *Der Kleine Pauly—Lexikon der Antike*. München: Deutscher Taschenbuch Verlag GmbH & Co. KG, 1979.

Ziegler, S. *Ptolemy—Geography, Book 6*. Wiesbaden: Dr. Ludwig Reichert Verlag, 1998.

Zohary, D. "Notes on Ancient Agriculture in the Central Negev." *IEJ* 4/1 (1954): 17–25.

INDEX OF TEXTUAL PASSAGES

Index of Geographical Sites

SUBJECT AND AUTHOR INDEX

date of,, 9, 10–13, 16, 20–22
historicity, 8–23
Israelite (northern) story, 110, 118,
137, 193–98, 247 n.15
mythology, 8, 23–26
source of story, 147, 193–98, 250 n.46

F

Faiman, D., 19
Finkelstein, I., 17, 19–23, 28, 118, 195
Freedman, D.N., 8–9, 13–14
Friedman, R., 31, 78, 183–87, 218–22,
229–31

G

Gemser, B., 102–3
geographical memory, 77–78, 195–96
Gevirtz, S., 12, 195
Giveon, R., 10
Gottwald, N., 16

H

Halpern, B., 237–38
Hapiru, 10–11
Haran, M., 92
historical-geography, 1, 3, 8, 26–28
and authors' perspective, 27–28, 99
literary, 1–5, 77–78
Hoffmeier, J.K., 22, 59–61
Houtman, C., 19
Hyksos, 11–12, 17–22, 28
entry into Egypt, 17–19
as source for the exodus, 11–13, 19,
21–22, 28–30
hypothesis, 1, 193–95

I

Ideological Israel, 247 n.15
Israel (Northern Kingdom), 118
borders, 85–86

YHWH as god of, 237 n.82, 247 n.15

K

King, T.J., 93–94
Kuan, J.K., 139

L

Lagrange, F.M.-J., 22
Lambdin, T.O., 82
learning to walk, xv
Lemche, N.P., 21
Levine, B.A., 33, 101–2, 129, 146
Littauer, M.A., 234 n.30
Lucas, A., 236 n.70

M

Malamat, A., 10
Manetho, 17, 21
Mastin, B.A., 234 n.29
McCarter, P.K., 161
Merneptah Stele, 10–11
and the exodus, 10–11
date, 10–11
Meyer, E., 20
Montgomery, J.A., 59–60
Moritz, B., 59–60, 242 n.7
Moses, 7, 13, 23, 28
mythologies
and the song of the sea, 13–14
and Yam Sûp, 25–26
relationship to exodus account, 23–26

N

Na'aman, N., 78
Noth, M., 25, 29, 31, 78, 93, 177–82,
210–17, 226–28, 238 n.89

O

Oblath, M.D., 95, 195, 247 n.15, 248 n.18

Studies in Biblical Literature

This series invites manuscripts from scholars in any area of biblical literature. Both established and innovative methodologies, covering general and particular areas in biblical study, are welcome. The series seeks to make available studies that will make a significant contribution to the ongoing biblical discourse. Scholars who have interests in gender and sociocultural hermeneutics are particularly encouraged to consider this series.

For further information about the series and for the submission of manuscripts, contact:

Hemchand Gossai
Department of Religion
Muhlenberg College
2400 Chew Street
Allentown, PA 18104-5586

To order other books in this series, please contact our Customer Service Department:

(800) 770-LANG (within the U.S.)
(212) 647-7706 (outside the U.S.)
(212) 647-7707 FAX

or browse online by series at:

WWW.PETERLANGUSA.COM